MW01125699

"The type of 'catholicity' that governs Mercersburg theology is one which sees the Incarnation as the integrating medium for the whole of Christian theology. That is what makes this book so promising for contemporary dialogue between the Eastern Orthodox and Reformed traditions. Juridical categories will still have their value to Reformed theologians, but the author has uncovered a new horizon in the history of Reformed theology. As part of its fine survey of the Mercersburg theology's intersection with other theological traditions, this book lays the groundwork for achieving a creative synthesis between the Reformed and Orthodox traditions. It is a pioneering work, highly recommended."

—BRADLEY NASSIF
co-author of *Three Views on Eastern Orthodoxy and Evangelicalism*

"In this impeccably researched, beautifully written monograph, Brad Littlejohn, one of the brightest young scholars in the church in our generation, brings the Mercersburg movement into the twenty-first century. What does Mercersburg have to offer us? Littlejohn demonstrates that at a time when many in the church are looking to the past to help navigate the challenges of the future, Mercersburg is more relevant than ever . . . He provides a remarkable synthesis of theology, history, and contemporary application, reminding us that sometimes the surest way forward includes a glance backward. I hope Littlejohn's work will receive a wide and receptive audience in the church. We will all be better off if it does."

—RICH LUSK
author of *Paedofaith*

"It is a pleasure to welcome into print Littlejohn's excellent study on the Mercersburg theology and its relation to other Christian traditions. There is much here to reflect on, as we ourselves seek to discover what unity lies beneath our divisiveness, to listen to the voice of the Church spoken through the centuries on the basis of God's Word."

—DONALD FAIRBAIRN
author of *Life in the Trinity* and *Grace and Christology in the Early Church*

"While perhaps not as sanguine about some of John Williamson Nevin's soteriological distinctives as the author, I can heartily commend this study of the Mercersburg ecclesiology. By his detailed examination of key texts and interlocutors, and his careful placement of Nevin and Schaff in the broader context of nineteenth and twentieth-century discussions regarding the nature of the church, Littlejohn has performed a distinct service both to the Reformed community and the broader church."

—WILLIAM B. EVANS
author of *Imputation and Impartation: Union with Christ in American Reformed Theology*

The Mercersburg Theology
and the Quest for Reformed Catholicity

The Mercersburg Theology
and the Quest for Reformed Catholicity

W. BRADFORD LITTLEJOHN

PICKWICK *Publications* · Eugene, Oregon

THE MERCERSBURG THEOLOGY AND THE QUEST FOR REFORMED
CATHOLICITY

Pickwick Publications
A Division of Wipf and Stock Publishers
199 W. 8th Ave., Suite 3
Eugene, OR 97401

www.wipfandstock.com

ISBN 13: 978-1-60608-241-6

Cataloging-in-Publication data:

Littlejohn, W. Bradford.

    The Mercersburg theology and the quest for reformed catholicity / W. Bradford
Littlejohn ; foreword by Peter J. Leithart.

    xviii + 196 p. ; 23 cm.

    Includes bibliographic references and index.

    ISBN 13: 978-1-60608-241-6

    1. Mercersburg theology. 2. Theology, Doctrinal—United States—History—
19th century. I. Title.

BX 9571 .L58 2009

Manufactured in the U.S.A.

This book is dedicated to Dr. Peter J. Leithart,

a wise teacher and a faithful mentor

Contents

Foreword

FOR AN INCREASING NUMBER of Protestants, the dismemberment of Protestantism is a scandal, an oozing wound in the body of Christ, leaving behind a twisted Christ as painful to behold as the Isenheim altarpiece.

But what is a Protestant to do? The Reformation was itself a rent in the vesture of Christ, so how can Protestants object to the tin-pot Luthers and Machens who faithfully keep up the Reformation tradition of fissure and fragmentation? The problem is sharper for Protestants convinced, as I am, that the Reformation assault on liturgical and soteriological idolatry was necessary in the sixteenth century and remains thoroughly relevant in the twenty-first. Can Protestants be Protestants, and yet also be committed to the unity of the Church? Is there such a thing as a catholic Protestantism, a Protestant catholicism?

I teach my theology students to be "because of" theologians rather than "in spite of" theologians. God is immanent not *in spite of* His transcendence, but *because of* His transcendence. The Son became man not *in spite of* His sovereign Lordship, but *because* He is Lord, as the most dramatic expression of His absolute sovereignty. Creation does not contradict God's nature, but expresses it.

So too with Protestant catholicism: Protestants must learn to be catholic *because* they are Protestants, and vice versa.

To say this is, in part, to make a historical claim. In its origins and at its core, Protestantism is, as Philip Schaff saw and many recent students of the Reformation have confirmed, a thoroughly catholic enterprise. David Yeago sums it up nicely: Luther's aim was to address idolatry, and he ultimately addressed it in a way that "anchored [him] more deeply than ever before in the traditions of catholic dogma, catholic sacramentalism, and catholic mysticism."[1]

It is also a theological claim. Protest ought not be aimed at permanently dividing the Church. Luther, Calvin, and the rest insisted that the disarray of the late medieval Church came from fundamental corruptions of worship and doctrine. Their work divided the Church, and that was necessary, but the goal of that division was always reunion in truth and love. Genuine Protestantism seeks to unite the Church in Christ alone, as He offers Himself to His people in the Spirit through Word and Sacrament. To be Protestant is to aspire to a purified catholicity.

Especially in American Protestantism, this Protestant body is unrecognizable beneath the cancers of revivalism, rationalism, pietism, individualism and subjectivism. A churchly Protestantism is as alien to American soil as high tea. This historical amnesia is nothing new in American Protestantism, and is evident even in the best of American Protestant theologians. As Brad Littlejohn points out in this fine monograph, Charles Hodge, truly a giant of American Presbyterianism, defined the material principle of the Reformation as "our continued protest against the error of a mediating church or priesthood." This is, to put it mildly, hard to square with Luther's emphasis on the sacraments, or with Calvin's insistence, following Cyprian, that we "cannot have God as our Father unless we have the church as our mother." Hodge, for all his erudition, could not shake himself loose from his American context and as a result missed a central feature of the Reformation. In this respect, the Mercersburg theologians breathed more of the spirit of the Reformers than their opponents who styled themselves as defenders of the Protestant tradition. Schaff knew that the Reformation was continuous with many trends of medieval Christianity, and Nevin grasped the heart of Calvin's Spiritual sacramental theology.

We need an American Reformation that recovers the original catholic vision of Protestantism, and in pursuing this, American Protestants do well to take a page from early twentieth-century Catholics and embark on a program of *ressourcement*, and to this program Littlejohn's book is a valuable contribution. In this his first book, he displays the analytic skill, conceptual clarity, and readable style I have long admired in his work as a student. Here he explains the Mercersburg Theology fairly and thoroughly,

1. David S. Yeago, "The Catholic Luther," in *The Catholicity of the Reformation*, edited by Carl E. Braaten and Robert W. Jenson (Grand Rapids: Eerdmans, 1996) 13–34, at 29.

and shows how Mercersburg interacts not only with nineteenth-century Reformed theology but with the developments in Catholic, Orthodox, and Anglican churches over the past two centuries. Above all, Littlejohn is deeply conscious that historical theology is never an end in itself, never an exercise in mere antiquarianism. We remember so that we can know how to go forward, and we seek to recover lost resources so that we can pave a fresh future. He demonstrates how Mercersburg, and especially Nevin, can assist in forming an American Protestant churchliness.

This book is being published in 2009, the five hundredth anniversary of the birth of John Calvin. Calvinists will honor Calvin with lectures and symposia and collections of essays, but Littlejohn's book points us toward a different sort of commemoration. It suggests that Calvin's memory can best be honored by embracing and practicing the fullness of Calvin's hope for a Church catholic and Reformed.

Peter J. Leithart
Advent 2008

Preface

I FIRST DISCOVERED NEVIN, Schaff, and the riches of the Mercersburg Theology more than four years ago, and I have been mining eagerly ever since. My own theology, and my purposes for studying Mercersburg, have changed considerably during that time, yet every time I return to read my well-marked (now rainbow-colored) pages of *The Mystical Presence*, or glance through grainy photocopied sheets from *The Mercersburg Review*, I find new insights and new inspiration. It is unlikely that my reader shall care overmuch about my own journeys with Nevin and Schaff, but perhaps an account of them will help make more sense of the oddities and idiosyncrasies in the pages to come.

I was first introduced to the name John Williamson Nevin in the summer before my freshman year by Keith Mathison's brief account of his clash with Hodge in *Given For You*. My interest was piqued by the resemblance of that 150-year-old debate to one then raging within my own denomination, the Presbyterian Church in America, over the same issues: church, sacraments, imputation and union with Christ, and all the baggage that goes along with these. So I wrote my first paper at college (for the class History of American Presbyterianism) on the subject, and, finding that a great deal of research material had gone unused, I decided to employ it later in the writing of my senior thesis. This led me into much more research than I had expected, and I soon found myself in dusty library basements on the other side of the country. But the original flame of excitement that my first glimpse of Mercersburg had kindled continued to burn bright through long hours of research and what seemed at the time to be many pages of writing. The final product, assessing the relationship between Mercersburg's paradigm of Reformed ecclesiology and Princeton Seminary's, was successfully defended in April of 2007.

Friends and at least one panel member suggested that I seek a publisher for the thesis, relevant as it was to the current debates in the Reformed churches and the current revival of interest in the Mercersburg Theology. After letting this idea lie dormant for nearly a year, I decided to go ahead with it, and Wipf and Stock, having published a number of books relating to Mercersburg, picked it up.

Of course, some expansions would be necessary. A number of topics for such expansion had suggested themselves to me from my studies in the past couple years, which had ventured out of the little enclave of Reformed theology into other traditions as well, particularly the Catholic and Anglican. The obvious thing to do was to show that the theology of Nevin and Schaff was not merely Reformed but really catholic, offering fruitful points of dialogue with the Anglican, Catholic, and Orthodox traditions. Only the first of these had received any attention in Mercersburg studies, and so these three areas of exploration proved very exciting, and the parallels that emerged were often more striking that I had ever imagined. Indeed, the new content threatened to overwhelm the old, but a suitable organizational scheme soon presented itself. The original thesis comprises part of the Introduction, as well as most of chapters 1–3, which are particularly interested in the relation of Mercersburg to the Reformed tradition. Chapters 4–6 contain the new avenues of exploration, focusing on the relation of Mercersburg to the three catholic traditions just mentioned.

Throughout, I very often allow Nevin and Schaff to speak for themselves, quoting generously whenever the best summary is the one that is in their own words. For some, this may seem irksome, as if I were merely anthologizing; they may ask, "Why don't I just go and read *The Mystical Presence* straight through if I'm getting so much of it here?" I certainly recommend that they do; the value of that book is hard to overstate. But I hope that something more than that is offered, in the careful arrangement of Mercersburg doctrines in dialogue with friends and foes. My hope, by laying the insights of the Mercersburg Theology before the reader, is to offer to him, if Reformed, the same two things Mercersburg gave me: the understanding of a better, truer way to be Reformed, and the understanding that being Reformed is not a quarter as important as being Christian and part of the one, holy, catholic, and apostolic Church. To other readers, in other parts of that Church, I hope I may offer the opportunity to find allies in a theological territory long perhaps deemed hostile.

I have many to thank for the successful launching of this book into the world (though they are all quite innocent of its remaining defects, which are mostly due to my failure to consult them more). My History of American Presbyterianism professor, and eventual thesis advisor, Chris Schlect, deserves a big share of thanks, for encouraging me in my initial research, and wading through a long thesis that was waist-deep in footnotes, offering valuable sources and suggestions the whole way through. I also thank Douglas Wilson for grilling me throughout the thesis defense to make sure that Nevin and I passed the test of Reformed orthodoxy; I hope I have not disappointed him overmuch since. The third member of my thesis panel, Wesley Callihan, has repeatedly spurred me on with this project, by his shared enthusiasm for Mercersburg, his repeated suggestions that I get it published, and his intriguing insights that eventually led to what is now chapter 5 of this book, for which I thank him especially. Rich Lusk, who helped introduce me to much of the world of Mercersburg and many valuable sources, who reviewed every chapter draft I sent him, and who repeatedly helped set me straight when I was on a false trail, deserves particular thanks. Bill Evans, Donald Fairbairn, and Bradley Nassif also contributed valuable comments, suggestions, and sources. I thank my friends Brad Belschner and Donny Linnemeyer for offering witty and incisive critiques and suggestions on early drafts, and for keeping me firmly rooted to earth throughout. My young friend Isaiah Paradis helped do the no-fun work of manuscript-editing and footnoting when I was getting sick of it; but for him, this book might have taken much longer to see the light of day. My dear wife, Rachel, bore with me for months as I stayed up far past midnight to work on this book after completing the homework for my regular studies, and it will take me long to repay her support and patience. Finally, the greatest thanks goes to my wise mentor, Dr. Peter Leithart, who has talked through many of the thoughts that went into the new chapters with me, and has kept me spiritually and theologically grounded as I managed this and all life's other responsibilities.

Pro Christi Ecclesia Testamentoque
Moscow, Idaho
St. Andrew's Day (The First Sunday in Advent), 2008

Introduction
The Silenced Seers

PROTESTANTISM IN AMERICA TODAY is in trouble; or rather, it might be more accurate to say, protestantisms in America are in trouble. Liberal, Evangelical, Reformed, Charismatic—as we look around, it is apparent that the Protestant Church has lost a clear sense of its own identity. Denominations continue to proliferate, and many churches, too independent even to feel at home in one of these new micro-denominations, choose to act as their own "non-denominational" body. Even Reformed Presbyterians, with a supposedly "higher ecclesiology," have so thoroughly lost sight of the deeper issues of the Church that they are reduced to wrangling with their Baptist brethren over the superiority of their presbyterial form of polity (which they then proceed to demonstrate eloquently by leaving it every few years and setting up a new one with "tighter doctrinal standards"). An increasing number of exasperated and disillusioned Protestants, in the search for something at least vaguely resembling the mystical Body of Christ, have turned to Catholicism or Eastern Orthodoxy.

This unhappy turn of events is not as new as it may seem. More than 150 years ago, it was foreseen and prophesied by the great Reformed theologian John Williamson Nevin. In his day, for the most part, the Reformed churches of America still had enough lingering sense of the high majesty and history of the Church that they remained outwardly the stalwart heirs of the Reformation that they claimed to be. But Nevin knew that the reigning Reformed scholasticism did not possess the theological resources to cope with the swelling tide of sectarian subjectivism and arid rationalism, the twin daughters of the Enlightenment which

1

threatened to overwhelm American Christianity. He saw that Princeton Seminary's great war against revivalism was no more than a little scrap between consistent individualism and schizophrenic individualism. On his reading of the American religious climate, the only solution to the woes coming upon American Christianity was a return to the historical Reformational faith in the visible Church as the true Body of Christ, and an embrace of the whole of that Body's history and members, including Catholicism. And, so far as he could tell, there was no one left in the American Reformed corridors of power who would still stand for such a faith, or venture such an embrace.

So, in 1843, from the tiny German Reformed seminary in Mercersburg, Pennsylvania, he wrote a series of lectures published as *The Anxious Bench*, a devastating critique of revivalism in all its forms, turning a few heads, but failing to generate a large response from a religious public already saturated with pro- and anti-revivalism tracts. But the following year, with the arrival of Philip Schaff, a twenty-five-year-old prodigy fresh from the great universities of Germany, Nevin and his young colleague began to put Mercersburg on the map with their fierce critiques of sectarianism in American Protestantism. Nevin's publication of *The Mystical Presence*, a full-blown historical vindication of a richly sacramental and ecclesiocentric Reformed faith, in 1846, drew Charles Hodge, the Colossus who bestrode the narrow world of Reformed orthodoxy, into the fray. For the next four years, and intermittently thereafter, a fierce war of pens was waged between Mercersburg and much of the rest of the American Reformed world. From Nevin's perspective, it was a battle for the soul of American Protestantism, one that, in his own day, he lost.

The prevailing Reformed orthodoxy of Charles Hodge and Princeton Seminary ensured that the Mercersburg Theology always remained a fringe movement, both in the churches and the history books. Many Reformed Protestants have tended to view the nineteenth-century Church according to the paradigm of Princeton's self-perception: a long war between the conservative heirs of the Reformation and their innovating opponents, the revivalists, followed by the beginning of a war against their still more innovating opponents, the liberals. When the arch-conservative Hodge encountered Nevin's theology, he was for once flummoxed, for at last he had met an opponent who was, in many ways at least, more conservative than he. From Nevin's perspective, it was Hodge who was innovating. Thus neither Hodge nor the history books have been sure quite what to do with the Mercersburg Theology, and its defiance of the traditional paradigm has resulted in its near extinction in both modern church life and academic studies.

While the legacy of the Mercersburg Theology has been largely forgotten, and few church historians have given Nevin's distinctive thought more than a passing glance, the movement has attracted a few isolated scholars throughout the past century. During the past decade, indeed, scholarly works and popular discussions on Mercersburg have been cropping up more and more frequently, offering hope that Nevin and Schaff will finally get the hearing they deserve. I hope that this study may be part of such a renaissance, but I should perhaps take a few pages to discuss other significant interpretations of Mercersburg, and how the present work differs from them.

Mercersburg in the History Books

From the publication of Nevin's biography by Theodore Appel in 1889, until 1953, almost no literature on Mercersburg can be found. In 1953, Luther Binkley wrote a little book on the Mercersburg Theology which was quickly forgotten, and deemed insignificant by later Mercersburg scholars. Finally in 1961, the prominent church historian James Hastings Nichols published an outstanding summary of Mercersburg thought, *Romanticism in American Theology*, and shortly afterward, an anthology, *The Mercersburg Theology*. Unfortunately, however, no one picked up on his work, and both works went out of print (until being republished by Wipf and Stock just recently). The next book-length study of Nevin and his theology to be published was Richard Wentz's *John Williamson Nevin: American Theologian* in 1997. This didn't set off a flurry of interest either, but in 2004, Reformed church historian Darryl Hart published an excellent biography of Nevin, *John Williamson Nevin: High Church Calvinist*. This work is significant and deserves particular attention, since Hart is the first scholar in the conservative Presbyterian churches to break from Hodge's dismissal of Nevin, and to pay close attention to his work, and because Hart is one of the most respected conservative church historians of our day.

Despite the merits of each of these three works, they leave the reader with the impression that perhaps Albert Schweitzer's wry assessment of the Quest for the Historical Jesus applies here: each historian sees in

Nevin only his own face reflected back at him. But of course, such is always the temptation in historical study of this kind, a temptation I dare not claim to have entirely avoided.

Hart summarizes previous scholarship on Nevin at the outset of his work rather negatively. Most mentions of Nevin in historical literature, he says, peg Nevin as "an intellectual innovator breaking outside the predictable ranks of Scotch-Irish philosophy and the theological categories of Reformed Scholasticism." Scholars like Nichols, he says, portray Nevin as an open-minded ecumenist influenced by European Romanticism. Hart is unhappy with this picture: "As accurate as interpretations are that stress Nevin's innovative views, they slight his fundamental identity and contribution as a Reformed theologian."[1] For Hart, Nevin was essentially a firm opponent of innovation, not an innovator himself.

This, I believe, is a basically accurate portrait, but the question is what innovation he opposed. Hart portrays Nevin as a "high-church Calvinist," that is, essentially a Reformed Protestant, an heir of the Reformation who held true to the early Reformed emphasis on church and sacrament. Hart thus tends to emphasize Nevin's critique of Protestantism as a critique aimed at recent low-church innovations, rather than a questioning of Protestantism as such.[2] Hart sees much of Nevin's theological vision as no more than an attempt to reclaim and develop the Old School Presbyterian confessionalism of his youth. While no doubt some of this is valuable as a corrective to views of Nevin that lose sight of his Reformed identity and conservative temperament, I am afraid that it leads Hart to distort his account of Nevin's thought somewhat. Nevin's main purpose, according to Hart, was "saving the church for Protestants by recovering the older Reformation sense that church membership was necessary for salvation."[3] This was certainly part of Nevin's agenda, but he was also interested in recovering for Protestantism not simply early Protestantism, but early Christianity, an understanding of the theological emphases that had mattered to the early and medieval Church. Hart is so determined to see in Nevin a return to early Reformed doctrine that, in many of the

---

1. Hart, *John Williamson Nevin*, 33.

2. See, for example, page 59, where he critiques Nichols for conflating Nevin's critique of Puritanism with a critique of Presbyterianism. In Hart's mind, Nevin is seeking to vindicate true, old-school Presbyterianism against Puritan innovations; Nichols, I think, is more correct in seeing a much more sweeping condemnation of the Reformed tradition, at least since the seventeenth century.

3. Ibid., 236.

areas where Nevin is also tapping into medieval or patristic ideas, such as his theology of the ministry, Hart sees nothing but a recovery of the Reformed heritage.[4] This tendency in Hart's analysis manifests itself in what seems a failure to take seriously the roots of Nevin's near-conversion to Catholicism. Hart seems almost to attribute this phase in Nevin's life to a sense of rejection and disillusionment after earlier controversies, and to a period of personal physical and emotional breakdown. While these were no doubt major factors, the fact remains that Nevin's doubts were based on serious study of the early Church and earnest doubts as to the legitimacy of Protestantism. Perhaps more seriously, Hart pays almost no attention to Nevin's ecumenical interest, but portrays him as an earnest partisan of Reformed theology. This neglects one of the most central themes in Nevin's thought and life—a passionate catholicity that sought a way of unifying all the great branches of the faith, not merely the Reformed.

Moreover, it is not evident that Hart has really entered into the mind of Nevin, as he often characterizes aspects of Nevin's thought as oddities or oversights, which were in fact absolutely central to his theological vision. For example, in discussing Nevin's *magnum opus, The Mystical Presence,* Hart calls Nevin's notion of the mystical union with Christ "the hardest part of his argument to decipher,"[5] and later patronizingly grants that it "had a degree of plausibility," and "was not as bizarre as it might at first have sounded."[6] He concludes that "[Nevin's] views in *Mystical Presence* were not clear."[7] While of course they are not *perfectly* clear (what book ever is?), this admission by Hart that he doesn't really understand Nevin's most central exposition of his thought (which has been hailed by many Reformed scholars since as one of the finest ever expositions of Reformed Eucharistic theology) seems problematic.

Later, he offhandedly refers to "Nevin's quirky idea of historical development,"[8] without ever explaining what is so "quirky" about it. Again, given that this notion formed an integral part of Nevin's theological and historical outlook, and had been developed at some length by him and

4. Ibid., 167, 235.

5. Ibid., 120.

6. Ibid., 125.

7. Ibid., 129. These comments all have a striking and amusing resemblance to the comments Hodge made about Schaff's *Principle of Protestantism* (see chapter 2 below).

8. Ibid., 160.

Schaff, Hart's dismissal of it with such an adjective betrays a carelessness to the contours of Nevin's thought. Toward the end of the book, he suggests a criticism of Nevin:

> In an effort to recover the church catholic as a means of grace, he had ignored a central feature of the Reformation, which was to make the word and preaching central in worship. The word could have easily supported Nevin's understanding of the church as a mediator of salvation. But his interest in sacramental teaching and practice bordered on obsession and so obscured the prominence of pulpit over table (not altar) in historic Reformed worship.[9]

Hart here actually suggests that Nevin's emphasis on sacraments, as opposed to the word, represents a sort of irrational aberration, an "obsession" that was unnecessary to accomplish his theological goals. Such a suggestion is rather odd given that, for Nevin, the recovery of robust sacramentology and the centrality of the Eucharist in all of Christian life and worship, were the chief goal and main pillar of his whole ecclesial vision.

A final, somewhat comic, touch is added when Hart, at the very end of his biography, attempts to enlist Nevin under Hart's idiosyncratic banner of the radical spirituality of the Church. Hart dichotomizes between the Church as "mainly a transformer of culture," and as "primarily an agency of grace through word and sacrament,"[10] and then suggests that Nevin stood as a bulwark for the latter: "Nevin's abiding insight [was that] Christianity's primary influence needs to be evaluated not by the church's ability to influence society, but by its performance of sacred rites and recitation of holy words through which the body of Christ grows."[11] It is hard to see how anyone can read articles like Nevin's "Catholicism" and fail to see how passionately he believed that the Church should and would transform every area of culture and human endeavor.

So, while Hart offers an excellent biography of Nevin, and helpfully establishes the Reformed Presbyterian context of his life and work, he fails, I think, to do justice to the depth and catholicity of Nevin's thought. He fails to understand the sacramental center of his thinking, derived from patristic as well as Reformation sources, and he ignores the ecumenical impulse that drove so much of Nevin and Schaff's work.

9. Ibid., 214.
10. Ibid., 237.
11. Ibid., 238.

Richard Wentz's *John Williamson Nevin: American Theologian*, I fear, fails much more conspicuously to capture the spirit of Nevin's theology. Wentz seeks to interpret Nevin as "very much an American theologian, and not merely a romantic misfit unable to find a home in the American intellectual landscape and without resource to become an expatriate"[12] (it is unclear whether this is intended as a critique of Nichols's reading). Central to this portrait is Nevin's embrace of what Wentz calls "the public character of theology," though it is not always quite clear what Wentz means by this. Wentz sees Nevin's theology as peculiarly shaped by his American context—by American anti-intellectualism, the uniquely democratic nature of American society, the individualistic sect mentality, ethnic diversity, and the "tension between the claims of past and present, history and immediacy, tradition and subjectivity, universality and particularity."[13] While this perspective offers some valuable insights, it has the result that the exposition of Nevin's thought is organized not so much according to the spirit and chief interests of Nevin's theology, but according to the spirit and chief interests of Wentz and what he considers to be the *ethos* of American theology. Part of the problem here, as with Hart, but much more seriously, is a failure by the author to really enter into the mind of the man whom he is explaining. Wentz is clearly a theological liberal, and, instead of admitting his differences with Nevin and then doing his best to explain Nevin on Nevin's own terms, he persists in a rather unsuccessful and patronizing attempt to make Nevin a forerunner of the liberal agenda, along the way ignoring critical distinctions and commitments that Nevin was at pains to make.

It is oftentimes revealing when an author claims to know the man he is expounding better than the man knows himself, repeatedly saying something like, "he doesn't seem to quite realize it himself, but what he must really be trying to say is . . ." Of course, this is certainly not always illegitimate (indeed, it is sometimes an important part of good historical work, and I do something like this myself a couple times in this book), but it does make one suspicious.

For example, Wentz says,

> Perhaps he failed to understand sufficiently that there may be a sense in which not just Christ and the *believer* are one, but that the *world* has its life from Christ. Perhaps Nevin's thought was

12. Wentz, *John Williamson Nevin*, 8.
13. Ibid., 7.

still too much controlled by Reformation paradigms, too religiously concentrated on what are called believers and belief. The significance of Christianity may well be found in its philosophy of history, not in a salvationism that nourishes believers.[14]

Along similar lines, he sees in Nevin's concept of the mystical union exactly what Nevin was at pains to deny—that is, a dissolving of the individual into the general life of Christ in some pantheistic sense. Wentz goes so far to say, "Nevin's theology here reveals a sophistication quite beyond its time. Although he would not have understood it so, there is a sense in which it offers to dialogue with a Buddhism that insists on the necessity of transcending the experience of ordinary, particular selfhood."[15] Later, he quotes a passage from Nevin on the mystical union and boldly rephrases it as a mystical union between Christ and humanity (instead of between Christ and the believer, in Nevin's original quote). He admits patronizingly, "Unfortunately, this reconstruction of theology is not always clear to Nevin himself, at least as I read him. Yet I would maintain that it is consistent with the heart and systematic direction of his thought."[16]

A couple of chapters later, he suggests that Nevin's view of catholicity (which for him was thoroughly centered on the orthodox confessional Church), if understood properly, taught the participation of all religions in the new creation. "Nevin's thought has creative implications for the relationship of Christianity to other religions. Here again, however, he is unable to accept those implications because Western history was not yet willing to release many thinkers from the imperialistic and exclusionary claims of culture and religion."[17] And after surveying Nevin's theology of history, he says, "As some twentieth-century thinkers, such as Teilhard de Chardin and Paul Tillich, have shown, the understanding of Christ as center does not require a commitment to Christianity as superior religion. . . . Somehow, I find this not out of harmony with the spirit of John Nevin's theology of history."[18]

It is not, of course, impossible for a liberal, or anyone with a radically different agenda from Nevin, to read him sympathetically and offer

14. Ibid., 25.
15. Ibid., 40.
16. Ibid., 43.
17. Ibid., 74.
18. Ibid., 96–97.

an accurate exposition of his theology, but a certain amount of honesty and realistic differentiation is necessary. But Wentz's approach, in which he suggests that if Nevin had really known what he was saying, he would have shined forth as one of the finest proponents of liberalism and universalism, results in a sad distortion of the historical Nevin. Though aspects of his thought are brought out admirably by Dr. Wentz, the reader is left to wonder whether he is hearing Nevin's views or Wentz's, and does not ever get a satisfactory portrait of John Nevin's life and theological vision.

James Hastings Nichols's portrait of the Mercersburg Theology,[19] which I have saved for last though it came first, is thoroughly admirable. Although Hart (and perhaps Wentz) suggests that Nichols sees Nevin too much as a German romantic and a theological innovator (as we might infer from the title), this critique misses the thorough and nuanced portrayal that Nichols gives of the development of Nevin and Schaff's thought. He is keen to show their intellectual development and the sources upon which they drew for each focus of their theology. In particular, he does not treat Nevin's theology as a static whole, but as a constantly evolving and growing struggle with particular problems, especially the nature of Protestantism. He writes as a true historian, maintaining a careful distance between himself and the object of his study, so as to offer a careful and objective portrait. Moreover, he has an impressive mastery of the worldwide theological milieu of the nineteenth century, so that he can plot Mercersburg with remarkable precision on the map of global theology. Nor do I think that Nichols depicts Nevin as unduly influenced by German romanticism and idealism; rather, he links him to other leaders of the mid nineteenth-century high-church revival in Germany, Denmark, and England, and examines his ideas primarily in that context.

However, there is at least one area where Hart has a fair complaint, one which I second. Though perhaps not so liberal as Wentz, Nichols comes from a broader tradition and is thus very critical of the narrow sectarian orthodoxy of Nevin's opponents. Moreover, armed with a twentieth-century knowledge of church history, he is quick to belittle their striking ignorance in this area. There is, of course, nothing wrong with this *per se*; they certainly deserved such criticism. But in his zeal to depict Nevin and Schaff as open-minded men ahead of their time, breaking free

19. Nichols, *Romanticism in American Theology.*

from the prejudices of their contemporaries, he is quick to write off men like Hodge and the heritage he represented as ignorant and backward, without seriously interacting with their tradition. If Wentz and Hart are weak in really entering into the mind of Nevin, Nichols is perhaps a bit weak in really entering into the mind of Nevin's opponents. Even if his critiques and dismissals are strictly accurate, they are not likely to win a sympathetic hearing for Nichols (or for Mercersburg) among Reformed Christians. To really understand Mercersburg, it is necessary to really understand Princeton, what they stood for, and why Nevin's language rang so false in their ears.

Having surveyed the strengths and weaknesses of these three past discussions of Mercersburg, perhaps I should now clarify the purpose of this present work and how, hopefully, it fills a bit of a gap in the existing literature. In this study, I hope to do justice both to the Reformed center of Nevin and Schaff's thought as well as to the full catholicity of Nevin and Schaff's thought. This latter I mean in two senses: first, catholicity in the sense (or similar to the sense) of ecumenism—a passionate desire that all believers may be truly one, one in spirit and one in visible union; second, catholicity in the sense of an embrace of what I am calling the "catholic heritage," that is, the sense of motherhood of the Church, the mysterious power of the sacraments and the liturgy, the divine authority of the ministry, and the rest of the spiritual worldview that character-ized the first five and even the first fifteen centuries of the Church. It is important, therefore, to see that Nevin's ambitions to recover a truly Reformed heritage were accompanied (at least as his thought matured) by a desire to root that heritage in older, broader catholic traditions, and if necessary, reshape the heritage accordingly.

In line with Hart's goal, I shall analyze the Mercersburg Theology as a recovery of the Reformed tradition in dialogue with Princeton's al-ternative version of Reformed theology. In doing this, I hope to remedy a weakness of Nichols's otherwise excellent study. In chapter 2 I will use the interaction between Mercersburg and Princeton on two particular issues as case studies to illuminate their differences, and in chapter 3, I will outline their opposing paradigms more fully. It is not my purpose to offer an extended historical vindication of Mercersburg as the truer heir of the Reformation, though I will suggest that in many ways it was. In particular, I suggest that Mercersburg's recovery of the centrality of the visible Church, more than Princeton's rigorous dichotomy between the true invisible Church and the dubious visible Church, represents a more faithful heritage of the Reformation. As such, Nevin's theology can be very instructive to the Reformed Church today, which is currently undergoing a severe identity crisis, particularly when it comes to these same issues of church, sacraments, and history.

Having rooted the Mercersburg Theology in its historical and Reformed context in the first three chapters, I will allow it to branch out and bear fruit in dialogue with other traditions in the next three. Chapters 4 through 6 shall be in line with Wentz's goal, as I seek to show the ecumenical power of the Mercersburg Theology. By recovering a sense of the catholic heritage of the Church, Nevin's theology offers, I think, an excellent bridgehead for ecumenical dialogue with the Anglican, Catholic, and Orthodox traditions. Unlike Wentz, however, I believe this can be emphasized without giving up Nevin's core identity as a Reformed Protestant theologian—you can't build bridges unless you have some firm ground to start from. In this, I believe, lies much of the enduring value of the Mercersburg Theology: perhaps more than any other movement in Reformed history, it sought to bring Reformed theology out of its self-imposed isolation to listen to the broader Church (especially in its more Catholic manifestations), and, indeed, to speak to the broader Church on its own terms.

While I make some attempt to trace some of the philosophical influences upon the Mercersburg Theology, my main purpose, unlike Nichols, is not to trace the development of different aspects of Nevin and Schaff's theology, but to present it as a coherent whole. This is not, of course, to deny the value and validity of most of Nichols's analysis, nor to obscure the fact that very rarely does a good, creative theologian maintain a single, static position that dictates his stance on every issue. It is quite true that Nevin's thought evolved (and not always in a single direction), and to trace this evolution is very valuable. However, it is also true that among these changes, we may discern consistent themes and emphases, and also a halting progress towards a mature synthesis, and that it is also very valuable to uncover this underlying vision and framework. It is my goal in this book, especially in chapter 3, to present such a static underlying framework, and in chapters 4–6, to survey the Mercersburg perspective on various theological *loci* without particular attention to the development of their articulations of these doctrines. Again, I do not in any way deny the existence of shifts and developments within this model I am calling "the Mercersburg Theology," but I will leave most of them to the side in my discussion, lest we lose the forest for the trees. Also, I should perhaps mention another oddity of my method in this book (though the same phenomenon appears in the other books on Mercersburg): while "the Mercersburg Theology" technically includes both Schaff and Nevin (as well as a few lesser figures), I shall much more often simply focus on Nevin's thought, and indeed sometimes use "Nevin" and "Mercersburg" interchangeably. This is simply because, despite Schaff's valuable contribution, Nevin was undoubtedly the theological leader at Mercersburg, he wrote more in developing the theology during this period, and it was his work that generated the most controversy and offered the most trenchant critiques of the Reformed churches. Perhaps I should have simply followed Hart and Wentz in self-consciously focusing on Nevin alone, but Schaff's contribution to the discussion at certain points is indispensable, and so I have included him in places throughout the book.

Nevin and Schaff, I believe, offer a unique contribution for Protestants today, especially Reformed Protestants. Their sparring with Hodge, as well as other vehement opponents in the Reformed churches, was a war over who the true heirs of the Reformation were: the last rear-guard of those who held to a sacramental and churchly system of religion, or the individualist sons of the Enlightenment. Reformed Christians will benefit from hearing their attempt to recover Reformational thinking, and may be surprised how far their own "Reformed" tradition has strayed from it. But Mercersburg's legacy is not simply to establish a proper Reformed theology, but a truly catholic theology. The Reformers, they realized, were not infallible; indeed, they had sometimes thrown the baby out with the bathwater. The Mercersburg Theology represents an attempt, even if one that was hesitant, evolving, and in the end ambiguous, to tap into the riches of historic catholic tradition without surrendering the crucial claims and protests of the Reformation. As such, it is deeply relevant to a Protestant church that is, in many ways at least, attempting to blindly stumble back toward an older understanding of the Church, and to Catholic and Orthodox churches that are now looking on their Protestant brothers with new sympathy and yearning for reunion. In this book, I hope to allow Nevin and his fierce love for Mother Church to speak to a new generation, a generation in dire need of his urgent warnings and burning questions.

CHAPTER 1

Situating the Mercersburg Theology

Nevin's Early Life

JOHN WILLIAMSON NEVIN WAS born on February 20, 1803, in rural Pennsylvania, to a family of traditional Scotch-Irish Presbyterians.[1] As a child, he quickly imbibed the churchly, Calvinistic faith of Middle Spring Presbyterian Church, only to find his faith challenged upon entering Union College, a Puritan institution in upstate New York. There he encountered the revival preaching of Asahel Nettleton, one of the great conservative leaders of the Second Great Awakening. While strongly opposed to the extreme revivalism of fanatics like Charles Finney, Nettleton and his insistence on the necessity of a personal conversion experience threw Nevin into doubt and confusion over the validity of his childhood faith. He later recounted the experience:

> I, along with others, came into their hands in anxious meetings, and underwent the torture of their mechanical counsel and talk. One after another, however, the anxious obtained "hope"; each new case, as it were, stimulating another; and finally, among the last, I struggled into something of the sort myself, a feeble trembling sense of comfort—which my spiritual advisers, then, had no difficulty in accepting as all that the case required. In this way

1. Hart's biography is easily the best resource for understanding Nevin's early life and pre-Mercersburg career, though Nichols's *Romanticism in American Theology* also has some helpful chapters.

I was converted, and brought into the Church—as if I had been altogether out of it before—about the close of the seventeenth year of my age.[2]

In 1821 Nevin graduated with honors from Union College and returned home. Two years later, he determined to renew his preparation for the ministry by attending the young but thriving Princeton Seminary, where he came under the tutelage of his future nemesis, Charles Hodge. Hodge had been born in 1797, and like Nevin, had been raised in the Presbyterian faith. Also like Nevin, he encountered challenges to his faith while at the College of New Jersey, in the form of Archibald Alexander's preaching. However, Hodge saw no contradiction between this newer, more experiential faith and his Presbyterian heritage, and he thrived under Alexander's preaching. After graduating, Hodge attended Alexander's seminary in Princeton as well, and then joined him on the faculty there in 1822.

Despite continuing spiritual confusion, Nevin excelled as a student and soon earned Hodge's approbation and friendship. Indeed, when Hodge left to study in Germany from 1826–28, Nevin was appointed to fill his teaching position.[3] Following Hodge's return, Nevin took up a post as professor at Western Theological Seminary in Pittsburgh, where, though a prominent local religious leader, he had little involvement in denominational politics or theological disputes.

During these ten years the stresses of revivalism began to take their toll on the Presbyterian Church. Finney's "New Measures" and the questionable New England theology they represented were loudly decried by

2. John Williamson Nevin, *My Own Life*, 9–10, quoted in Hart (45). Hart also records Nevin's eloquent and significant lament, "Alas, where was my mother, the Church, at the very time I most needed her fostering arms? Where was she, I mean, with her true sacramental sympathy and care?" (59). Hart summarizes, "Nevin tried to take sustenance from the revivalistic Protestantism that undergirded both the Presbyterian and Congregationalist communions. What he found was a spiritual diet rich in subjective experience but lean on the essentials of historic Christianity" (60).

3. Hart's interesting remark on this is worth quoting in full: "The poignancy of Nevin's tenure at Princeton deserves comment no matter how small. Here was Nevin, who over the course of his life would lose most of Hodge's confidence in him as a reliable theologian, substituting for arguably the most conservative Calvinist in nineteenth-century America. Moreover, here was Hodge, whose major critique of Nevin would be that his former student dabbled too much in doctrines German, going off to Germany to study in the presence of theologians whom Nevin would appropriate much better, even if only studying with them secondhand through their books and articles" (51).

the "Old School" Presbyterians, led by the likes of Charles Hodge, while the "New Schoolers" just as loudly castigated their brethren for their stiff traditionalism and indifference to evangelism. At the General Assembly of 1837, many of Hodge's compatriots (though without the support of Hodge himself) succeeded in ousting hundreds of "New School" churches from the denomination, creating a schism that was to last until 1869.[4] Interestingly, Nevin, though no friend of revivals, was one of only a few members of his presbytery to reject the General Assembly's resolution, objecting to the overly dogmatic and divisive nature of the decision. This difference between Hodge's rigid, dogmatic adherence to orthodoxy and Nevin's vigorously catholic, anti-sectarian attitude was to become very prominent in their later debates.

Ironically, though, it was Nevin who became a member of the small, backwoods denomination, joining the German Reformed Church in 1840 to take up the post of theology professor (and subsequently headmaster) at their seminary in Mercersburg, Pennsylvania, and of the denominational college, Marshall College. It was there that he published his first major work, a short but potent critique of revivalism called *The Anxious Bench* (1843). While many other such works had been written before Nevin's (including some by Hodge and his stalwart Princeton compatriots), *The Anxious Bench* soon gained attention for the piercing insight with which Nevin unmasked the ecclesiological assumptions at the root of revivalism. However, few grasped the full implications of the new paradigm of church and liturgy that Nevin was propounding. That would have to wait until the arrival of his new colleague, Philip Schaff, the following year.

The Controversy Years

Schaff, who was later to gain a name for himself as the greatest church historian of the nineteenth century, was only twenty-five years old when he sailed over from Germany to join Nevin at Mercersburg. However, he had already earned a brilliant reputation among the distinguished theologians under whom he had studied in Germany, and came to America brimming over with zeal and knowledge. His inaugural address, "The Principle of Protestantism," embodied Schaff's strong sense of catholicity and historic continuity, and took fierce aim at the common (then

4. For more on nineteenth-century revivalism and its effect on the Presbyterian Church, see Murray, *Revival and Revivalism* and Marsden, *Evangelical Mind.*

and now) notions that Protestantism was a complete rebellion against Roman Catholicism and that, as it had continued to free itself of remaining Romish superstitions, it had continued to grow into apostolic purity. The address was soon translated into English by Nevin, and created quite a stir within the denomination and without, even catching the attention of Charles Hodge.[5] Between 1844 and 1847, the ranks of the German Reformed Church became increasingly polarized, with those more favorable to the New Measures rallying behind the critiques of minister Joseph H. Berg , while others supported Nevin and Schaff's ecclesiological vision, which soon came to be known as the "Mercersburg Theology."

Several more publications by Nevin and Schaff culminated in Nevin's *magnum opus*, *The Mystical Presence* (1846), a historical vindication of the Reformed or Calvinistic doctrine of the Lord's Supper, and of the entire Christocentric, ecclesiocentric view of religion which that tradition embodied. The book eventually drew the criticism of Charles Hodge, who published a 50-page response in *The Princeton Review* in 1848. In his article, Hodge questioned Nevin's orthodoxy and his loyalty to Reformed Protestantism, and attempted to marshal his own historical arguments for a very different view of the Reformed eucharistic doctrine. Nevin and Schaff responded by creating the *Mercersburg Review* in 1849, from which Nevin and his colleagues launched stinging attacks on sectarianism and the low ecclesiology of the Princetonians and other opponents. When Nevin published his 128-page rebuttal of Hodge's view of the Eucharist, Hodge never directly responded, probably because there was very little response he could offer. Most scholars have concluded that, whatever the virtues of Nevin's theology, he manhandled Hodge on the historical question; indeed, many consider his rebuttal of Hodge to be the best historical survey of the doctrine that had yet been published.[6]

Hodge's disengagement from this debate certainly did not mean the end of controversy for Nevin. The pages of the *Princeton Review* saw several more anti-Mercersburg articles over the next few years, including a piece by Hodge entitled "What is Christianity?" where he sought to cast Nevin as a heretical disciple of Schleiermacher. Even twenty years later, Hodge did not miss the opportunity to take some potshots at Nevin from the pages of his *Systematic Theology*. But Nevin's fiercest opponents were closer to home. Though he had gained a number of allies in the

---

5. See chapter 2.

6. Cf. Mathison, *Given For You*, 155.

seminary and throughout the German Reformed Church as he developed more fully his incarnational and sacramental system of theology in the early issues of the *Mercersburg Review*, he soon ventured onto even more controversial ground. As Nevin embarked on a thorough study of the early Church Fathers (the fruits of which appeared as three articles on "Early Christianity" in 1851 and four on "Cyprian" in 1852), and called more of the Protestant heritage into question, many opponents felt vindicated in their early warnings against Mercersburg's "Romanizing." Joseph Berg grew more and more shrill in his attacks, finally resigning his pastorate in the German Reformed Church with a rhetorical flourish in March 1852. The Dutch Reformed Church, a sister denomination to the German Reformed, cut their ties with the denomination when it failed to repudiate Nevin's teachings, while publications like the *Lutheran Observer* and the *Puritan Recorder* loudly sounded their alarms. Indeed, considering the very controversial tenor of these articles (though Schaff himself confessed them historically above reproach), Nevin was lucky to find as many allies as he did. His powerful personality and tremendous labors for the denomination and the seminary had won him many disciples among students, ministers, and fellow faculty, and even when they did not share his doubts or conclusions, most stood behind him.[7]

And indeed, at this time, his doubts were mounting rapidly. Stung and disillusioned by Hodge's attacks and disgusted with the vapidity of American Protestantism, Nevin began to wonder if he really could maintain his theological views as the true heritage of the Reformation. His study of the early Church, which he hoped would reassure him, prompted deeper doubts, as he found little hint of Protestant theology in the writings of those first few centuries. Indeed, he was forced to conclude that the theology of the Fathers was much closer to Catholicism than to any form of Protestantism. The Reformation could still be justified on the theory of historical development, but what guarantee was there that it was a legitimate advance and not a mere rebellious innovation? These doubts, coupled with ill health and family bereavement, drove Nevin into near-retirement by early 1853, as he resigned from his posts at Marshall College, Mercersburg Seminary, and the *Mercersburg Review*. In the end, though, despite personal urgings from Roman Catholic leaders such as

---

7. For an excellent analysis of this tumultuous period of the Mercersburg Theology, chapter 8 of Nichols's *Romanticism* is an excellent guide.

Orestes Brownson, he chose to remain Protestant and began to resume active service in his denomination by the end of 1854.

However, the heyday of the Mercersburg Theology and the debate it generated was over. While he eventually went on to write more articles and even a new liturgy for the German Reformed Church (1867), and in 1866 became president of the recently merged Franklin and Marshall College, his most creative work was done, and he shied away from taking center stage. The sole exception, a heated debate over the new liturgy which broke out in 1867, saw him back to his polemical brilliance once again, this time in debate with the famed German theologian Isaak Dorner. However, this was short-lived and the rest of his days as a teacher, writer, and denominational leader were remarkably uneventful. In 1863, Schaff moved on to a brilliant career at Union Theological Seminary in New York, and never returned to Mercersburg. Though he gained great fame as a church historian and stood by many of his early teachings, he rarely emphasized Mercersburg distinctives and few of his later admirers remembered his early career. By 1870, it was clear that the Mercersburg Theology would never gain much influence outside of the German Reformed Church. Even there its influence rapidly declined soon after Nevin's death, and the denomination eventually became part of the liberal United Churches of Christ.

Hodge, meanwhile, continued to enjoy a brilliant career at Princeton Seminary, and, by his death in 1873, after a fifty-one-year tenure at the seminary, reigned supreme as the guardian of Reformed orthodoxy in America. His low sacramentology and ecclesiology had triumphed over Nevin's by sheer weight of numbers and reputation, and his harsh critiques ensured that few of his Presbyterian compatriots would take Nevin seriously as an orthodox Protestant theologian for the remainder of that century and the next.

Before embarking on a detailed study of what Nevin and Schaff taught, and what their opponents thought, we must first have some idea of the historical and intellectual milieu they were working in, and of the problems which they were trying to confront. So in the following section I will attempt to paint, in broad, hopelessly oversimplified brushstrokes, a mosaic of the theological, philosophical, and historical landscape preceding the theological firefight of 1840s Mercersburg.[8]

8. Much of the following will be based on the excellent background sketch in Evans, "Imputation and Impartation." For more on the philosophical background, Linden DeBie's recent work, *Speculative Theology and Common-Sense Religion* is a thorough study.

Setting the Scene

As the dust settled in the aftermath of the Reformation and the Wars of Religion, a host of new intellectual and religious movements began to take shape in the nations of northern Europe. In the mid-1600s, Turretin in France and the Westminster divines in England sought to systematize their scholastic versions of Calvin's teachings, while men such as René Descartes (1596–1650) were busy fashioning their own systems of thought, on quite different premises. Descartes's rationalism, doubt, and dualism sparked an intellectual tradition that was to revolutionize the Western mind. Faced with the breakdown of the medieval synthesis of philosophy and theology, Descartes began with the one certitude—the contents of his own mind—and built his system accordingly. In the process, he introduced a radical dualism between mind and body, severing the realm of experience from the realm of spirit and intellect. The question of how to relate mind and matter, thought and experience, vexed Western philosophy as never before, and spawned a wide array of attempted answers in the following century.

The dualist answer, some feared, put too great a chasm between natural and supernatural, allowing the world of matter to function autonomously apart from God. George Berkeley (1685–1753) and with him American theologian Jonathan Edwards (1703–1758) proposed a radical solution: there was no matter as such—there was only spirit, the realm of ideas. God creates all ideas, which He conveys directly to us and thereby enables us to experience the "world," such as it is. This approach destroyed the problem of dualism, to be sure, since there was only one kind of substance—spiritual—but it merely exacerbated the product of dualism, namely, the tendency to undervalue the material world. It also erased the wall between natural and supernatural, since God's direct action was needed for any human knowledge or action.

Meanwhile, Reformed theologians were struggling with a related nexus of issues. God's grace comes to man in human vessels, our faith teaches—or does it? As questions of covenant and election, union with Christ and the means of grace, continued to evolve, theologians struggled with how to reconcile the role of God's invisible, spiritual grace with the material means and agents which conveyed that grace to believers. In a similar vein, systematic theologies were vexed with the relationship between natural and supernatural. Are natural elements such as those in the sacraments mysteriously imbued with the supernatural, or are they merely an occasion for the operation of our natural spiritual faculties? The growing Pietist movements at this time, perhaps influenced by the trends of Cartesian dualism (or perhaps itself influencing them, or more likely, both), increasingly saw a rift between spirit and flesh, to the detriment of the latter, and emphasized subjective inward piety rather than traditional visible exercises of religion.

All of these issues were background to the Mercersburg controversy in one way or another. Central to Nevin's critique of Hodge were the problems created by dualism, both of soul and body and of natural and supernatural; likewise, Hodge fiercely criticized Nevin for what he saw as an overly integralist approach which broke down all these distinctions. Nevin and Schaff, moreover, were to mount a significant critique of modern Protestantism which revealed the close connections between the rationalist impulse and the pietist impulse.

These two impulses developed side by side throughout the momentous eighteenth century, which saw such diverse but related events as the Great Awakening, Immanuel Kant's "Copernican Revolution," and the French Revolution. During this time, Pietism came to full flower in the American colonies, where the loose political organization and separatist religious impulse were conducive to Pietism's emphasis on an individual, rather than corporate, expression of Christianity. This shift came with surprising suddenness, transforming the American religious scene in a decade of revivals known as the Great Awakening (c. 1735–1745). Though moderated by conservative figures such as Jonathan Edwards and Jonathan Dickinson (1688–1747), this movement saw a turn away from reliance on the traditional means of grace for salvation to, instead, an individual conversion experience. Its emphasis on the immediate, subjective encounter of the believer with God set the stage for a more anthropocentric, unchurchly, and unsacramental style of religion.

The colonies were not alone in their struggle with Pietism; indeed, in the Old World, the movement was bearing, if anything, more sinister fruits. In Europe the established ecclesiastical structures and traditions were too strong to give way to full-blown individualism. Nevertheless, the subjective, naturalistic emphases of Pietism suggested that the essentials of Christianity lay in moral uprightness, and many of the traditional trappings of Christianity could be safely dispensed with. This move can be clearly seen in the central figures of the Enlightenment such as David Hume and Immanuel Kant, who denied the value of the Church and most of the central doctrines of Christianity but still valued its moral teaching. The trend toward subjectivism and opposition to tradition manifested themselves most vividly in Hume's radical skepticism, whereby he denied our ability to have real knowledge of apparently obvious processes in the external world. This dramatic move spawned two great reactions in European philosophy.

The first was a movement known as "Common Sense Realism," propounded by Hume's fellow Scotsman Thomas Reid (1710–96). Reid argued that there was no need to posit the existence of intermediate "ideas" which are the objects of our knowledge, as Locke, Berkeley, and Hume had; rather, the mind "apprehends reality directly and unmediated."[9] The reliability of this knowledge is insured by the "common sense" which all men share, which arises "from the constitution of the human mind itself."[10] Reid's ideas quickly spread to America via the influence of John Witherspoon, an early president of Princeton College, and his followers at the College and later at the Seminary embraced this methodology wholeheartedly.

Of crucial importance for theology was Common Sense Realism's thoroughly dualistic outlook. These thinkers adhered to the Cartesian mind/matter dualism, as well as a number of other dualisms implied in this: "subject and object, body and soul, flesh and spirit, finite and infinite, natural and supernatural, creator and creation, cognitive faith and religious experience."[11] This emphasis on discontinuity rather than continuity related also to another facet of Common Sense Realism's epistemology, that is, particularity. According to this epistemology, knowledge was first and foremost of a truth in its particularity, and general principles were then inductively derived from empirically known particularities. For Hodge and others Common Sense Realists at Princeton Seminary, this led to a very scientific approach to theology, perhaps best illustrated by Hodge's statement in the introduction to his *Systematic Theology*:

> If natural science be concerned with the facts and laws of nature, theology is concerned with the facts and principles of the Bible. If the object of the one be to arrange and systematize the facts of the external world, and to ascertain the laws by which they are determined; the object of the other is to systematize the facts of

9. Evans, "Imputation and Impartation," 157.

10. Ibid.

11. Ibid., 160.

> the Bible, and ascertain the principles or general truths which those facts involve.[12]

The effects of this emphasis on "common sense," a dualistic view of the world, and the particularity of knowledge will become readily apparent as we see Hodge's responses to the Mercersburg theologians.

Meanwhile, in Germany, Immanuel Kant (1724–1804) articulated another response to Hume, which was called "transcendental idealism." In it, he famously distinguished between the *noumenal*, or the realm of real things, and the *phenomenal*, the realm of things as we know them. It is the subjectivity of the mind that is responsible for determining the way things are in our experience; the actual essence of things is unattainable by the finite. In this "Copernican Revolution" of philosophy, in which the whole world was subjected to the consciousness of the individual, Kant sought to uphold the cornerstone of his philosophy, *individual* human autonomy. It is worth noting what a short step this was from his pietistic upbringing, where *individual* access to God was stressed above all. But it was here that the child came of age and devoured its mother, for in Kant's philosophy, the entire project of traditional Christian theology was radically undermined. Theology is committed to finding out the essence of things, particularly of transcendent entities, and in Kant's philosophy, this was no longer possible or even desirable. Kant's successors in Germany sought new ways of addressing this problem.

Friedrich D. E. Schleiermacher (1768–1834), accepted the Kantian emphasis on subjectivity, and sought to move the discussion "beyond the Kantian noumenal-phenomenal and metaphysical-moral dualisms by finding a level antecedent to cognition and morality—feeling (*Gefühl*)—where God is immediately present to pretheoretical human consciousness."[13] Hegel and Schelling, meanwhile, forged a philosophical system which viewed all of finite reality as the self-realization of the Absolute Reason throughout history. In this system, as Evans describes, "Traditional epistemological distinctions—subject and object, *a priori* and *a posteriori*—are transcended, as is the absoluteness of metaphysical distinctions such as the finite and the infinite, matter and spirit, natural and supernatural, etc."[14] Such an approach overturned the traditional Christian divide between God and the world, and returned to a sort of

12. Hodge, *Systematic Theology*, I.18.
13. Evans, "Imputation and Impartation," 167.
14. Ibid., 168.

Neo-Platonic view of the world as an emanation from God. It likewise spawned a new era in historical studies in Germany. Inspired by the Hegelian concept of dialectic, German historians began to characterize history as a process of organic development, the progressive unfolding of the Absolute. As we will see, the German idealist emphases on the presence of God within the world, and the developmental character of truth throughout history, gave the Mercersburg Theology a distinctive color which brought it into conflict with the much more static, black-and-white theology of Common Sense Realism and Princeton Seminary.

However, despite the wide differences between the prevailing philosophy of Scotland and that of Germany, both tended to deemphasize the supernatural in favor of the natural, and at least until Hegel, the communal in favor of the individual. These emphases were paralleled by the products of Pietism taking root in America.

As hinted at above, after the death of Jonathan Edwards, leader of New England Congregationalism and president of the Presbyterian College of New Jersey, some disturbing trends began to gain momentum in American theology. This is first particularly seen in the New England successors of Edwards such as Samuel Hopkins (1721–1803) and Joseph Bellamy (1719–90), who tended to rework his theology in a more anthropocentric and moralistic direction. This so-called "New Divinity," catering to the new prevalence of revivalism on the one hand and rationalism on the other, robbed fundamentals of Reformed theology such as the atonement and the sacraments of their objective force and turned them into merely subjective moral phenomena. For Hopkins, union with Christ itself merely "consists in the actual agreement of the heart with Christ, and suiting and adapting itself to him and redemption by him."[15] Naturally, Hopkins thus also transforms the Church into a mere voluntary society of believers, and exalts the role of private judgment in religion.[16] In this rationalistic, unchurchly theology of the New Divinity, one can recognize the objects of some of Nevin's most ferocious later criticism.

Nor was this the worst of it. The next generation of New England theologians, led by Nathaniel William Taylor of Yale, pushed theology in an even more subjective and anthropocentric direction, making the attainment of salvation entirely into a matter of the will, and thus robbing it

15. Hopkins, *System of Doctrines*, II.40, quoted in Evans, "Imputation and Impartation," 245.

16. Evans, "Imputation and Impartation," 249.

of any supernatural character. This theology was popularized and applied by the radical revivalist Charles Finney in the 1820s and '30s, dissolving the whole complex process of justification, sanctification, spiritual nourishment by the means of grace, etc., into a one-time ecstatic conversion experience. Finney, a preacher in the somewhat more conservative Presbyterian Church, soon created enormous controversy in that denomination, leading to the schism of 1837, when a large body of its churches were expelled and went on to form the New School Presbyterians.

Princeton Seminary and leaders like Charles Hodge had been leaders in the opposition to Finney, considering the revivals of the Second Great Awakening as dangerous innovations. Princeton saw itself as the leading conservative force in American Presbyterianism, standing for tradition and the Reformation, wielding as its chief weapon the sword of systematic theology, fortified by the armor of Common Sense Realism. It was theirs to hold the fort against the tide of revivalism sweeping the nation's churches and the ripples of apostasy emanating from New England. So it is not hard to imagine their surprise and consternation when a couple of upstart theologians from a backwoods seminary duly informed them that they were actually part of the enemy. While rejecting radical revivalism, they still maintained the basic pietistic/rationalistic principles of dualism, subjective individualism, and the preeminence of the particular over the corporate. These unbiblical principles, contended Nevin and Schaff, had to be purged from the diseased ranks of Protestantism if the Church was to survive. The ensuing battle was fierce and in many ways still hangs in the balance. It is to an exploration of the contended doctrines that we now turn.

CHAPTER 2

Hodge Offers His Two Cents
Two Case Studies

A S MENTIONED IN THE Introduction, I believe it is crucial to understand Nevin and Schaff in their Reformed context. Of course,
their fellow Reformed often had little use for their theology, but this
was not so much due to Mercersburg's abandonment of the Reformed
heritage, but to their stubborn refusal to leave it behind and join the rest
of their American contemporaries in desacramentalized, individualistic
Christianity. In the course of the conflicts over the Mercersburg Theology,
it became clear that a chasm had opened between Mercersburg's vision of
what it meant to be Reformed and Princeton Seminary's vision.

Two crucial reviews by Charles Hodge shed light on the nature
of this chasm, one written in 1845 in response to Schaff's *Principle of
Protestantism*, one in 1848 in response to Nevin's *Mystical Presence*. These
two essays pose an interesting contrast to one another because of their
radically different tones. In the first, a confident and unconcerned Hodge
expresses general approbation for the young Schaff's work, while offering
some patronizing suggestions on how he could improve and clarify some
of his statements (apparently failing to perceive that a fundamentally
different theological worldview was at work). In the second, the tone is
completely transformed (except, perhaps, for the occasionally patronizing air); now we see a theological guru sternly setting the record straight
in response to the dangerous babblings of a wayward student. This second

essay, unsurprisingly, has received a fair amount of historical attention (though still not a great deal); the first, very little. In this chapter, I shall briefly examine both of these reviews (and the books which provoked them), and use them to throw into sharp relief some of the key points of difference between the two theological visions they represent.

Schaff delivered his inaugural address, "The Principle of Protestantism," shortly after his arrival in America, before the Synod of the German Reformed Church, upon whom it made a strong impression.[1] Schaff's message differed sharply from that of Joseph Berg. Earlier during the synod, Berg had preached a sermon on the history of the denomination, which he saw not as the offspring of the Catholic Church, but of the various sectarian movements of the Middle Ages. Indeed, Berg sought to free the history of the German Reformed Church from any defiling link to the Catholic Church that for hundreds of years served as the visible representative of the Body of Christ on earth.[2]

As we will see, Berg's account stood in almost polar opposition to Schaff's view of Church history, and it is no wonder that conflict soon developed between the two, eventually leading Berg to leave the denomination. Schaff's address was promptly published the following year in German, and shortly thereafter in an English translation by Nevin. Later that year the book prompted an ecclesiastical examination into Schaff's orthodoxy, but he was vindicated by a vote of 40 to 3.[3] Meanwhile, the book reached the attention of Charles Hodge at Princeton Seminary, who soon reviewed it in *The Biblical Repertory and Princeton Review*. This review provides some fascinating insights into Hodge's theological outlook and the reasons for his opposition to Mercersburg. The question that emerges as the key point of contention is: what is the nature of the Church? Particularly, the old debate about visible vs. invisible church seems to loom over this whole discussion. Schaff, apparently seeing the two as closely intertwined, never raises the distinction, but uses the term "church" interchangeably for both. Hodge, for whom the distinction is far more important, is puzzled by Schaff's ambiguity, and says as much. His inability to come to grips with Schaff's less dualistic approach provides us with some key insights about his theological outlook, and foreshadows the future development of the controversy.

1. Schaff, *Principle of Protestantism*, 7.
2. Ibid., 7–13.
3. Ibid., 16.

Schaff's Argument in The Principle of Protestantism

In *The Principle of Protestantism*, Schaff contends above all for a unified view of Church history. After all, if the Church is one, then its history should be one history. Furthermore, since this unity is a visible unity, Schaff thought, its unity through history should be a visible, historical phenomenon. In light of the strong anti-Romanist tendencies among American Protestants of his day, Schaff particularly focused on the relationship of the Reformation to the medieval Roman Catholic Church. Was the Reformation an altogether new phenomenon and the churches it founded an altogether new state of affairs, a complete separation from the apostate ecclesiastical body that had gone before? Or was it perhaps a mere restoration of the apostolic Church, an excision of errors and a return to an earlier, proper state of affairs? Both as a theologian and as a historian, Schaff rejected both of these alternatives. He set forth his philosophy of "reformation" in the very first words of the address as follows:

> To be true to its own idea, a *reformation* must hold its course midway, or through the deep rather, between two extremes. In opposition on the one side to *revolution*, or the radical and violent overthrow of an existing system, it must attach itself organically to what is already at hand, and grow forth thus from the trunk of history, in regular living union with its previous development. In opposition to simple *restoration*, on the other side, or a mere repetition of the old, it must produce from the womb of this the birth of something new.[4]

The Protestant Reformation, declares Schaff, was indeed a new development in the history of the Church, but one that grew out of a foundation within the existing Church. To deny this would indeed be an injustice to its greatness, as Schaff says, "No work so vast as the Reformation could be the product of a single man or a single day."[5] Indeed, it was not merely a growth out of the Catholic Church, but its fulfillment:

> [It] carries upon its standard the sacred field motto: "I am not come to destroy, but to fulfill!" And thus neither the unhistorical radical on the one hand, nor the motionless slave of the past on

4. Ibid., 57.
5. Ibid., 59.

the other, can find in the true representatives of the Reformation either precedent or pattern.[6]

Schaff goes on to explore some specific areas in which the Reformation had built on existing movements within the medieval Catholic Church. Among these he lists the movements of the Waldenses, Lollards, and Hussites, the inward piety emphasized by mystical movements like that of à Kempis, the reforming conciliarist movement, and the foreshadowings of the Protestant doctrine of justification found in thinkers like John Wessel. All of these, Schaff argues, bear witness to the fact that the Reformation sprung from tendencies already latent within Catholicism, tendencies that indeed must inexorably boil forth at some point. Were this not so, it would be hard to account for the fact that reforming movements arose almost simultaneously all throughout Europe as Martin Luther began his reformation. A prominent example of this that Schaff points to was the "Oratory of Divine Love" in Italy, the heart of Romanism, where, at the time of the Reformation, many leading men in the Roman Church "had come to the very threshold of the evangelical doctrine of justification."[7] As Schaff puts it, "[Luther] gave utterance to what was already darkly present to the general consciousness of his age."[8]

It is important to be clear again about what Schaff is doing with these examples. Above all, he is not pointing to these movements as hidden, underground bearers of truth in the midst of an apostate age, like Elijah in Baal-worshipping Israel. Indeed, this was Berg's perception of the Middle Ages, which Schaff was so eager to refute. Schaff's Reformation was the natural growth to maturity of the medieval Catholic Church itself, and these various pre-Reformations testify to this organic unity. Key to understanding this is Schaff's idea of historical development. The Church, as a living, Spirit-animated organism, must grow and evolve through history. While this idea has often been abused by liberals, Schaff, as a true historian, emphasized the necessity of continuity with the past. He sees in the secular history of Europe a helpful parallel to its spiritual history: "The papacy is a Christian universal monarchy, erected on the popular spirit of ancient Rome."[9] Just as the Roman Empire, with its authoritarian infrastructure, filled the important role of bringing

6. Ibid., 58.

7. Ibid., 68.

8. Ibid., 59.

9. Ibid., 61.

peace and order to Europe while the barbarians slowly grew civilized, so
the Roman Church brought spiritual peace and order while the people
grew toward greater freedom and maturity. In both, the later stage was
ultimately a higher development, but in both it rested upon the foundation laid by the earlier stage, which was itself necessary and beneficial in
its own age. Schaff considered this concept of historical development to
be essential to a proper understanding of Church history.

In summarizing the relationship between the Reformation and the
Catholic Church, Schaff lays forth the following proposition as "vastly
important and even indispensable for the vindication of Protestantism":

> The Reformation is the legitimate offspring, the greatest act of
> the Catholic Church; and on this account of true catholic nature
> itself, in its genuine conception: whereas the Church of Rome,
> instead of following the divine conduct of history has continued
> to stick in the old law of commandments, the garb of childhood,
> like the Jewish hierarchy in the time of Christ, and thus by its
> fixation as Romanism has parted with the character of catholicity
> in exchange for that of particularity.[10]

Having argued for the connection of Protestantism with the past,
its "retrospective aspect" as he calls it, Schaff proceeds to set forth its
"prospective aspect," or the nature of its historical advance. This takes
place, not as a creative act, in which the Church invents altogether new
doctrines, Schaff is quick to clarify, but as an "apprehension always more
and more profound of the life and doctrine of Christ and his apostles."[11]
This apprehension had taken place most notably in the early ecumenical
councils, when the Church first formulated a clear doctrine of the Trinity
and of the Incarnation. In the case of the Reformation, the development
was not in Trinitarian or Christological theology, but in soteriology.
Thus, the Reformation maintained all the essential creedal statements
of the faith, and moved the Church forward by developing doctrine in
another, relatively unexplored direction. The doctrine of justification by
faith, Schaff emphasizes, was not the sole property of the Reformers, but
had been foreshadowed by earlier Christian thinkers such as Augustine,
Anselm, and Bernard of Clairvaux.[12] However, it fell to the Reformers to
bring this principle to a fuller, clearer scriptural exposition.

10. Ibid., 73–74.
11. Ibid., 76.
12. Ibid., 77.

However, his exposition of this "material principle" of the Reformation does not necessarily align with traditional Protestant versions. Too often, Schaff believed, the Reformation was seen as the triumph of individual conscience over Church authority. According to Schaff, the essence of the Reformation was not the attempt to overthrow papal authority or the Church hierarchy, and was certainly not a proto-Enlightenment crusade for the emancipation of the mind of the individual. "[The Reformers'] object was rather to bind man to the grace of God, and to lead his conscience captive to God's word."[13] Schaff's reinterpretation on this point provided Mercersburg with one of its sharpest weapons against revivalism and sectarianism, which, they charged, were in complete departure from the principles of the Reformation. Though the Reformation did in the end result in a greater freedom of conscience, the condemnation of papal authority was a *secondary* principle of the Reformation, stemming from the failure of the Church authorities to give Luther's message a hearing.

Having made this preliminary distinction, Schaff enters into an extended discussion of the nature of the "material principle," the Protestant doctrine of justification. He summarizes the various facets of the doctrine, and emphasizes repeatedly that the foundation of the doctrine lay in a proper understanding of man's depravity. The Catholic Church, though operating within an Augustinian tradition, had not adequately appreciated the corrupting powers of sin, that man "is unable to produce from himself anything that is good."[14] The doctrine of justification by faith, according to Schaff, throws us back upon the grace of God, rather than the strength of man, for our salvation and spiritual growth.

The same principle applies to the "formal principle," that is, the sufficiency of Scripture. Schaff's understanding of the relationship between the two is striking and insightful and warrants being quoted in full:

> As the doctrine of justification refers back to the doctrine of sin as its necessary presupposition, so does the doctrine of the authority of the Scriptures also to a corresponding view of the relation of the natural reason to revelation. The more favorable the view that is taken of the will of man in its natural state, the less will be the account made of the blindness of the understanding as going hand in hand with sin and the higher the consequence attached to the word of man, as well as to his works, in the business of

13. Ibid., 79.
14. Ibid., 86.

salvation; and so the reverse will hold also in every point. Hence Romanism, as it makes faith and works to be parallel sources of justification, and lays the main stress in fact practically upon the last, is only consistent with itself, when it invests, here also in the sphere of the formal principle, the word of God and human tradition with equal authority as sources of religious knowledge, and gives the second in reality the preference above the first.[15]

So, in articulating the authority of Scripture, the Reformers were protesting against an overvaluation of man's word, rather than God's. The Catholic Church had subjected Scripture to man-made traditions, and claimed infallibility for an institution that, though the divinely authorized bearer of truth, was after all made up of fallen and fallible men. Protestantism insists that "infallibility belongs to Christ and his word alone, and to all else so far only as it may be joined to him in living union."[16] The traditions of the institutional Church are then indeed a source of truth, but a subordinate and fallible source, worthy of respect and often submission but not above criticism. In one respect, however, Schaff allows normative authority to a kind of tradition, that is, the formal dogmatic tradition contained in the creeds and taught throughout the history of the Church. That is because this does not constitute a testimony separate from Scripture, "but the contents of Scripture itself as apprehended and settled by the church against heresies past and always new appearing; not an independent source of revelation, but the one fountain of the written word, only rolling itself forward in the stream of church consciousness."[17]

As we have seen then, Schaff takes a fairly standard approach in his general formulation of the nature of the Reformation, but in the process, subverts in many ways the traditional narrative. The Reformation, he insists, must be understood as an outgrowth of medieval Catholicism, and its protest as one against too much human authority, not too much authority of God's Church. If we become confused about who the actual enemy was, Schaff warns, we are sure to misunderstand the principles at stake. But Schaff's argument does not end here. In Part II of *The Principle of Protestantism*, he applies his understanding of the Reformation to the present day, to see where and how Protestantism has gone wrong.

15. Ibid., 98.
16. Ibid., 104.
17. Ibid., 116.

Consistent with the method he applies to Catholicism, Schaff treats the "diseases of Protestantism," as he calls them, as arising out of the fabric of Protestantism itself, rather than as entirely alien elements. Likewise, their solution will not be a restoration of the sixteenth century or a radical new revolution, but a new reformation growing out of the true Protestant spirit and moving the Church forward into its triumphant future. The critique of rationalism and sectarianism in this section of the book underlies all of Nevin and Schaff's later polemics, and is thus crucial for understanding Mercersburg's decade-long attack on American Protestantism. Schaff's diagnosis of the roots of these two problems is one of the most insightful portions of the work, but will have to be stripped down to a brief summary here.

Though rationalism might seem rather straightforward, Schaff's definition of it points in interesting and instructive directions: "one-sided theoretic subjectivism." Instead of treating rationalism as the direct outgrowth of dry scholasticism, Schaff roots it in the subjective moralistic pietism that developed in the later seventeenth century. Once Christianity was divorced from the objective historical basis of the institutional Church and her sacraments, rationalism became inevitable. As Schaff insightfully describes the shift, "The undervaluation of the church and her symbols led gradually to the undervaluation of the apostles and their writings, and terminated finally in a denial of the divinity of Christ himself."[18] The Pietists began by shifting the emphasis to man subjectively considered and away from Christ and the objective Church; the end result of this, Schaff says, was that "the whole supernatural world is drawn over into the present life as a mere product of the religious fancy without all objective reality, and the infinite Godhead itself must shrink into the finite spirit of man."[19] This is not, as the rationalists claim, the necessary result of Protestantism, which insists adamantly on the distinction between God and man, but a corruption based on an overemphasis of the subjective aspects of Protestantism.

What should this mean for American Protestants? Schaff acknowledges that rationalism in its complete and extreme form was, at that point at least, primarily a European phenomenon. However, the main principle of rationalism, that is, "the general standpoint of a cold, abstract intellection, to which all that is mystical or supernatural in Christianity is

18. Ibid., 131.
19. Ibid., 133.

found displeasing,"[20] was already entrenched in American Protestantism, and the rest was likely to follow soon. Therefore, Protestants should leave off their anti-Romanism for the time being and make common cause against the greater enemy: "Let us first with united strength expel the devil from our own temple, into which he has stolen under the passport of excessive toleration, before we proceed to exorcise and cleanse the dome of St. Peter."[21]

The second disease of Protestantism, sectarianism, is diagnosed by Schaff as the flip side of rationalism, "one-sided practical subjectivism." This one is more dangerous, "because it appears ordinarily in the imposing garb of piety, Satan transformed into an angel of light,"[22] and is the particular curse of the Reformed churches.[23] Sects, Schaff is careful to clarify, were not the product of the Reformation, but of human depravity, and have always existed in the Church; however, the new freedom of the Reformation gave more scope for sects to flourish. "Still they were held back, at the beginning, by the thunder of Luther's voice, and the colossal weight of his person. Calvin too had such a religious horror of heresies and sects that he hewed to pieces without mercy the unprincipled Libertines of Geneva with the sword of his spirit."[24]

Schaff traces the history of American sectarianism to the Puritan movement, with its opposition to established forms and insistence on a purely spiritual Christianity, which of course led to a devaluation of the historical, institutional Church. This, combined with the disestablishmentarianism engendered by the American Revolution, gave the sect spirit freer rein in American Protestantism than it had ever before had, leading to a seemingly endless multiplication of religious bodies. Schaff's invective against this process is too eloquent not to quote in full:

> Where the process of separation is destined to end, no human calculation can foretell. Anyone who has, or fancies that he has, some inward experience and a ready tongue, may persuade himself that he is called to be a reformer; and so proceed at once, in his spiritual vanity and pride, to a revolutionary rupture with the historical life of the church, to which he holds himself

20. Ibid., 137.
21. Ibid.
22. Ibid., 140.
23. Ibid., 141.
24. Ibid., 144.

immeasurably superior. He builds himself of a night accordingly a new chapel, in which now for the first time since the age of the apostles a pure congregation is to be formed; baptizes his follow- ers with his own name, to which he thus secures an immortality, unenviable it is true, but such as is always flattering to the natural heart; rails and screams with full throat against all that refuses to do homage to his standard; and with all this though utterly unprepared to understand a single book, is not ashamed to ap- peal continually to the Scriptures, as having been sealed entirely, or in large part, to the understanding of eighteen centuries, and even to the view of the Reformers themselves, till now at last God has been pleased to kindle the true light in an obscure corner of the New World! Thus the deceived multitude, having no power to discern spirits, is converted not to Christ and his truth, but to the arbitrary fancies and baseless opinions of an individual, who is only of yesterday. Such *conversion* is of a truth only *perversion*; such *theology*, *neology*; such *exposition* of the Bible, wretched *imposition*. What is built is not a church, but a chapel, to whose erection Satan himself has made the most liberal contribution.[25]

Though some may defend this as legitimate and helpful diversity, Schaff laments this spirit of divisiveness as utterly foreign to the teaching of the New Testament. "The sect system, like rationalism," he concludes, "is a prostitution and caricature of true Protestantism, and nothing else."[26] It is this corruption that has allowed the forces of Romanism to gain ground, and so sectarianism, not Romanism, should be the first concern of true Protestants. He ends the section with the stirring call, "Away with human denominations, down with religious sects! Let our watchword be: One spirit and one body! One Shepherd and one flock! All conventicles and chapels must perish, that from their ashes may rise the One Church of God, phoenixlike and resplendent with glory, as a bride adorned for her bridegroom."[27]

The remainder of the work may be summarized very briefly. In chap- ter 4, Schaff addresses the question of Puseyism, or the Oxford Movement. This was a high-church movement in the Anglican Church beginning in the 1830s, which had tremendous influence on the Church of England and caused great concern among many English and American Protestants because it was feared to be on the road to Rome. Many of its teachings

25. Ibid., 149–50.
26. Ibid., 153.
27. Ibid., 155.

bore an uncanny resemblance to those of Mercersburg, and some of this similarity will be discussed in chapter 4. At this time, though, Schaff sought to distance his objectives from those of Oxford. Schaff here does this by characterizing, with some fairness, Puseyism as a mere backward-looking reaction to the diseases of Protestantism, not a forward-looking reformation. In chapter 5, he sets forth a sketch of a proper Protestant understanding of Church history, which shall be explored more later in this book. Finally, chapter 6 comprises a set of 112 "Theses for the Time," echoing perhaps the Oxford Movement's (in)famous *Tracts for the Times.* These pithy declarations summarize everything that is said in the rest of *The Principle of Protestantism,* and are very helpful for gaining a clear synoptic understanding of the Mercersburg Theology.

Schaff, as we have seen, is eager to root the advent of Protestantism in a proper respect for, rather than rebellion against, the institutional Church. By mistaking its true principles and deserting the objective Christ and His Church for subjective experience, Protestantism had fallen into the twin ditches of rationalism and sectarianism. Both diseases shared a common disdain for the institutional Church, its liturgy and its sacraments, and could not be remedied without a return to a more historical, catholic spirit. So much for Schaff's view of Protestantism. Now we will examine Charles Hodge's thought on these issues, as expressed in his fascinating review of *The Principle of Protestantism* that appeared in the 1845 issue of *The Princeton Review.*

Hodge's Response

Unlike his later review of Nevin's *Mystical Presence,* Hodge is basically positive towards Schaff, but the misgivings that he does express betray deep-seated differences that would in time boil over into open controversy. At the outset of his review, Hodge confesses his inability to fully understand what Schaff is getting at, because of his "obscure" and "German" mode of discourse.[28]

Specifically, Hodge professes confusion over Schaff's use of the term "church": "Is it the body of professors? or the body of true believers? or the

28. Hodge, "Schaff's Protestantism," 626. In reality, it often appears that Hodge probably did understand what Schaff was saying, but found it alarming, and was seeking to read it in the most charitable light possible (something which, incidentally, he was rarely to do later with Nevin).

two in inseparable union as one body?"[29] For Hodge, the classic Reformed distinction between the visible and the invisible church is rigid and all-important. However, no such distinction appears in Schaff's *Principle of Protestantism*, where the visible, historical church is assumed to be the true, real Church, and, as shall be examined later, this integration of visible and invisible was central to the whole Mercersburg endeavor. Unless this is understood, Schaff's work does indeed dissolve into confusion, for the invisible church of necessity endured in continuity throughout the Middle Ages, and the visible church undeniably was severed at the Reformation. However, if understood as a more organic union of inward and outward, the Church can indeed be spoken of as enduring in one body throughout history.

Moving on to address Schaff's points specifically, Hodge accepts Schaff's general contention that "the middle ages were no doubt pregnant with the Reformation,"[30] though we might wonder if he really caught the polemic force of what Schaff was trying to say. In reviewing Schaff's exposition of the material and formal principles of Protestantism, Hodge professes agreement with Schaff but sneaks in a rather different viewpoint, though again it is unclear to what extent Hodge realized the difference. It is this section that provides the most instructive and historically fascinating illustration of the fundamental and growing divide between Mercersburg's and Princeton's understanding of the Church. Hodge defines the material principle, justification by faith, as "our continued protest against the error of a mediating church or priesthood."[31] Anyone who has actually read Schaff's exposition is likely to stop short, puzzled, at this point; whether or not this was what the Reformers meant by justification by faith, it certainly does not sound the same as Schaff's definition: that man "is unable to produce anything from himself that is good."[32] Hodge clearly sees in the idea of justification by faith exactly what Schaff emphasized was not in it—a fundamental opposition to the authority of the institutional Church. Hodge goes on to say,

> So long as [the fact that all men have access to Christ by faith]
> is asserted, do we protest against the great error of Rome, that
> men can only come to God through the church, or through the

29. Ibid.

30. Ibid., 627.

31. Ibid.

32. Schaff, *Principle of Protestantism*, 86.

mediation of other men as priests, by whose ministrations alone
the benefits of redemption can be applied to the soul. The reverse
of this is true, and the reverse of this is Protestantism. *We are in
the church because we are in Christ, and not in Christ because we
are in the Church.*[33]

Though it is certainly an oversimplification, it is not altogether inaccurate to characterize this last sentence as the key disagreement between Mercersburg's and Princeton's ecclesiologies, for in later writings, we find Nevin saying exactly the opposite: that we are in Christ because we are in the Church.

Hodge, on the contrary, asserts that the Reformers insisted that the Church did not have "the custody of the blessings of redemption"; on the contrary, "we can and must, each one for himself, lay hold on [Christ] by faith, and we know that whosoever believes on him hath eternal life, though he has never heard of the church, or of a priest, or of the sacraments."[34] Fortunately, Hodge did recognize some of the difference between what he and Schaff were saying about justification by faith, though he tried to be charitable. Schaff had "failed to render prominent" the aspect of justification that Hodge had described, and Nevin, he said, had apparently denied it,[35] though, he was quick to say, it was probably only *apparently*. In summary, Hodge generally applauds Schaff but feels that he "presents this doctrine too exclusively 'in opposition to all Pelagian and Semi-Pelagian error.' He does not present it sufficiently in its opposition to the doctrine of a mediating church, which was historically its most prominent aspect."[36]

His remarks on the formal principle, the authority of Scripture, follow a similar pattern. He begins by professing his concurrence with Schaff's exposition and then gives his own definition: a "protest against the doctrine of an inspired church to whose teaching we are obliged to bow."[37] On this point, Hodge feels, Schaff's fuzziness about the invisible/visible church distinction gets him into trouble. For, if we are talking about the visible church, a mere body of professing believers, says Hodge, its teaching may be little different from that of the world, whereas that

33. Hodge, "Schaff's Protestantism," 627–28 (italics mine).
34. Ibid., 628.
35. Ibid., 628–29.
36. Ibid., 628.
37. Ibid., 629.

of the true, invisible church must be infallibly true, and thus cannot be departed from.[38] Hodge again insists that he is not necessarily disagreeing with Schaff, but only with what Schaff *appears* to be saying. He also points out that Schaff's apparent approval of the traditional rituals of the Church "will find few American Protestants to agree with him."[39]

He is also amiable toward, but not altogether comfortable with Schaff's diagnosis of the diseases of Protestantism. As to the emphasis on the dangers of rationalism, Hodge patronizingly remarks, "This is a very natural view to be taken by a theologian born and educated in Germany," and himself considers "in reference to the state of the church in America, Romanism to be immeasurably more dangerous than infidelity."[40] Here he seems to betray more than anywhere else either a poor reading of Schaff or an intentional evasion of the main force of Schaff's argument. For when Schaff speaks of rationalism, he makes it clear that he means more than the philosophical skepticism and atheism of the universities; he means the pervasive subjective naturalism of the average Protestant churchgoer. Likewise, Hodge makes no specific rebuttal to Schaff's clear exposition of the reasons why Romanism was the secondary threat.

But it is not until Hodge turns to address sectarianism that the real point of tension becomes clear:

> The section relating to "sectarism" we consider as more marred by false principles and false views of facts and of their historical relations, than any other part of the book. Here we think our author betrays erroneous principles as to the unity of the church, too much forgetting that it is a spiritual unity, arising from the union of believers with Christ and from the indwelling of his Spirit; and which manifests itself in unity of faith, of love, and of communion.[41]

Hodge, for whom the invisible church is everything, cannot see any point in Schaff's emphasis on visible, historic unity. From his perspective, Schaff's doctrine of visible church continuity and solidarity are unintel-

---

38. Of course, it will appear that if Hodge is really saying here what he appears to be, his view of tradition becomes meaningless. For if the tradition of the invisible church is the only tradition that is trustworthy, we may well question how this is to help us if we can't see it.

39. Ibid., 630.

40. Ibid.

41. Ibid., 630–31.

ligible. On the historical question, he cannot agree with Schaff's claim that the Reformers would have preferred to remain in the Roman communion, had it been possible, and believes that the principle of secession from unsound church bodies is indispensable. Where Schaff attributes the formation of a new sect to religious pride and scrupulosity, Hodge blames it on the faults of the unscriptural practice of the parent religious body, and even when it is the result of scrupulosity, he admires the "assertion of the supremacy of conscience."[42] Again Hodge seems unable to grasp the essential point at issue when he declares that he is unsure what Schaff means by a sect: "Why are the Congregationalists, or Baptists any more a sect than the German Reformed, or the Episcopalians?"[43] The answer is, of course, that for Schaff the nature of a sect lies not so much in the fact of a body's distinct denominational polity as in that body's attitude toward the historic, catholic nature of the Church and its traditions. Hodge again betrays a somewhat patronizing attitude toward the young foreigner, and seems to have a low view of Schaff's extraordinary perceptiveness: "In this account given by Dr. Schaff . . . we think he shows he is from home. He is speaking of events, which as they did not occur in Germany cannot be supposed to be so well understood by a scholar so thoroughly German."[44] Hodge concludes his review by summarizing Schaff's remarks on Puseyism and concluding that Mercersburg was not in danger of going in that direction, though he was less than comfortable with the German philosophy behind their confidence in the Church's future. He ends the review with a very skeptical review of the merits of German theology, and cautions against putting any faith in any supposed contributions from that direction.

What may we conclude from this summary of an obscure and forgotten theological exchange? First of all, it is instructive to observe that here, as seems to occur in many theological debates, Hodge seemed remarkably unable to understand the thought-world of his opponent. If we are to take Hodge at his word and not accuse him of intentional dissimulation, it would appear that he really fails to understand Schaff's entire perspective regarding the nature of the Church and its role in history. This constant misunderstanding was to plague the interactions between Mercersburg and Princeton throughout the controversy; though

42. Ibid., 632.
43. Ibid.
44. Ibid.

as it went on, Hodge, instead of misunderstanding and assuming the best of his opponents (as he does here), began to misunderstand and assume the worst.

More importantly, though, in this exchange we see the root of the disagreements between Mercersburg and Princeton: what is the nature of the Church? Specifically, the question might be posed (though it doesn't seem to have ever been explicitly framed in these terms during the controversy): what is the relationship between the visible, historical church, and the invisible, ideal church? How do we reconcile these, which is the more important, and to which should we ascribe the qualities that the New Testament attributes to "the Church"? The answers given to this set of questions have tremendous implications for one's entire system of theology, and in particular, one's view of the role of Church history, as we shall see in the next chapter. Before examining these questions further, though, let us take time to look at another fascinating exchange between Mercersburg and Princeton.

The Debate over The Mystical Presence

The debate between Charles Hodge and John Nevin on the Reformed doctrine of the Lord's Supper, while certainly failing to rank among even the half-dozen most famous debates in nineteenth-century Presbyterianism, is probably the most well-known moment in the story of the Mercersburg Theology, and justly so. The leading Reformed theologian in America publicly took his former star student to task, not only for bad history and bad sacramental theology, but for incipient Romanism, pantheism, Eutychianism, and Sabellianism, to name just a few of the theological maledictions Hodge employed in his review. This in itself is no doubt intriguing, but it gets much better when we find that historical authorities since Hodge have accused his article, in scarcely kinder words, of historical boneheadedness. Though historians have generally agreed that Hodge was "demolished"[45] by Nevin's response the next year, Hodge, cutting his losses, ignored it and continued in his stern and confident reprimands against the dangerous innovator in Mercersburg.

As historians have pretty well concurred in their view of the historical merits of Hodge's review,[46] it is not my purpose here to cover

---

45. Nichols, *Romanticism*, 89.

46. Nichols's assessment, perhaps the harshest of all, is worth quoting: "Hodge, in contrast, handled the history arbitrarily and without regard for chronology. He selected one

that ground. Rather, I want to use this review, like the last one, as an opportunity to discover the particular points at which Hodge's theology differs from Nevin's, and what this says about the underlying paradigms. In contrasting the two on the issue of Eucharistic theology, it is perhaps a bit too easy to assign to Hodge the bad-boy part of a mere Zwinglian. Nichols seems happy to categorize him so.[47] While this might be an accurate characterization for Hodge's Southern Presbyterian contemporary, Robert Dabney, it appears from Hodge's writings on the sacraments that he at least aimed to cling to some relics of a higher view, though it is doubtful whether the result was ever clear or consistent. Part of Nevin's point in *The Mystical Presence*, of course, was to show that decadent doctrines like Hodge's, if articulated consistently, would inevitably slide over into Zwinglian memorialism. But we must, like Nevin, be precise in defining the points of difference in Hodge's doctrine, if we are to uncover what was really at stake.

First, then, as with *The Principle of Protestantism*, I shall start off with a summary of Nevin's main argument.

Nevin believed that the issue of Christ's presence in the Eucharist, far from comprising a mere abstruse peripheral debate, was a decisive point at which all theologies must stand or fall. It was, he said, "one of the most important [questions] belonging to the history of religion. It may be regarded indeed as in some sense central to the whole Christian system."[48] Even here, at the first sentence of his exposition, he was parting ways from the prevailing winds of Reformed doctrine, in which most of the issues involved seemed small and insignificant. But Nevin saw that the change he witnessed in Protestant Eucharistic doctrine

---

set of formulations, which he found congenial, chiefly those derived from Zwingli, and another set with which he could not come to terms, those showing the influence of Calvin. He then arranged a third category of formulations exhibiting both emphases, which he interpreted as Zwinglian. Although he offered a pretentious parade of sources, all the important documentation, with one exception, he had borrowed without acknowledgment from *The Mystical Presence*. In effect, what he had done was to comb over *The Mystical Presence* in a fortnight or so, with no significant independent study, and to rearrange its historical evidence completely out of context in accordance with his own ideas of theological propriety. It was not that he was dishonest; he just lacked understanding of what history is. For him, the past was an armory of theological tenets, and a man had a right to pick and choose as he would" (90). As mentioned in the Introduction, Nichols's antipathy towards Hodge is a bit too palpable at times, and this is perhaps one of them, though he is not far from the mark.

47. Ibid., 90–91.

48. Nevin, *Mystical Presence*, 47.

must involve much more than the simple substitution of one
theory of the Lord's Supper for another. The doctrine of the eucharist is intimately connected with all that is most deep and central in the Christian system as a whole; and it is not possible for
it to undergo any material modification in any direction, without
a corresponding modification at the same time of the theory and
life of religion at other points.[49]

Why was it so central? Well, since this sacrament is the most intimate point of communion between Christ and the believer, Eucharistic
theology is intertwined with one's view of union with Christ, and indeed,
soteriology as a whole. Also, what sort of nature man has (anthropology)
and what sort of nature Christ had (Christology) are an unavoidable part
of the picture as well. Since the sacrament is an ordinance of the Church,
the account one gives of sacramental grace must include an account of
the grace offered in the Church more generally, thus involving ecclesiology as well. The ramifications of Nevin's sacramental theology in all these
areas shall emerge throughout this chapter and the next.[50]

The point about union with Christ, however, emerges quickly at the
forefront of Nevin's sacramental discussion: "Any theory of the eucharist
will be found to accord closely with the view that is taken, at the same
time of the nature of the union generally between Christ and his people.
Whatever the life of the believer may be as a whole in this relation, it
must determine the form of his communion with the Saviour."[51] His
point, therefore, in recovering the Reformed doctrine of the Eucharist,
is to recover in full a right understanding of the Christian's union with
Christ: "the idea of an inward living union between believers and Christ,
in virtue of which they are incorporated into his very nature, and made
to subsist with him by the power of a common life."[52]

49. Ibid., 48.

50. No claim is being made here regarding the order of cause-and-effect. Did Nevin
embrace a certain notion of sacramental theology which then led him into new convic-
tions about Christology and anthropology, or was it vice versa? Such questions are rarely
answerable, because the mind rarely works that simply, and its workings are often hidden to the historian's view. In any case, my point here is merely to show the relationships
between the different elements in the theological paradigm, not to posit any particular
account of their development.

51. Ibid., 50.

52. Ibid.

Nevin conveniently enumerates four crucial tenets of the Calvinistic doctrine of the Lord's Supper, which I shall summarize carefully.

First, he says, "the union of believers with Christ is not simply that of a common humanity, as derived from Adam."[53] For many, the mere fact that Christ became man, and therefore shares our human nature, is a sufficient ground of our solidarity with Him. Nevin held to a strong view of the natural unity of all men in Adam (discussed below in chapters 3 and 6), but the unity of Christ and believers, he contended, was much more than this. The shared humanity is indeed a prerequisite for our union with Christ, but this union takes place on another plane as well, "on the ground of our participation in His own nature as a higher order of life." This sharing in His nature exists only "in a direct connection with his person."[54]

Second, "the relation is more again than a simply *moral* union."[55] Nevin uses this word "moral" as a pejorative term rather frequently, and its meaning is not always self-evident. Here he offers an example of what he means: "Such a union we have, where two or more persons are bound together by inward agreement, sympathy, and correspondence."[56] This is a union of friendship, a unity of mind and heart, the sort of union with Christ that contemporary evangelicalism makes so much of. Of course this unity exists between the believer and Christ—"The Saviour lives much in his [the believer's] thoughts and affections. He looks to him with an eye of faith, embraces him in his heart, commits himself to his guidance, walks in his steps, and endeavours to be clothed more and more with his very mind itself."[57] But this is simply a consequence of a much deeper, fuller union, "a common life, in virtue of which Christ and his people are one even before they become thus assimilated to his character."[58]

This distinction is of crucial relevance for understanding the Lord's Supper, which for many was understood as merely an opportunity for a believer to perceive Christ with the eyes of faith and bend his heart and will into closer conformity with Him. If this is all there is, Nevin insists,

53. Ibid., 51.
54. Ibid.
55. Ibid.
56. Ibid.
57. Ibid.
58. Ibid., 51–52.

then the only efficacy in the sacrament is that which the worshipper puts into it. If the believer is really focused, then he is really united to Christ; if his spiritual faculties are underdeveloped, then the union is vague and ineffectual. Nevin will not stand for this.

> [The Supper] is not simply an occasion, by which the soul of the believer may be excited to pious feelings and desires; but it embodies the actual presence of the grace it represents in its own constitution; and this grace is not simply the promise of God on which we are encouraged to rely, but the very life of the Lord Jesus Christ himself. We communicate, in the Lord's supper [sic], not with the divine promise merely, not with the thought of Christ only, not with the recollection simply of what he has done and suffered for us, not with the lively present sense alone of his all-sufficient, all-glorious Salvation; but with the living Saviour himself, in the fulness of his glorified person, made present to us for the purpose by the power of the Holy Ghost.[59]

It is still perhaps not quite clear what this union with the "Saviour himself," or the presence of his "very life" means, but for Nevin, this must be so from the nature of the case—it is a mysterious presence, not one that is easily described, as a merely "moral union" might be. Nevin's last remark about the agency of the Holy Spirit is worth noting, as it will become quite significant in understanding the difference with Hodge's perspective.

The third key point Nevin notes about the union with Christ is that it is more than "a simply *legal* union."[60] This point is made in the context of the federal theology tradition, which, building from early formulations of Reformed scholasticism, had articulated the various elements of soteriology in rigorously forensic and federal categories. The believer was united to Christ in the sense that Christ legally or federally represented the believer, as all the stockholders in a corporation might be said to be federally united to the board members, or, perhaps better, as the members of a family are federally united to the father. Nevin does not intend to deny the truth of any of the legal or covenantal relations that this system posited, but again, he says, they must be rooted in something deeper and more real. Christ federally represents the believer because the believer truly shares in His life (as perhaps we might say of the family example,

---

59. Ibid., 52.
60. Ibid., 53.

but not the corporation example). This means that the benefits of Christ, while of course they are given to the believer, never come separately from his person. An individual may participate in the benefits that come from a corporation he is invested in, without any concrete relationship to its board members or officers. Nevin is on guard against any such model for understanding the imputation of Christ's benefits to His people:

> Our interest in Christ's merits and benefits can be based only upon a previous interest in his person; so in the Lord's Supper, we are made to participate, not merely in the advantages secured by his mediatorial work, the rewards of his obedience, the fruits of his bitter passion, the virtue of his atonement, and the power of his priestly intercession, but also in his true and proper life itself. We partake of his merits and benefits only so far as we partake of his substance.[61]

Fourth, the union is not merely with "Christ in his *divine nature* separately taken or with the *Holy Ghost* as the representative of his presence in the world."[62] The Spirit, of course, is essential in uniting the believer to Christ, in the Supper as well as elsewhere, but the Spirit cannot be divorced from Christ. To use another imperfect analogy, the Spirit is more like a minister who by his power unites bride and groom together in their marriage relationship; he is certainly not like a proxy whom the groom sends in his place to say his vows and conclude the marriage covenant on behalf of the absent groom. Of course, neither is quite an apt characterization, for no analogy can capture the intimate union between the Spirit and Christ. Nevin describes the three-way (or rather four-way) relationship this way:

> It is by the Spirit indeed we are united to Christ. Our new life is comprehended in the Spirit as its element and medium. But it is always bound in this element to the person of the Lord Jesus Christ himself. Our fellowship is with the Father and with his son Jesus Christ, *through* the Holy Ghost. As such it is a real communion with the Word made flesh; not simply with the divinity of Christ, but with his humanity also; since both are inseparably joined together in his person, and a living union with him in the one view, implies necessarily a living union with him in the other view likewise. In the Lord's Supper, accordingly, the believer

61. Ibid.
62. Ibid.

communicates not only with the Spirit of Christ, or with his divine nature, but with Christ himself in his whole living person, so that he may be said to be fed and nourished by his very flesh and blood. The communion is truly and fully with the *Man* Christ Jesus and not simply with Jesus as the Son of God.[63]

These four points, Nevin says, are necessary to define the right Reformed doctrine over against rationalism (of the sort that Nevin saw rampant in the Reformed Church of his day). Nevin also briefly defines the Reformed view against the "figment of *transubstantiation*," affirming, with all the Protestant Reformers, that "Bread remains bread, and wine remains wine."[64] Against Lutheran *consubstantiation* he is likewise firm, declaring that "the elements cannot be said to comprehend or include the body of the Saviour in any sense. It is not *there,* but remains constantly in heaven. . . . The manducation of it is not oral, but only by faith. It is present in fruition accordingly to believers only in the exercise of faith."[65] The Reformed doctrine, he clarifies, is one of the "spiritual real presence" in which the body of Christ remains in heaven but is, by the power of the Holy Spirit, made to commune with the believer on earth, "for the real nourishment of his new life."[66] This is not, as for the Catholics and perhaps the Lutherans, a material mingling with Christ's material body, but "a participation of the Saviour's life. Of his life, however, as human, subsisting in a true bodily form. The living energy, the vivific virtue, as Calvin styles it, of Christ's flesh, is made to flow over into the communicant, making him more and more one with Christ himself, and thus more and more an heir of the same immortality that is brought to light in his person."[67]

Nevin summarizes the significance of this whole doctrine under two key points. First, the sacrament in itself has an objective force. It is not merely an occasion for the subjective operations of the believer to make of it what he will. Faith is of course the essential instrument for taking hold of the objective grace thus offered, and making use of it unto eternal life. Despite this subjective element, however, the sacramental sign necessarily includes the reality—Christ; it is not merely a pointer to

63. Ibid., 53–54.
64. Ibid., 54–55.
65. Ibid., 55.
66. Ibid., 56.
67. Ibid., 57.

a Christ who is who is no more present here than anywhere else. Second, the grace here offered is the life of Christ Himself, God and man; not merely the benefits He has gained for us by His work. Nevin is right in identifying these two points as crucial, for we shall see them coming up over and over in Hodge's review.

After this introduction, Nevin offers an extended historical survey of early Reformed sources, proving that the view just sketched was indeed the historical Reformed view. Then he shows how this doctrine fell into gradual declension and ended in a completely different doctrine, more Zwinglian than Calvinistic, which he calls "the modern Puritan view." After these surveys, he summarizes the differences between the two, again helpfully enumerating the key points.

First, in the old view, Christ's presence in the Supper was "*specific* in its nature, and *different* from all that has place in the common exercises of worship."[68] The Eucharist does not simply provide another pointer to Christ or instruction about Him, as the ministry of the Word does, nor does it simply strengthen faith and religious feelings, as prayer; it offers a profound grace and participation in Christ that cannot be found elsewhere in the Christian life. In the new view, this is flatly denied; all the ordinances become merely different instruments for accessing the same grace.

Second, in the old view, "the sacramental transaction is a *mystery*; nay, in some sense an actual *miracle*. The Spirit works here in a way that transcends, not only the human understanding, but the ordinary course of the world also in every other view."[69] In marked contrast to the humble awe of the early Reformers at the power of the sacrament, the "modern Puritan" writers outdid one another with their patronizing expressions about the confusion and incomprehensibility of these early doctrines. In the view of the later theologians, the sacrament operates in a clear and intelligible way upon understanding and the affections of the believer.

Third, says Nevin, the old view held to an objective force in the sacrament, a real and necessary union between sign and thing signified. The sacrament was understood to really make present to the believer the signified grace. Now, he laments, the sacramental transaction merely pictures the grace of Christ to the believer; it is a substitute for an absent

68. Ibid., 111.
69. Ibid., 112.

Christ, and a promise to the faithful believer that Christ's blessings will be bestowed on him, in a different time and different form.

Fourth, as mentioned above, in the early Reformed view, the sacrament accomplishes a real union with the person of Christ, not merely a reception of His benefits, but a sharing in His life. The modern Puritan view, however, represents the union as moral only, or else as consisting only in the believer's union with the Spirit.

Finally, the two views differ as to whether the believer communes with Christ's divinity only, or with His humanity also. The old Reformed view insisted upon the latter, that Christ's "humanity forms the medium of his union with the Church. The life of which he is the fountain, flows forth from him only as he is the Son of Man. To have part in it at all, we must have part in it as a real human life."[70] The contemporary view, however, could see no distinction between this and the errors of transubstantiation and consubstantiation. Consequently,

> it will allow no real participation of Christ's person in the Lord's Supper, under any form: but least of all under the form of his humanity. Such communion as it is willing to admit, it limits to the presence of Christ in his divine nature, or to the energy he puts forth by his Spirit. As for all that is said about his body and blood, it is taken to be mere figure, intended to express the value of his sufferings and death.[71]

Nevin concludes his survey with stern words of warning,

> We have no right to hold [this change] unimportant, or to take it for granted with unreflecting presumption that the truth is all on the modern side. The mere fact is serious. For the doctrine of the eucharist lies at the very heart of christianity itself; and the chasm that divides the two systems here is wide and deep. . . . Only ignorance or frivolity can allow themselves to make light of it.[72]

Hodge's Response

Hodge does not seem to have shared Nevin's view of the pressing importance of the subject, confessing at the outset of his review that he had

70. Ibid., 117.
71. Ibid., 118.
72. Ibid., 119.

allowed *The Mystical Presence* to sit on his desk unread for nearly two years, and that "it requires the stimulus of a special necessity to carry us through such a book."[73] However, having once read it, he found the subject very pressing indeed, on account of the many grave errors, historical and theological, that he perceived in the book. "We differ from him indeed, essentially, as to the whole subject, not only as to the historical question, but as to what is the true doctrine," he declared, and suggests that "Dr. Nevin is tenfold further from the doctrines of our common fathers,"[74] than the "Puritans" he so criticized.

Hodge begins by summarizing what, on his reading, was the true Reformed doctrine. If we will remember Nevin's four initial points, Hodge would appear at first to be in agreement on one, though not necessarily on the other three. Nevin specified that the union was not a merely moral union, but a participation in the life of Christ Himself. Hodge appears to agree:

> If the union between Christ and his people were merely moral, arising from agreement and sympathy, there would be no mystery about it; and the Lord's Supper, as the symbol of that union, would be a perfectly intelligible ordinance. But the scriptures teach that our union with Christ is far more than this. It is a vital union, we are partakers of his life, for it is not we that live, but Christ that liveth in us.[75]

However, on the other three points, Hodge appears to differ. The union does take place upon the basis of a shared human nature, contrary to Nevin's first point. The union is a federal union, in possible contradiction to Nevin's third point. Remember that Nevin insisted that, while there is a federal element, it is only on the basis of a deeper union of life. It is not yet clear if and how Hodge might disagree with this statement. Finally, Hodge makes the Spirit the means of the union, in apparent contradiction to Nevin's fourth point. Nevin of course allowed that the Spirit was essential to the union, but not to the exclusion of the personal presence of Christ Himself, which appears to be excluded by Hodge here. I shall examine Hodge's statements in more detail shortly.

After his summary statement, Hodge enters in upon his own examination of the historical evidence. As already mentioned, most scholars

73. Hodge, "Doctrine of the Reformed Church," 227.
74. Ibid.
75. Ibid., 228.

consider this to be a pretty shabby examination indeed, and there is no need to go through Hodge's reconstruction in detail. The gist of it is to argue that Hodge's own view, roughly that of the Zwinglians, was held by most of the Reformed in the sixteenth century, and that the emphases Nevin highlighted were peculiar to Calvin, bizarre, and inconsistent with the Reformed system of doctrine. Therefore, the Reformed of Calvin's time and later rightly rejected these unique elements.

Hodge then systematically unfolds his view of the right doctrine of the Lord's Supper, appealing to the sources he has chosen and his own reading of them. Manifesting the same weakness we saw in his review of Schaff, Hodge tends to read his sources through his own preconceived notions and profess agreement with them when in fact his use of the same language clearly intends a radically different meaning. He articulates his own view in words borrowed from those of the early Reformed sources, so that he can seem to be not far from them or Nevin, but on closer examination, we see how these words often serve precisely the opposite agenda.

Using Nevin's five points of difference between the "old Reformed view" and the "modern Puritan view," let us attempt to accurately pinpoint Hodge's position on the spectrum.

First, does Hodge believe that unique grace is offered in the Eucharist, or is it simply one of several equally valuable, and ultimately interchangeable, means of communing with Christ? Here he falls clearly on the side of the "modern Puritan view," and attempts to claim that so did the early Reformed.

> The question . . . whether there is any special benefit or communion with Christ to be had there, and which cannot elsewhere be obtained, the Romanists and the Lutherans answer in the affirmative; the Reformed unanimously in the negative. . . . On this point there was no diversity of opinion in any part of the Reformed church. There was no communion of Christ, no participation of his body and blood, not offered to believers and received by them, elsewhere than at the Lord's table and by other means. This is exalting the grace of God without deprecating the value of the sacraments.[76]

Hodge indeed goes further than this, maintaining that the grace received in the sacraments of the New Covenant, the grace of union with Christ,

76. Ibid., 247–48.

must be understood as no different than the grace available to Old Testament saints.[77] In a rather radical summarizing statement he says that the receiving of Christ's body "is not confined to the Lord's Supper, but takes place whenever faith in him is exercised."[78]

Second, on the question of whether the Supper should be viewed as a mystery and miracle, Hodge gives no precise answer. He does confess at the outset of his review that "the subject itself is mysterious," involving as it does the union between Christ and believers which "is declared to be a great mystery."[79] However, most of the rest of Hodge's exposition seems devoted to demystifying the subject and ridding it of the peculiar and incoherent expressions with which Calvin had muddled it. Indeed, the point just made, that the grace of the sacrament is no other than that which faith receives at any time, seems to constitute a fairly clear decision against imputing any particular mystery to the matter. Here too, it would seem, Hodge has espoused the "modern Puritan view," though the lip service to an older view remains.

On the third question—whether there is an objective force in the sacrament—Hodge also embraces the modern view, though here we must be careful to be precise in identifying the point of difference. "All agree," he assures us, "that they [the sacraments] have an objective force; that they no more owe their power to the faith of the recipient than the word of God does."[80] The question here, he insists, is not objective divine power vs. subjective human feelings. Hodge is careful to reject the view that the sacraments are "mere badges of profession, or empty signs of Christ,"[81] whose efficacy rests upon an exercise of religious feelings by the recipients. The question, Hodge says, "is what is the source to which the influence of the sacraments as means of grace, is to be referred?"[82] The Reformed, he says, reject the Roman view, that the sacraments "contain the grace they signify, and that they convey that grace, by the mere administration, to all who do not oppose an obstacle," as well as the Lutheran view which, though resting the sacraments' efficacy on the attending word of God, makes them "nevertheless always operative, pro-

77. Ibid., 252.
78. Ibid., 255.
79. Ibid., 227–28.
80. Ibid., 274.
81. Ibid., 256.
82. Ibid., 274.

vided there be faith in the receiver."[83] The Reformed do not deny that they are "efficacious means of grace"; however, "their efficacy, as such, is referred neither to any virtue in them nor in him that administers them, but solely to the attending operation or influence of the Holy Spirit, precisely as in the case of the word."[84]

Nevin, of course, would hardly disagree (nor, most likely, would many Catholics or Lutherans)—of course the efficacy of the sacraments rests upon the operation of the Spirit. So it seems that the question is not, as Hodge claimed, the source of the efficacy. Rather, as he goes on, we see that that the question concerns the Spirit's mode of operation. "Their power . . . to convey grace depends entirely, as in the case of the word, on the co-operation of the Holy Ghost. Hence the power is in no way tied to the sacraments. It may be exerted without them. It does not always attend them, nor is it confined to the time, place, and service."[85] This is indeed a great leap. Nevin makes clear that sacramental grace depends upon the work of the Spirit, but this by no means implies that the grace is not always present, or that it may appear in a different time, place, or way. After all, the Spirit is always present and uniquely working in the sacrament. Hodge seems to believe that, because the Spirit is needed to make the sacrament effectual, He randomly skips out of church, showing up to do the job sometimes and not others, and sometimes deciding to do it at home instead. Hodge's conclusion that this power of the Spirit may be exerted without the sacraments presupposes, of course, that the grace of the Supper is not unique in any way, but is merely the grace of faith that may operate wherever the Spirit stirs it up. Here, too, though he seeks to guard against utter subjectivism, Hodge has essentially departed from the old Reformed view as Nevin saw it.

The fourth question—whether we participate in Christ Himself or merely in His benefits—is clouded by Hodge's fuzzy use of terminology, but the end result is the same. As quoted at the beginning, Hodge does declare that "we are partakers of his [Christ's] life, for it is not we who live, but Christ who liveth in us,"[86] implying an agreement with Nevin, but his subsequent remarks move steadily away from this. Christ is certainly present in the sacrament, but, with typical scholastic precision,

83. Ibid., 256.
84. Ibid.
85. Ibid., 256–57.
86. Ibid., 256.

Hodge reminds us that "the word presence . . . is a relative term. . . . For presence is nothing but the application of an object to the faculty suited to the perception of it."[87] Spiritual things, then, are present "when they are presented to the intelligence so as to be apprehended and enjoyed," and therefore "may be present as to efficacy and virtue" even when spatially distant. Christ's presence in the sacrament, therefore, is "a presence of virtue and efficacy not of propinquity."[88]

Despite a rather different tone, these statements are perhaps not irreconcilable with Nevin's, which also deny a local presence and emphasize the participation not in Christ's material flesh as such, but in the power or virtue of its life. But Hodge goes on a few pages later to delineate two ways of understanding this "virtue and efficacy." One way saw it as "a vivifying efficacy imparted to the body of Christ by its union with the divine nature," which was shared with the believer by the power of the Holy Ghost. This, which Hodge admits to have been Calvin's idea, he rejects. Rather, we should understand "the virtue of Christ's body and blood as . . . a body broken and of blood as shed, that is, their sacrificial, atoning efficacy,"[89] in other words, as the remission of sins. Hodge here consciously rejects the Incarnation as a basis for Christ's presence in favor of the Atonement,[90] underlying a characteristic and recurring contrast between his theological paradigm and Nevin's. In effect, Hodge has said, with much circumlocution, "Christ is truly present in the sacrament in the sense that, by faith in his sacrifice, we receive forgiveness of sins," a full denial of the personal presence of Christ in the sense that Nevin and the early Reformed understood it. It is clear that, despite again giving lip service to the confessional language, Hodge sees participation in Christ as a participation in His benefits, not His life. Or does he?

In the next section of his review, he appears to renege, affirming "all the Reformed agreed . . . that we receive Christ himself and not merely his benefits."[91] But the meaning of this for him will become clear when we examine the final question: is our communion with Christ a sharing in His humanity, or only in the divine nature or Spirit? Here, Hodge minces no words in denying the former. "Do the Scriptures teach . . . that we are

87. Ibid., 244.
88. Ibid., 245.
89. Ibid., 249.
90. Ibid., 252.
91. Ibid., 254.

partakers of the human nature, of the real flesh and blood of Christ? . . .
This the whole Reformed church denied."[92] And later he insists that, since
the Old Covenant saints necessarily received Christ in just the same way
that we do, that it is impossible "that our union with Christ involves a
participation in his human body, nature, or life."[93] Indeed, there does not
seem to be any real communion with the divine nature of Christ, either,
but there is a genuine union with Him by the Spirit. Hodge explains the
Reformed statements that we receive Christ Himself by saying, "we receive the substance of Christ, i.e. as they explain it, Christ himself, or
the Holy Spirit, by whom he dwells in his people."[94] "Christ himself" is
interchangeable, it seems, with "the Holy Spirit," His proxy. Hodge goes
on, explaining Paul's analogy of the union between husband and wife:

> If the intimate relationship, the identification of feelings, affec-
> tions and interests, between a man and his wife, if their spiritual
> union, justifies the assertion that they are one flesh, far more may
> the same thing be said of the spiritual relation between Christ
> and his people, which is much more intimate, sublime and mys-
> terious, arising, as it does from the inhabitation of one and the
> same Spirit, and producing not only a union of feeling and affec-
> tion, but of life. The same apostle tells us that believers are one
> body and members one of another, not in virtue of their common
> human nature, nor because they all partake of the humanity of
> Christ, but because they all have one Spirit.[95]

Though the terminology is often similar to Nevin's, Hodge clearly understands the Spirit as a representative who is present to us *in lieu* of
Christ, rather than the means of making Christ, body and soul, divine
and human, present to us.

Hodge follows this statement of the doctrine with an overview of
the general contours of Nevin's theology of the Incarnation, Church, and
sacraments, which in general appears quite accurate. But, having concluded this summary, to which Nevin would likely have few objections,
Hodge declares, "It is in all its essential features Schleiermacher's theory,"
showing again a failure to attentively hear and understand his inter-
locutor. Whatever German elements might have contributed to Nevin's

92. Ibid., 229.
93. Ibid., 255.
94. Ibid., 254–55.
95. Ibid., 256.

exposition, the theological system in general, if it is un-Reformed, is at least roughly Eastern Orthodox (as Chapter 5 shall begin to explore). In any case, this proves the least of the insults Hodge is prepared to hurl at Nevin's theology, which, in the concluding section, he links with a host of heresies, ancient and modern.

But this final section is very helpful for seeing where, in Hodge's eyes, some of the key battle lines lay. As seen above, Hodge sees it as very important to emphasize the Spirit, not the divine-human body of Christ, as the means of the mystical union, and he spends several more pages hammering in this point, especially with reference to the status of Old Testament saints. This concern highlights Hodge's de-emphasis on the Incarnation, as well as the same dualism of spirit and flesh that contributed to his view of the visible and invisible Church. Hodge also again lays great stress on the need not to attribute any special efficacy or power to the sacraments themselves, but rather to view them as merely potential means, equal to the preaching of the Word or whatever else the Spirit may choose to use (or not to use), to quicken faith and imparting Christ's benefits.

All this, I believe, manifests the same tendency: a resistance to the incarnation of grace. Grace must remain free-floating, invisible, and unpredictable if it is to be grace. Therefore, the true Church must be invisible (as we saw above in the review of Schaff), since God would never entrust anything so precious to a visible institution, subject to the vicissitudes of history. Therefore, the Spirit alone, and not the incarnate flesh of the God-man, can serve as a vehicle for eternal life. Therefore, the visible forms and rituals of the sacraments can be only an invitation for Christ to show up, but no promise of His presence. We shall see this fear of incarnated grace, of the supernatural made historical, throughout Hodge's view of Christology, ecclesiology, and Church history in the next chapter. Nevin, however, as we shall see in all the remaining chapters, insists constantly on the non-contradiction of supernatural grace and natural history, of spirit and matter, of invisible power and visible agent. It is to a more systematic analysis of these issues, that we shall now turn.

CHAPTER 3

Paradigms in Collision
What Was at Stake in the Mercersburg-Princeton Debate

IN THIS CHAPTER, I hope to show how some of the paradigmatic differences between Mercersburg and Princeton, gestured at in the preceding two chapters, play out in detail. This section, of course, only scratches
the surface of all the issues under debate and all the arguments raised,
but I have chosen to focus on three major loci of Mercersburg thought,
which together offer a broad and coherent mosaic of the Mercersburg
Theology and Princeton's reaction to it. This section will begin with a
discussion of the Incarnation, the beginning of the Christian faith and a
foundational doctrine of the Mercersburg Theology. This leads naturally
into a discussion of the nature of the Church, particularly in terms of
its relation to the Incarnation—that is, how the physical Body of Christ
and the ecclesial body of Christ relate—and to the question of visible vs.
invisible church. Finally, I will analyze how the two different paradigms
of the Church articulated by Mercersburg and Princeton inform each's
approach to Church history. This will in some ways bring the discussion
full circle, showing the groundwork for Schaff's historical approach in
The Principle of Protestantism and the opposite paradigm under which
Hodge is operating.

Throughout this discussion, certain themes will recur. Methodologi-
cally and philosophically, we will find that where Nevin and Schaff are
more concerned with the general, Hodge always prefers to focus on the

particular. Moreover, where Nevin and Schaff see continuity, particularly between inner and outer, spiritual and physical, Hodge sees radical discontinuity. Additionally, it is worth noting how, for Hodge, who sees theology as a Baconian science, everything tends to be static and compartmentalized, while for Nevin and Schaff, theology, like history, is characterized by living, organic flow. These differences, which reflect their philosophical precommitments, have radical implications for their theological outlook. We can also see in this section how some of the theological points of tension that were identified in the last chapter play out in these three areas. The relationship of invisible divine action and visible human action arises repeatedly. Both Nevin and Hodge use the Incarnation as a model for understanding this, but, as they do not agree at this starting point, they are similarly divided in their ecclesiology, with Hodge ending up with what Nevin calls a docetic or Nestorian concept of the Church, one in which the divine never really unites with the human. Hodge throughout resists incarnated grace, that is, the idea that grace, which as divine action is properly invisible, should ever truly operate through visible means.

The Incarnation: Christ Comes to Earth

The doctrine of the Incarnation was the keystone of the Mercersburg Theology and one of the primary battlegrounds between Nevin's German theology and Hodge's Scottish Presbyterianism. Nevin believed and passionately argued in his *Antichrist* that every theological error ultimately stems from a failure to properly understand the nature of the God-man. The Incarnation, as the point at which God and Man meet, must be the starting point for all Christian theological reflection.

In *The Mystical Presence*, Nevin begins his "Biblical Argument" for his sacramental theology with an exposition of the Incarnation, and thinks it impossible to overstate its importance. He eloquently opens:

> *"The Word became flesh!"* In this simple, but sublime enunciation, we have the whole gospel comprehended in a word. From the glorious orb of light which is here made to burst upon our view, all that would else be dark and chaotic becomes at once irradiated with the bright majesty and everlasting harmony of truth itself. The incarnation is the key that unlocks the sense of all God's revelations.[1]

---

1. Nevin, *Mystical Presence*, 187.

The nature of creation itself, Nevin argues, points to the Incarnation, as the necessary fulfillment and completion of the great pyramid of nature. Man is the pinnacle of creation, and in the government of Man the rest of creation finds its proper place and purpose. But man himself lacks his proper fulfillment without the God-man. "The Incarnation then is the proper completion of humanity. Christ is the true ideal man," Nevin boldly declares.[2] A statement like this might seem to echo the dangerous tendencies of later liberal theology, or its predecessors, the German theology of Schleiermacher's school. Hodge's concerns might here seem valid. But if we follow the rest of Nevin's argument, we see that he is in no danger of dissolving the divinity of Christ. Christ is the ideal man in the sense that in Him we see fulfilled that for which man was created, a life of communion with God Himself. "History, like nature, is one vast prophecy of the incarnation, from beginning to end," says Nevin.[3] All the religions of paganism attempt to bridge the gap between the human and the divine, and heroes such as Gilgamesh and Hercules represent man's desire to attain godhood. But ultimately, paganism, as man's attempt to raise himself up to divinity, fails to provide an answer. Old Testament Judaism, on the other hand, though it did indeed provide a real means of communication between God and man, yet was not sufficient in itself to bridge the gap. As Nevin aptly diagnoses it,

> God drew continually more and more near to men in an outward way. But to the last it continued to be only in an outward way. The wall of partition that separated the divine from the human, was never fully broken down . . . the revelation to the end, was a revelation of God *to* man, and not a revelation of God *in* man.[4]

The Incarnation provided the answer to the ages of longing, pagan and Jewish, to heal the breach made by man's Fall and restore man to the communion and union with God for which he was created.

Two key issues emerge from this discussion in *The Mystical Presence*, which betray Nevin's philosophical assumptions (as mentioned above), and which will dictate the course of his entire theology. First, in opposition to Hodge's dualism, Nevin sees man's nature as an integral unity of body and soul. Second, Nevin asserts that there is a sort of general life of

2. Ibid., 188.
3. Ibid., 189.
4. Ibid., 191.

humanity considered as a whole, above and beyond the mere aggregate life of all its members.[5] The following pages will set forth the implications of these points for the doctrine of the Incarnation.

The first key point of Nevin's incarnational theology is that, as human nature is a true unity of body and soul, so the Incarnation must involve a true unity of God and man: "It was no phantom or show only, but a true body joined with a reasonable soul. . . . The union of the two natures, while it leaves them distinct, must be regarded as organic, involving a strict personal unity in the form of a common undivided consciousness."[6] If it were anything less, a merely outward means of communication between divinity and humanity, it would not progress beyond what Judaism offered. An undervaluation of either the divinity or the humanity of Christ would deprive Christianity of its distinctive character and value, for

> in the first case, Christianity is shorn of its dignity as a strictly new creation, and simply carries on the process of history as it stood before; in the other case, it is such a creation as comes to no organic union whatever with the world's previous life, and runs out accordingly into the form of magic.[7]

The union between divinity and humanity accomplished in Christ cannot be merely a contractual mediation, two parties being brought together by agreement, but must be a true life-union. Puritan Christology gives us an atonement, but fails to bring us to a true "at-one-ment," Nevin says.[8]

Moreover, to have any lasting importance, it must not merely be the union of God with one man considered as an isolated individual, but must affect the whole race of mankind. This principle might not seem particularly controversial, but Nevin develops it in a way that takes direct aim on the prevailing "Puritan" theology of his day. Above all, Nevin lambasts any construction that makes the Incarnation a mere means to the end of the atonement, lacking real significance in itself:

> The incarnation is [to be] viewed not simply as an outward contrivance, to open the way for the work of redemption, but as the

5. Hodge's nominalism, on the contrary, strongly emphasizes the individuality and separateness of individual men and denies that humanity as such exists as an entity, rather than a mere name.

6. Nevin, "Sartorius," 158.

7. Nevin, "Antichrist," 23.

8. Ibid., 38.

real foundation in which the entire mystery not only starts, but continues also to hold from beginning to end. It is the union of divinity and humanity in Christ, which not simply qualifies him for the work he was appointed to perform, but of itself involves in his person that reconciliation between heaven and earth, God and man, which the idea of redemption requires, and for which there could be no room in any other form. He is in his very constitution our PEACE, in whom first the sundered worlds just mentioned are made one.[9]

How does the Incarnation possess this comprehensive force to thus give life to the whole world? It is here that Nevin's theory of a general life of humanity, mentioned above, becomes crucial. Since humanity is more than merely the sum of individual men, since it is, as it were, the greater life from which all individual men receive their humanness. Christ's Incarnation, by glorifying humanity, becomes the vivification of the human race, not merely of individual men:

> Christ's human life is] the comprehension in truth of man's life as a whole, the actual lifting up of our fallen nature from the ruins of the fall, and its full investiture with all the glory and honor for which it was originally formed. Humanity, as a single universal fact, is redeemed in Christ, truly and really, without regard to other men, any farther than as they are made to partake of this re-demption by being brought into living union with his person.[10]

Just as Adam, the Father of the race, had in his person, as it were, this general humanity, and by his sin brought death upon it, so the Second Adam unites in His person the whole human race and imparts life to humanity. The typology of Christ as the Second Adam is, of course, present in Scripture and a commonplace of Christology. But Nevin's use of it in *The Mystical Presence* is striking. For it is not as if Adam stood as merely the covenantal representative of the human race, from whom death was imputed, and Christ stood as the covenantal representative from whom life was imputed. Rather, as Adam's headship is true and organic, as encompassing in himself the future life of mankind, so Christ's headship is equally organic, and the new life which flows from Him is not some magical grace dispensed by His divinity, but the overflowing of His superabundant, glorified human life. Nevin emphasizes this point: "The

9. Nevin, "Sartorius," 154–55.

10. Nevin, "Wilberforce on the Incarnation," 175.

humanity of Christ is the repository and medium of salvation for the rest of mankind."[11]

However, in emphasizing the universal significance of the atonement, Nevin is careful to affirm its particularity and avoid asserting a general incarnation of divinity in humanity, as Hodge charged him with asserting, and as perhaps some contemporary German theologians were doing.[12] Nevin remains fully orthodox here, understanding that man is too fallen to be reconciled to God without a perfect mediator.[13] Indeed, he suggests that those who generalize the Incarnation actually undermine its universal force, and he quotes the conservative German theologian Ernst Sartorius's brilliant remarks:

> In the body of the sun, light is not concentrated, to remain there fixed, but rather that all the world may be enlightened by it; whereas when many stars twinkle in place of the one orb of day, we have at best but the dusk of night. Into such night dusk [*sic*] would those lead us, who rob the planets of their sun, while in room of the one God-man, who is the Saviour of all and the Light of the world, they affect to proclaim *all* men, and especially, the heroes of the race, an incarnation of deity. They deny both, the personal oneness and glory of Christ, as well as his true universality; for the last consists just in this, that as the *one* divine head of his Church, he comprehends under himself *all* its members, and communicates to them his truth, grace and righteousness forming them thus into one body.[14]

Nevin's strong ecclesiology enables him to avoid a pantheistic heresy on this point. For the new life which Christ brought to humanity in His Incarnation is not merely diffused throughout mankind, but is concentrated in the new humanity, the Church. It is to this new humanity that He gives His own life, and through which He transforms the world. But before enlarging on this point, we must examine Hodge's critique of

---

11. Ibid., 179.

12. Building off of Hegel's notion of the Absolute Spirit that pervades the whole world and all men, many of the more liberal German theologians tended to steer Christianity toward a sort of pantheism, in which the Incarnation stands for mankind's becoming divine. Hodge often seems to have identified Nevin's theology as falling in with this pantheizing tendency.

13. Nevin, "Sartorius," 157.

14. Ibid.

Nevin's incarnational outlook, and the more dualist theory of the hypostatic union that colors his Christology and ecclesiology.

Hodge's Perspective

In his article, "What is Christianity?" published in 1860, about a decade after the direct interaction between Princeton and Mercersburg, Hodge mounts a comprehensive critique of Nevin's anthropology, Christology, and ecclesiology. His main intent is to show that Nevin's incarnational theology and the apostasy of Hegelian idealistic pantheism, along with all forms of German theology in between, are essentially the same doctrine. On the whole, this critique appears skewed and off base, and reveals more of Hodge's own presuppositions than Nevin's.

Hodge understands, like Nevin, that one's anthropology will dictate one's incarnational theology, since "If Christ took upon him our nature, we cannot agree what he assumed, unless we are agreed to what human nature is."[15] But he disagrees with Nevin on the two main points emphasized above. First, the German anthropology, he claims, denies an essential dualism between body and soul, which is "everywhere assumed in the Bible."[16] That Schleiermacher, many German theologians, and Nevin did deny such a dualism seems rather certain; Hodge quotes them clearly to this effect, and they would have been the first to admit it. That this dualism is "everywhere assumed in the Bible" is less clear, and Hodge here offers no defense for this assertion. On the second point, he disputes the "mystical system's" (as Hodge dubs it) claim that there is an objective generic life of humanity above and beyond the mere aggregate existence of individual men. He is surely right to identify this as a linchpin of Nevin's theology, but the conclusion he draws from it, namely, that it entails "the essential oneness of God and man,"[17] seems to depend on certain assumed premises which Hodge neither mentions nor defends.

As Hodge moves on to critique the Mercersburg doctrine of the Incarnation itself, we see the same pattern. Hodge correctly identifies Nevin's emphasis on the necessity of the Incarnation, but then seems to draw unwarranted conclusions from it. As discussed above, Nevin believed that the need for union between God and man was built into

15. Hodge, "What is Christianity?" 124.
16. Ibid.
17. Ibid., 126.

creation, and the Incarnation, therefore, was the necessary climax of history. Hodge quotes many of the preceding passages and concludes that, according to Nevin, "Humanity includes in its original constitution the idea of that union with God which is found in the person of Christ, *and it reaches that end according to a law immanent in its own nature,* by a regular process of historical development."[18]

On these points, the philosophical differences discussed earlier come quite clearly to the surface. As Nevin's doctrine clearly evinces his reliance on a German idealism of sorts, so Hodge's response shows him to be firmly in the grip of Common Sense Realism. A dualism between body and soul must exist because "this is a fact revealed in the common consciousness of men."[19] The idea of a generic human life is not to be trusted because "there can be no direct evidence of its existence."[20] Also, whereas Nevin claims that Adam's sin was imputed to all humanity on the basis that the life of all humanity was contained in him, Hodge flatly asserts the contrary:

> Thus in the case of Adam, he was an individual man, with no more of the generic life of the race than any other man. He transmitted to his children his own nature, just as in any other case of reproduction in the animal or vegetable kingdom. The race were no more physically in him, than the Hebrews were *in* Abraham, or the Ishmaelites *in* Ishmael. His act was no more the act of the race, except on the ground of a divine covenant, than an act of Abraham was an act of all his posterity.[21]

Given Christ's identity as the Second Adam, such a statement is tremendously significant. Nevin feels comfortable in repeatedly appealing to Adam and his organic, perichoretic relation to his descendants in order to illustrate the relationship between Christ and His members. For Hodge, however, the analogy between Christ and Adam implies no such thing.

Moving on to discuss Christology *per se,* Hodge accuses Nevin of precisely what Nevin is at pains to deny, that the Incarnation of Christ is an incarnation in humanity as a whole, not in an individual man.[22] It is

18. Ibid., 130 (italics mine).

19. Ibid., 133.

20. Ibid., 135.

21. Ibid., 137. Never mind that Scripture often speaks in exactly this way, such as Heb 7:10.

22. Ibid., 140. On this point, his critique may have some force, though it is certainly

perhaps instructive here to quote in full Hodge's "paraphrase" of Nevin's doctrine on this, in which he claims to get at Nevin's "real meaning":

> The world is an organism. Men are not units. Humanity is a stream of life. Individual men stand related to that stream as the waves to the sea. The Son of God became incarnate, not in one of those waves, but in the stream itself. Jesus alone did not become God in virtue of the incarnation. The race becomes God. Humanity is deified and flows on, not as of old, a stream of mere human, but of theanthropic life.[23]

Had Nevin indeed taught such, he would have deserved all the abuse heaped on his "heretical system." But Hodge here does both himself and Nevin a disservice by indiscriminatingly lumping Mercersburg's orthodox incarnational theology together with apostate pantheism, and thus radically distorting the actual substance of Nevin's words. This misunderstanding again betrays the nominalist Hodge's inability to come to grips with Nevin's idealist metaphysic and careful use of the idea that Christ's Incarnation has force for humanity as a whole.

Likewise, the integralism of Nevin's anthropology transfers over to his Christology: "As in man there is no dualism between soul and body, so in Christ there is no dualism between his divine and human nature. They are one life."[24] To this integralist view of the hypostatic union Hodge is implacably opposed; in his review of *The Mystical Presence*, he accuses Nevin of Eutychianism (to which Nevin replied that Hodge's dichotomous view tended towards Nestorianism).

If we turn from this polemical article to Hodge's *Systematic Theology*, we see a bit more of a positive exposition of Hodge's own thinking, and the underlying difference is the same. For Hodge, who has already shown himself to be a dualist in his understanding of body and soul, is likewise committed to a dualist Christology, with a rigid separation of the divine and human natures in Christ. Such, indeed, Hodge argues, is the necessary conclusion of common sense and human reason. He sets forth these "axiomatic principles" at the outset of his statement on the hypostatic union: 1) attributes imply a substance or nature of which they can be predicated;

---

oversimplistic. Nevin's attempts to distinguish between particular Incarnation and universal force as opposed to universal Incarnation are sometimes a bit unclear; though, in principle, the distinction seems valid.

23. Ibid., 142.
24. Ibid., 146.

2) where attributes are incompatible, the natures must be distinct; 3) attributes cannot exist separate from a substance; 4) the attributes of one substance cannot be transferred to another.[25] Since these principles are indisputable, he believes, he can go on to construct a perfectly rational explanation of the hypostatic union. This means that, since the incompatibles of divine and human cannot in any way be mixed in the same substance, the two natures of Christ remain entirely distinct, unmixed, and unchanged. There is no union of the two into a theanthropic nature, nor is there any transfer of attributes from one nature to another. There is no indwelling between the two natures.[26] There is, he says, a "personal union" and a "communion of attributes," but all that is meant by this is that we can ascribe both the divine and human attributes to the (somewhat abstract) person of Christ, which possesses both natures.[27]

Throughout this discussion, he invokes his dualistic anthropology to support and illustrate his Christology: "As therefore the human body retains all its properties as matter, and the soul all its attributes as spirit in their union in our person, so humanity and divinity retain each its peculiar properties in their union in the person of Christ."[28] "We cannot mingle mind and matter so as to make a substance which is neither mind nor matter."[29] "As speaking in man is a joint exercise of the mind and of the body, so the mediatorial work in Christ is the joint work of his divinity and humanity."[30] Here also he is fiercely critical of more integralist accounts, condemning them both as violations of the creeds and of common sense.

In summary, then, we find Nevin embracing a more mystical approach that seeks throughout to integrate and unify, while Hodge desires a more empirical scientific method, distinguishing and separating. The Incarnation, for Nevin, is the point at which divine life merges into human, the "at-one-ment" for which mankind has been longing, and in Christ's person the whole human race is represented and enlivened. Hodge sees this as simply pantheism, and insists that divine and human were kept separate within the person of Christ, and that moreover, what

25. Hodge, *Systematic Theology*, II. 387.

26. Ibid., 388–91.

27. Ibid., 392.

28. Ibid., 389.

29. Ibid.

30. Ibid., 458.

Christ did, He did as a unique individual, separately from the rest of mankind. For Hodge, then, the Incarnation is a very localized phenomenon, and its effects are restricted to the acts of Christ which are imputed to us through His covenant headship. Nevin's Incarnation held universal force and significance, particularly as mediated through the Church, to which we shall now turn.

The Church: Christ Remains on Earth

Having examined what the Incarnation meant to these two schools of theology, we must next consider how it colors each's doctrine of the Church. Naturally, for Nevin, it will play a much larger role, as the Church is the vehicle by which the theanthropic life of Christ is carried forward through history and imparted to mankind. If Christ's Incarnation has indeed brought a new life-force into the world, how do we participate in this? This is perhaps the point at which Nevin's departure from some of his more liberal German predecessors becomes clear and crucial. For the rejuvenation of spiritual life offered in Christ is not automatic; it does not become merely merged with the life of the world in such a way to lose its distinctive, otherworldly character, but must be imparted to each individual as he is united to Christ. Moreover, this union must take place by the agency of the Church, not merely by men autonomously communing with the divine. So, despite the apparently pantheistic tendencies of his theology, Nevin's high ecclesiology maintains a sharp distinction between the Church, the locus of divine life, and the world, the object that must be transformed by that life.[31]

It is here that Nevin's doctrine of the "mystical union" becomes important.[32] The objective restoration of mankind accomplished in the Incarnation, death, and resurrection of Christ is not complete until it is subjectively fulfilled in the union of men with their Redeemer, that they might partake of that life. This union is not, Nevin emphasizes,

---

31. This of course is what Wentz refuses to take note of in his reading of Nevin.

32. On this doctrine, William Borden Evans' thorough study, already quoted in earlier sections, is crucial to a full understanding. In it, he documents the development of the theology of union with Christ within Reformed theology from Calvin through the nineteenth century. In particular, he notes how, within Reformed scholasticism, finally brought to its climax in the Princeton theology, union with Christ was bifurcated into an abstract spiritual union and an abstract covenantal union, as opposed to the earlier Reformed theology which had articulated a single union, which was real, mystical, and covenantal.

Paradigms in Collision 67

merely spiritual, or only with Christ in His divinity, but with Him in His manhood, the only medium of union with the Godhead. "Every single Christian [must] be joined in the way of real life directly with the Word absolutely taken, and not with the Word only *through* the flesh which it has already assumed in Christ."[33] Because we must unite with Christ the God-man, the only mediator between God and men, in order to be saved, it is necessary that Christ be continually present to man in the world:

> The Mediation of Christ, then, is not something past and gone, nor yet something that lies wholly beyond the actual order of the world, with which we are to communicate only in the way of memory or thought; it lives always, with perennial force, in the actual presence of Christ's manhood in the world. . . . The Incarnation cannot be held as real, if the being and working of the Mediator in the world be not apprehended as the presence in it still of the living power of the true Human Life.[34]

As stated before, Nevin is not so careless as to allow this continual presence of Christ to degenerate into a pantheistic identity between Christ and the world, or an indwelling of all men by Christ, but confines it to the Church, God's ordained agent for the perpetuation of the Incarnation. The Church thus becomes far more than a mere society of the redeemed (as often in evangelicalism) or even an apparatus for redemption (as often in Romanism), but is truly the mystical Body of Christ Himself:

> If Christ be the principle of a new creation, the point in which the earth and heavens have been brought into permanent living conjunction as never before, it follows at once plainly that the Church in which is comprehended the power of this fact, and which of this very reason is declared to be his BODY, the fullness of Him that filleth all in all, must carry in itself a constitution of its own, as really objective and enduring, to say the least, as the course of nature, on which as a basis it is made supernaturally to rest.[35]

As the first Adam was head over the old creation, so Christ, the Second Adam, has become the author of the new creation, which is begun and carried forward in the Church: "The creation itself becomes

33. Nevin, "Wilberforce on the Incarnation," 182
34. Ibid., 185.
35. Nevin, "Antichrist," 40.

complete only in the Church, the life of nature in the life of the Spirit."[36] All that Christ was and all that He did are carried on in His Body, which is animated by His Spirit.[37] Moreover, it is important to note, because Christ's life is carried over and transmitted to us in the Church, and not dispensed from on high through some kind of ethereal one-on-one relationship between Christ and the believer, an individual Christian becomes an oxymoron. Properly understood, we become Christians, not separately and on our own, but by union with the Body of Christ, and Christianity is thus an organic, corporate affair, as pictured in the scriptural metaphors of "body" and "vine."[38] Despite all the grand claims that he makes for the Church, therefore, Nevin insists that we not allow it to degenerate into an ideal abstraction; the Church is the corporate body of believers, and is as visible and real as Christ himself when He walked on earth.

The doctrines of Christology and ecclesiology are not separable from one another, as Nevin argues forcefully in *Antichrist*. A docetic Christ will lead to a docetic church, "an election of living units, the pneumatic order of human spirits, each attracted for itself towards Christ, and all uniting by aggregation to form the idea of his kingdom."[39] It is perhaps at this point that Nevin's argument is most revealing and compelling: if Christ is to be truly the God-man, a genuine union of divine and human, Spirit and flesh, then the Church, as His Body, that which carries forward His life, must likewise be a union of divine and human, Spirit and flesh, visible and invisible. A fully human Christ will not allow for an abstract, invisible Church. If the Church is invisible, and is the Body of Christ, then it follows that Christ is the Invisible Man![40] This may sound like sophistry and equivocation, but Nevin clearly has a point. One's Christology will dictate one's ecclesiology, and if "the tabernacle of God is with man . . . humanity itself has become the Shechinah of glory, in the person of Immanuel,"[41] then the same must be said of His

---

36. Nevin, *Mystical Presence*, 204.

37. Nevin, "Church," 59.

38. Nevin, *Mystical Presence*, 216–17. Note that here too, Nevin's idealist metaphysic manifests itself. Just as there is a generic human life above and logically prior to individual men, so in the new humanity, the Church, there is a generic new life above and logically prior to individual believers.

39. Nevin, "Antichrist," 41.

40. Credit for elucidating this sublime syllogism must go to my friend Brad Belschner, who scribbled it in the margins of my research notes.

41. Nevin, *Mystical Presence*, 201.

visible Body, the Church. That means the ivy-covered building down the street, the men and women in the pew next to you on Sunday morning, the "heretics" in the other denomination, however unfitting it may seem that God would condescend to commune with man through so lowly a medium.

This brings us to the next question: what is the relationship between the Church visible and the Church invisible? This problem has plagued the Reformed churches for the last four hundred years, and here, more than anywhere, Mercersburg's teaching becomes highly relevant to the Reformed Church of today. This is also one of the most fascinating facets of Mercersburg theology; it seems to be the point of fundamental divergence between them and most of their contemporaries, yet they almost never explicitly focus on this as a key point of difference or treat it with the same polemic vigor seen in Nevin's works on the Incarnation, for example. The same is true of Hodge's treatment of the issue. In one way, this is an advantage, since it allows us to compare and contrast the two positions more dispassionately and clearly.

In his "Theses for the Time" at the end of *The Principle of Protestantism*, Schaff shows the connection between the Mercersburg view of the Incarnation and of the Church in Thesis 7:

> [The Church] possesses, like her Founder, a divine and human, an ideal and a real, a heavenly and an earthly nature; only with this difference, that in her militant stage, freedom from sin and error cannot be predicated of her in the same sense as of Christ; that is, she possesses the principle of holiness and the full truth, mixed, however, still with sin and error.[42]

Two key points emerge from this quote. The first is the analogy between the Person of Christ and the nature of the Church, already touched upon. The second is that the two natures of the Church are just that: two natures of the same organism, the same Body, rather than two separate bodies. These two natures are distinguished as the divine, ideal, heavenly nature vs. the human, real, earthly nature. The juxtaposition of "real" with human and earthly, rather than divine and heavenly, stands out as a striking deviation from much common thinking (then and now) about the Church, and its departure from Hodge's paradigm will soon become clear. Though the distinction of "ideal" and "real" is somewhat

---

42. Schaff, *Principle of Protestantism*, 220.

more complicated (to be discussed below), Schaff here affirms that the earthly aspect of the Church is by no means artificial or illusory, but is undeniably, inseparably, really part of the Body of Christ. As such, she is still riddled with imperfections, admittedly, in her "militant stage," but will one day be glorified.

Another way of looking at this question, articulated in Theses 3–5, speaks of the Church as the Body of Christ in two "respects": "her communion with her Head, and also the relation of her members to one another."[43] The first respect pertains to her role as a supernatural institution through which the life of Christ is communicated to her members and to the world. The second pertains to her role as a society of members communing with one another and working together by the same Spirit. Note that the first basically corresponds to the typical notion of the invisible church, the second to the visible, but here, they are merely "respects"—different roles of the same Body.

This notion is further developed in Nevin's remarkable sermon on Ephesians 1:23 ("Which is His body, the fulness of Him that filleth all in all") delivered at the convention of the Eastern Synod of the German Reformed Church in 1846. From the start, he declares, "The Church exhibits itself to us under two aspects, which are in many respects very different, and yet both alike necessary to complete its proper constitution. In one view it is the *Ideal Church*, in another it is the *Actual Church*."[44] Again, we see that these are merely two *aspects* of the one Body of Christ. Nevin goes on to develop each of these at some length, and I will uncover his definitions of each in turn. By "ideal," he qualifies (betraying his metaphysical precommitments once again) that he means not simply a mental construct but the "inmost substance of that which exists. . . . It is not opposed to what is actual, but constitutes rather its truth and soul."[45] Therefore, the Ideal Church, he concludes with a sweeping rhetorical flourish, "is the most real of all realities that God has established in this world, 'the pillar and ground of the truth' (1 Tim 3:15); the basis, in one word, of the 'new heavens and new earth, wherein dwelleth righteousness' (2 Pet 3:13)."[46]

43. Ibid.
44. Nevin, "Church," 58.
45. Ibid.
46. Ibid.

Much of what Nevin says about the Ideal Church has already been considered above in the latter section about the Incarnation, but a few more excerpts are worth quoting: "It is a living system, organically bound together in all its parts, springing from a common ground, and pervaded throughout with the force of a common nature. In its very conception, therefore, it is catholic, that is, one and universal."[47] "In her Ideal character . . . the Church is absolutely holy and infallible, free from error and sin . . . the Church is represented to be the organ and medium by which the world is reclaimed from the power of error, and transformed into a holy life."[48] "In its very conception, it is the power of a common or general life, which can never appear, therefore, as something isolated and single simply, but always includes the idea of society and communion, under all its manifestations."[49] Since the Church is thus necessarily social, "The Church under its ideal character includes in itself the necessity of a visible externalization in the world."[50] However majestic this Ideal Church may be, however much the "truth and soul" of that which exists, it is not complete on its own, but must be manifested in an actual, incarnate form.[51]

This actual form is the visible Church historical which we observe and of which we are members. It can, says Nevin, be viewed merely in light of one or another period, as the second-century church, or the Reformation-era church, but it is more than that. "Through all periods the Church remains the same, and from beginning to end, her history is but the power of a single fact."[52] Of course, by saying "the same" he by no means intends a static, unchanging conception of the Church; far from it. In the very next sentence, he declares that the Church is a "process"—a process which "is always pressing forward to its completion, as this will appear in the millennium."[53] He goes on to clarify, as Schaff did, that this actual church necessarily falls short of its ideal perfection. But this

47. Ibid., 59.
48. Ibid., 59–60.
49. Ibid., 60.
50. Ibid.
51. Note here how everything so far discussed ties together. Just as Nevin's anthropology insists that man's soul must be externalized in a body, and the divine life had to be externalized in Christ, so the Ideal Church must be externalized in the actual. We shall see the exact reverse, but equally consistent, pattern in Hodge.
52. Ibid., 61.
53. Ibid., 62.

is by no means a diminution of its importance; on the contrary, "This lies in its very conception. The Church is a new creation for the world, complete from the first in Christ, but requiring a process of historical evolution, according to the law of all life, to actualize itself with final, universal triumph in the world as a whole."[54] Thus he undercuts both the Roman conception of an infallible visible church and the evangelical notion of a fallible and therefore meaningless visible church. Another result of this doctrine, which Nevin points out, is that just because the Church falls short of her ideal in some respect, such as perfect unity, she has not ceased to be the Church. The implications of this will become very important to Nevin and Schaff's conception of Church history, which will be discussed in the next chapter.

Hodge's Perspective

Hodge's doctrine of the Church is radically different. Needless to say, his disagreement with the Mercersburg doctrine of the Incarnation precludes for him any idea of the Church as some kind of extension of the Incarnation. Just as he undervalues the humanity of Christ in favor of the divinity and the flesh in favor of the spirit, so the Body of Christ for him is entirely a spiritual idea, an empty metaphor. His doctrine of the visible and invisible church is determined by his Cartesian dualism and his nominalist anthropology and follows directly from what we have already seen of his theology. Unsurprisingly, the doctrine of the Church plays almost no role in his *Systematic Theology*, but the collection of his writings on the Church, posthumously published as *Discussions in Church Polity*, gives us a very clear representation of his ecclesiology.

The very first article, "The Idea of the Church," leaves us in no doubt as to where Hodge stands on the visible/invisible question.[55] He states forthrightly at the outset, "The conception of the Church as the communion of saints, does not include the idea of any external organization.

54. Ibid.

55. Note that for Hodge's metaphysic, "idea" carries very different connotations than it does for Nevin's. For Nevin, the "ideal" is distinguishable from but never separable from the "actual"—they are two sides of the same coin. For Hodge, the "idea" of something is its abstract, non-physical essence, which, because it is really most actual, most true and real, is completely separable from its physical manifestation. Another way of putting this would be to say that for Nevin, both "ideal" and "actual" are necessary; for Hodge, the "ideal" is necessary, while the "actual" is contingent.

The bond of union may be spiritual. There may be communion without external organized union."[56] Note here how radically Hodge's spiritualizing approach reverses Nevin and Schaff's doctrine. We might not be surprised to find Hodge making invisible and spiritual that aspect of the Church which is the communion between the saints and Christ, but he also treats as invisible the communion of saints with one another, the second respect in which Schaff speaks of the Church (see above), and one which we might expect to be a very visible phenomenon. Now, in fairness to Hodge, his purpose here (and in many of his writings on the Church) is to preserve catholicity. In particular, he wants to dispute the Roman Catholic claim that the whole of the Church is to be found in one particular organization. The Church transcends the boundaries of any one denomination; it is not tied to any external organization, insists Hodge. If this were all that he said, he and Nevin would have been in firm agreement. However, Hodge felt that in order to safeguard the claim "The Church does not consist in any particular visible organization, to the exclusion of others," he had to claim "The Church does not consist in any visible organization at all," a claim with far more radical consequences.

Lest any should doubt whether he does indeed make such a radical claim, consider the following quote from "The Idea of the Church," directly following the section quoted above:

> The Church, therefore, according to this view, is not essentially a visible society; it is not a corporation which ceases to exist if the external bond of union be dissolved. It may be proper that such union should exist; it may be true that it has always existed; but it is not necessary. *The Church, as such, is not a visible society. All visible union, all external organization, may cease, and yet, so long as there are saints who have communion, the Church exists, if the Church is the communion of saints.*[57]

There is Hodge's clear statement on the subject. The Church as a visible body may exist, but the Church as such is not a visible body; for the two millennia since Christ's resurrection no visible body of believers may have existed, and yet the Church would have just as truly remained. On the other hand, Hodge is not denying the value of the visible church, which he strongly affirms in his *Systematic Theology*, calling it a "divine

56. Hodge, *Discussions in Church Polity*, 5.

57. Ibid., 5–6 (italics mine).

institution."[58] He elaborates, saying, "It is the will of God that such a Church should exist on earth. . . . God has imposed duties upon his people which render it necessary for them thus to associate in a visible organized body. They are to unite in worship; in teaching and propagating the truth, in testifying for God."[59] We may reconcile these two statements by clarifying that for Hodge the visible church is not necessary from the nature of the Church, but as a means of effectually accomplishing Christian duties.[60] Hodge does not deny that the visible church is important and valuable in many ways. But the point is that, whatever the significance of the visible church, visibility must not be considered part of the Church's *essence*. Hodge here is employing a rigid distinction between essence and accident: he wants to find out what the Church itself truly is, its essence; the Church may have other attributes, but these are accidents, and hence contingent, changeable, and dispensable.

This is made further clear in the article "The Visibility of the Church," comprising Chapter III of the *Church Polity*. Here he submits that, if the Church were, in its essence, an external, visible organization, then it would have all the attributes of other such organizations, like the nation of England, and hence be temporary and perishable.[61] But since its essence is otherwise, it is eternal, and "is visible only, in the sense in which believers are visible."[62] He fleshes out this remark by considering

58. Hodge, *Systematic Theology*, III.547. It is important to note that this discussion, the closest thing to a section on ecclesiology in the *Systematic Theology*, appears merely as a prefatory discussion to the question of infant baptism, the defense of which appears to be the motivation for his doctrine of the visible Church in this section: "In order to justify the baptism of infants, we must attain and authenticate such an idea of the Church as that it shall include the children of believing parents" (547). In this quote and others, Hodge appears to be patching together his theory of the Church to support a sacramental tradition that he has already accepted as a given. From Nevin's perspective, this is inverted: the doctrine of the Church must be the source from which your sacramentology necessarily flows out.

59. Ibid., 547–48.

60. Note that the bond, then, between Christ and the visible church is a merely incidental one; it is a tool that He often uses, not a part of His own body. For Nevin, however, the necessity of the visible Church flows out of the very nature of the Church and of Christ—Christ and His visible body are organically bound together.

61. Even assuming that his quest for "essence" is on target, Hodge here appears to set up for himself a false dilemma. The essence of the Church must either be that of a visible organization, or that of an invisible organization. Why is it not possible that the essence of the Church includes some qualities of both?

62. Hodge, *Church Polity*, 55.

four respects in which the Church is visible. First, because "it consists of men and women, in distinction from disembodied spirits or angels."[63] Second, "because its members manifest their faith by their works . . . goodness is an inward quality, and yet it is outwardly manifested, so that the good are known and recognized as such."[64] The third reason appears to be essentially the same as the second—namely, the Church is visible because believers are "separated from the world," they are new creatures, "they are visible, as a pure river is often seen flowing unmingled through the turbid waters of a broader stream."[65] Finally, "the true Church is visible in the external Church, just as the soul is visible in the body. That is, as by the means of the body we know that the soul is there, so by means of the external Church, we know where the true Church is."[66] This is particularly intriguing, because, as we have seen, Nevin has used a similar model to articulate the relationship of the *ideal* and the *actual* Church, which he seems to conceive of as analogous to a soul-body relationship. However, this metaphor means something very different for Nevin and Hodge; for Nevin, with his integralist anthropology, the visible body is the inseparable necessary form of the soul; while for Hodge's dualism, the connection is much looser and more contingent. So, in this last quote, the soul-body metaphor tells us that the visible church is not the true Church, but merely points to it; it is a symptom, as it were, indicating that the true Church is probably somewhere nearby.[67]

It hardly needs to be pointed out that this is a very weak account of the visibility of the Church, and few will find it a sufficient summary of biblical teaching on the subject. Hodge's persistent nominalism manifests itself again in this discussion, as the visibility of the Church is repeatedly made to rest in the visibility of individual believers, of which the Church is a mere aggregate assembly. Just as Hodge was so adamant that there was no higher existence of humanity *qua* humanity beyond the sum existences of individual humans, so there appears to be no higher existence of the Church *qua* Church beyond the sum existences of individual

63. Ibid., 56.

64. Ibid.

65. Ibid.

66. Ibid., 57.

67. Though this does not necessarily follow as well as Hodge wants it to. After all, according to Hodge, many eras and examples of the visible Church have been almost hopelessly corrupt, and have not necessarily been a sure sign that the true Church dwelt amongst them.

Christians. Some might object that since union with Christ, the Head, is what makes men Christians, Christ Himself is the higher existence of the Church, in whom the whole body holds together. However, in Hodge's nominalist system, this union with Christ is something that believers possess each one for himself, rather than as a corporate body; the corporate body is a mere by-product. Simply put, for Hodge, the logical order is: a man is justified and thus united to Christ, and hence, is in fellowship (spiritually) with other believers so united to Christ, and this communion constitutes the Church. For Nevin, on the other hand, a man is brought into the visible body of the Church and thus united to Christ, with all his saving benefits.

A brief recap is in order at this point. Nevin and Schaff define the Church as the historical perpetuation of the life of Christ, comprising a new humanity which is in life-giving union with its Head and shares this life with the world, transforming the old creation into the new. This body is perfect in principle, and will be perfect at the last day, but in its unfolding throughout history is tainted by error and apostasy, which it will only gradually overcome. The Church is one as truly as a human body is one because it is the unfolding of the one life of Christ, and is to embody this unity both outwardly and inwardly. Hodge, on the other hand, defines the Church as the spiritual fellowship of the elect, who are each united to Christ, the Head, and thus, through Him, to each other. In each believer, the old creation is superseded by the new, but this transformation is not a corporate, much less a cosmic matter. Because the visible church is tainted by error and apostasy, it is no true manifestation of the real, spiritual Church, but a mere society formed for the better achievement of Christian ends. The Church is one in the Spirit, but any physical or visible unity is accidental and unnecessary. Thus stand the two contrasting systems.

Church History: Christ Triumphs on Earth

This final section will bring our assessment of Mercersburg vs. Princeton full circle. We began by considering Schaff's view of Church history as expressed in *The Principle of Protestantism* and the controversy it created. Then we showed the principles which underlay his and Hodge's views, and uncovered the fundamental differences in anthropology, Christology, and ecclesiology which divided Mercersburg and Princeton into wholly different systems of theology. Having examined the foundation, we shall return to the question of Church history to demonstrate more fully the Mercersburg approach and distinguish it from the Princeton approach.

The most crucial and insightful work on this question to come out of Mercersburg was Philip Schaff's *What is Church History?* published in 1846. In this short book, he expands on the ideas which informed the theory of *The Principle of Protestantism* and offered a sweeping survey of the motivations and methods of studying Church history. At the outset, unsurprisingly, he insists on the intimate connection between ecclesiology and Church history:

> In proportion, however, as the Church is thus brought into prominent and principal view, her *History* must also become for theologians an object of attention and inquiry. Church and History altogether, since the introduction of Christianity, are so closely united, that respect and love towards the first, may be said to be essentially the same with a proper sense of what is comprised in the other. The Christian Church is itself the greatest fact in the history of the world, by which the ancient order of life both Jewish and Heathen has been overturned, and the way opened for a new course of existence altogether. Almost nothing has since occurred that can be counted great and important, which is not found to stand in nearer or more remote, friendly or hostile, connexion with the Church, and to acquire its true historical significance precisely from this relation. History, on the other hand, is the bearer of the Church; by whose means this last is made to possess a real existence, whereas, under any other form it could be nothing better than a baseless, fantastic abstraction, which for us who are ourselves the product of history, and draw from it all the vigour of our lives, would have no meaning or value whatever.[68]

In this quote, Schaff argues that the Church is, *by its nature,* visible and historical, and comes to maturity in history. Moreover, history, *by its nature,* is oriented by the Church. Therefore, not only is a proper understanding of Church history essential to any true idea of the nature of the Church, but it is necessary to give meaning to the lives of Christians today. The study of Church history, then, is as important as any area of doctrine, and those who neglect or abuse it endanger the project of Christian theology as a whole.

---

68. Schaff, *What is Church History?* 25–26.

This inseparable relationship between Church and history follows directly from the Mercersburg view of the visible/invisible church distinction, discussed above. For Nevin and Schaff, the visible, historical Church is inseparable from the invisible, timeless Church—it is indeed its necessary manifestation. There is no concept of a true Church existing in a transcendent realm beyond time and space, of which the Church we see is merely some vague corollary. No, if the Church is to have reality at all, it must be a reality which actualizes itself in space and time. And of course, we will remember that this is so because the Church springs out of the Incarnation, in which God declared that His saving power must be something which was actualized in space and time. But more importantly, the Church must be historical because God has a historical plan for His creation. Creation, Fall, Redemption, Consummation—the whole order of the world's life flows forward, first as a degeneration toward death and separation from God, then after the Incarnation and Resurrection, as an eternal regeneration towards life and union with God. God has willed neither that the glorification of mankind take place in an instant, nor that man be divorced from time and the world to be clothed with his glorified state. For it is not just man who is to be redeemed; the God-man came for the life of the world, and through His saving power in the Church, the whole world must be transformed into a new creation, to the glory of God the Father. This story of transformation is the story of History, and it is thus through history that the Church becomes the Church and accomplishes her God-given task to disciple the nations.

This idea comes out in Schaff's fondness for the scriptural image of the Church as the "kingdom of Christ on earth."[69] Just as any kingdom, it has citizens, it has a history, and it accomplishes its conquests in history, until it completes those conquests and history as we now know it shall cease: "The church is in part a pedagogic institution, to train men for heaven, and as such destined to pass away in its present form, when the salvation shall be completed."[70] Moreover, the Church is "the continuation of the life and work of Christ upon earth."[71] Therefore, because it is alive, animated by the life of Christ, "the church is not to be viewed as a thing at once finished and perfect, but as a historical fact, as a human society, subject to the laws of history, to genesis, growth, development. Only the

69. Schaff, *History of the Apostolic Church*, 164.

70. Ibid.

71. Ibid., 166.

dead is done and stagnant. All created life . . . is essentially motion, process, constant change."[72] Again, however, the distinction between ideal and actual plays a key role in this concept of development: "the church, in its idea, or viewed subjectively in Christ, in whom dwelleth all the fullness of the Godhead bodily, who is the same yesterday, to-day, and for ever, is from the first complete and unchangeable."[73] However, he says, we must distinguish from the *idea of the Church* its *"actual manifestation on earth; from the objective revelation itself we must discriminate the subjective apprehension and appropriation of it in the mind of humanity at a given time."*[74] This latter is necessarily gradual and progressive; the Church slowly grows to maturity through history.

Having established that Church and history are thus inextricably linked, Schaff moves on to discuss particular ways in which the Church evolves through history, and in which it is an object of historical study. First of all, the growth of the Church is "an *outward extension* over the earth, till all nations shall walk in the light of the gospel."[75] We may trace through time the geographical and institutional growth of the Church, from a loose collection of Near-Eastern house churches to a multitude of immense governmental structures spanning continents and cultures. Second, the history of the Church

> consists in an *inward unfolding* of the idea of the church, in *doctrine, life, worship,* and *government*; the human nature, in all its parts, coming more and more to bear the impress of that new principle of life, which has been given in Christ to humanity, and which is yet to transform the world into a glorious and blessed kingdom of God.[76]

Third, this history is necessarily organic:

> It is not an outward, mechanical aggregation of facts, which have no living connection. It is a process of life, which springs from within, from the vital energy implanted in the church, and which remains, in all its course, identical with itself, as man through all the stages of his life still continues man.[77]

72. Ibid., 167.
73. Ibid., 168.
74. Ibid.
75. Ibid., 169.
76. Ibid.
77. Ibid.

Moreover, it is a dialectical struggle, in which negative tendencies in each stage of development are succeeded by a new state of development, which builds upon what was positive in the previous stage.[78]

Essential in this organic concept of history is a common-sense, but significant, principle: "History properly allows no pause."[79] No matter how much we may categorize and periodize, history remains one unified story, one unbreakable stream. If the Church truly exists in history, we must allow that its history admits of no pause or division, but is one story. To be sure, Schaff admits, individual sects or even large branches of the Church may become severed from the one organic body, and dwindle away, "but the main stream of church history moves *uninterruptedly onward*, and *must* finally reach its divinely-appointed end. *Ecclesia non potest deficere*."[80]

This principle was to have a major influence on Nevin's and Schaff's understanding of the relationship between medieval Church and the Reformation, which was the question confronted at the outset of this thesis. This, however, is part of a larger question: how do we view the flow of Church history as a whole? Church history for Schaff, as already alluded to, necessarily consists of the unity of ideal and actual which underlies the Mercersburg conception of the Church. Through all its ages, the Church is animated by Christ and exhibits to us Christ, and His workings among His people. This is the ideal perspective. The history of the actual Church, however, presents us with a darker picture, full of schisms, apostasies, and human failures. The solution to this is not to insist that the actual Church is something entirely different from the ideal, but that, as one body, it is steadily growing into closer conformity with its ideal. As Schaff puts it:

> church history shews that this opposition, and that all errors and divisions, even though they may have a long and almost universal prevalence, must in the end serve only to awaken the church to her real world, to call forth her deepest energies, to furnish the occasion for higher developments, and thus to glorify the name of God and His Son Jesus Christ. All tribulation, too, and persecutions are for the church, what they are for the individual Christian, only a powerful refining fire, in which she

78. It is at this point that Schaff's Hegelianism shines through most clearly.

79. Ibid., 170.

80. Ibid.

is to be gradually purged from all her dross; till at last, adorned
as a bride at the side of her heavenly spouse upon the renovated
earth, she shall celebrate the resurrection morning as her last and
most glorious pentecost.[81]

Periods of division may indeed taint the Church's history, but they are
never more than periods, in Schaff's outlook. Schismatic elements either
lose all contact with the main body of the Church and wither away, or at
last, reunite with it, making it stronger and healthier than ever. Even in the
case of the centuries-long rift between Orthodox and Catholic, Catholic
and Protestant, Schaff was confident that Christ's triumph would at last
reconcile these bodies as well.

Such a perspective must overturn the common Protestant paradigm
of Church history. There can be no notion of a pristine and perfect apostolic Church, superseded after a short while by the abuses of prelacy and
popery, and at last overwhelmed by wholesale Romish apostasy, until the
true gospel was rediscovered at last by Luther and the Reformers. Nevin
satirizes this typical viewpoint in one of the most brilliant bits of polemic
writing ever to flow from his pen, saying,

> Hardly had the last of the apostles gone to heaven, before signs
> of apostasy began to show themselves in the bosom of the infant
> church, threatening to overthrow and defeat entirely its original
> design . . . till in the course of a single century from the death
> of St. John, perhaps indeed much sooner, the entire course of its
> life was changed from what it had been at first, and turned in a
> false direction. Traces of the original faith and piety are still to
> be found indeed in the third and fourth and fifth centuries . . .
> the power that prevailed, and that was fast carrying all things its
> own way, almost without question or protest, was the "mystery
> of iniquity," that same great anti-Christian apostasy in principle
> and drift, which in due time afterwards culminated in the Pope,
> and brought upon the world the darkness of the middle ages.
> . . . So in truth Satan in the end fairly prevailed over Christ. The
> church fell, not partially and transiently only, but universally, in
> its collective and corporate character, with an apostasy that was
> to reach through twelve hundred years. . . . So long as the Bible
> lived, there was still room for hope; and at last accordingly, "in the
> fulness of time," after centuries upon centuries of ecclesiastical

81. Ibid., 176.

chaos, God was pleased to say once more "Let there be light," and there was light.[82]

Obviously, this is a rather extreme view that Nevin is critiquing. Most intelligent Protestant theologians and historians would confess that the situation was more nuanced than that, and that many valuable truths were preserved through the general meltdown of the medieval Church.

However, the point remains that from the Puritan perspective, there is no reason why the view satirized above could not be true. If the essence of the Church lies in an unchanging, invisible union of the elect with Christ, there is no need to insist on continuity within the history of the visible body. Saints in the early Church had union with Christ, this Church ceased entirely to be a true Church, but there were still saints within the body who had union with Christ, and finally, at the Reformation, a new visible institution was formed which was more conducive to true faith. Christians who think this way need not think of medieval Christians as their brethren, part of the same body, but may rest content in critiquing them as hypocritical professors in an entirely different institution than their own. Not only were such destructive doctrinal effects as these to be feared, but this paradigm simply led to bad history, or, as Nevin puts it, with his distinctive vehemence, "it has not a syllable of true historical evidence in its favor."[83] As Nevin meticulously demonstrated in many of his writings,[84] it is simply false that the early Church was a pure apostolic institution, or that it was clearly distinct from the "Catholic" elements that came later—it was "Catholic" from the beginning. Thus, those who make Christianity to consist essentially in an individual religion, unmediated by the institutions of the Church, must admit that Christianity fell away from its true principle at its very inception. Nevin also denies that the Reformation was anything like a complete overturning of medieval theology and a return to the Early Church:

> However much of rubbish the Reformation found occasion to
> remove, it was still compelled to do homage to the main body
> of the Roman theology as orthodox and right; and to this day

82. Nevin, "Early Christianity," 518–19.

83. Ibid., 560.

84. Particularly his three articles on "Early Christianity," his sequence of articles on "Cyprian," and his carefully argued piece on "The Heidelberg Catechism." Nor is it to be forgotten that the bulk of *The Mystical Presence* and the many rebuttals to Hodge's critique of it were a historical argument about the nature of Reformation theology.

> Protestantism has no valid mission in the world, any farther than
> it is willing to build on this old foundation.[85]

Schaff too depends upon this principle of historical continuity, not only
in *The Principle of Protestantism*, but in all his writings on Church history, including his famed *History of the Christian Church*.

Hodge's Perspective

Indeed, Charles Hodge was sufficiently uncomfortable with the presuppositions of Schaff's Church history that upon the publication of the
first volume of the *History of the Christian Church*, he printed a lengthy
review and critique in the pages of *The Princeton Review*. By this point
Hodge understood the broader principles at stake in the debate, and uses
the review as an occasion to expose and critique the broader patterns
of Mercersburg theology, in the process revealing some of the key connections between their anthropology, Christology, and ecclesiology that
have been addressed here. Again, however, he seems less aware of the
principles underlying his own position, which rule out certain understandings of Church history *a priori*.

Most important of these is his understanding of the essential nature
of Christianity.[86] "Christianity," he says, "is a system of doctrines super-
naturally revealed and now recorded in the Bible."[87] This stands in contrasts to Mercersburg's theory, in which Christianity "is not a doctrine, it
is not a rule of conduct, it is not a feeling, but a life. . . . Christianity is not,
therefore, a system of truth divinely revealed, recorded in the Scripture
in a definite and complete form for all ages, but it is an inward living
principle, an entirely new form of life."[88] Since Christianity is essentially
a system of doctrine and, "of that system there can be no development"[89]
(lest we allow that truth be subjective), Hodge cannot hold to anything
like Schaff's idea of historic development. He professes to hold to some

85. Ibid., 532–33. At this quote Dr. Proudfit, writing in *The Princeton Review*, seems
quite flabbergasted, though his refutation of it consists of no more than placing two excla-
mations after the quote and calling it a "strange and sad spectacle" (Proudfit, "Heidelberg
Catechism," 132).

86. For more on this, see his article "What is Christianity?" discussed above in relation
to the doctrine of the Incarnation.

87. Hodge, "Dr. Schaff's Apostolic Church," 157.

88. Ibid., 171.

89. Ibid., 157.

idea of the historical development of the Church, but he then goes on to qualify this concept into oblivion.

For example, he admits that, "while Christianity, considered as a system of doctrine, is thus complete and unchangeable, the knowledge of that system as it lies in the mind of the individual Christian, or in the Church collectively, is susceptible of progress, and does in fact advance."[90] So we have two forms of historical development: 1) an individual's Christian progressive growth in his knowledge of doctrine; and 2) the growth of the collective body of Christians in knowledge of doctrine. As examples of the second, he cites the fact that the great Trinitarian and Christological declarations of the first five centuries were a great step forward, as was the Protestant doctrine of justification. Moreover, the evangelical Churches of his day, he claims, were far in advance of the authoritarian doctrines of the Reformers.[91]

However, this modest claim must be heavily qualified. The purity and knowledge of the Church may just as easily regress as progress, according to Hodge. Of course, Schaff and Nevin admit as much as well— the growth of the Church is a bumpy, not smooth upward slope. But in Hodge's account, it appears more like a series of hills, sloping downward as drastically as upward. Where Nevin and Schaff might have admitted that the fourteenth century was a regression from the twelfth, but on the whole, a progression from the sixth, for example, Hodge boldly declares, "the tenth century was far behind the second, and the state of the Romish Church before the Reformation *tenfold worse* than what it was in the days of Clemens Romanus."[92] Note the force of this declaration: the Church of the fifteenth century, guardian of the theological treasures of Anselm and Aquinas and all the great doctrinal advances of the first 1400 years, was tenfold worse than the Church riddled with Gnosticism, untaught in the doctrines of the Trinity, the Incarnation, Original Sin, the substitutionary atonement, etc. This is not far from Nevin's caricature: "So in the end Satan fairly prevailed over Christ." We might well reply that this leaves us with no historical development, implying as that does forward progress, but merely historical change. But Hodge has an answer ready:

90. Ibid., 158.

91. Ibid., 161–62. Here, ironically, Schaff might not agree that there had been historical progress.

92. Ibid., 162.

> In all these cases we must make a distinction between the true and the nominal Church, between sincere and professing Christians. The former may retain their integrity in the midst of the degeneracy and apostasy of the latter. The true Church may attain its highest state of spiritual excellence, in the midst of the general defection of the external body.[93]

What this boils down to, then, is that the elect will steadily grow in knowledge and purity, but the Church as a visible historical institution may well do the reverse. It could be contended that this theory, by essentially abstracting progress into the invisible realm, forfeits any right to be considered a notion of *historical* progress, given that visible, not invisible, institutions are the province of history. So Hodge's doctrine of the historical development of *doctrine* is weak. Perhaps this does not matter so much—doctrinal development is, after all, only part of the picture for Nevin and Schaff.

However, defining Christianity as a system of doctrines, Hodge has ruled out any other possible notion of historical development. Certainly it does not develop organically, as Mercersburg would have it—a growth and maturation of spiritual life, stemming always from Christ as the root and source of its life. He critiques the notion that Christians are connected to Christ through the Church as leaves on a tree to its root, arguing that, on the contrary, Christ is always and immediately present to believers: "the individual believer gets his life by immediate union with Christ, and not through the Church."[94] Moreover, since "the Church of the present does not derive its life by way of transmission from the Church of the past, but immediately from Christ by his work and Spirit," she may acknowledge and respect the teachings of former ages, but "her faith always rests immediately on the word of God."[95]

Whatever the integrity of Hodge's conclusion here, the way he reaches it certainly undermines any remaining notion of historical continuity in the Church. So then, are we left with any notion of continuity in the body of Christ? If there is a continuity, it cannot be of a particular visible organization, since we know that this has split many times. Nor can it be a continuity of doctrine, since we know that certain eras of the Church have

93. Ibid., 162–63.

94. Ibid., 163. It is curious that Hodge is so fierce and so undiscriminating in his critique of this metaphor, given that the tree metaphor derives from Scripture.

95. Ibid., 165.

backslidden into complete apostasy; moreover, our doctrinal authority, Scripture, comes to us immediately rather than historically, and hence, there is no fundamental sense in which our present doctrine grows out of past doctrine. Nor can it be a continuity of life, since the Church for Hodge, as we know, is in no sense a continuation of the Incarnation, or an organic growth, but a collection of believers each immediately united to Christ. The only remaining unity, then, is a unity of sympathy and feeling between believers of various eras,[96] or the spiritual union of the elect throughout all time. But, as mentioned before, neither of these can be in any way considered a historical continuity. Church history, then, is no longer an essential key to understanding what the Church is, the means by which the Church "is made to possess a real existence" and which gives "meaning" and "value" to believers' lives.[97] Instead, it is merely a profitable source for studying the various forms Christian doctrine has taken over the years and for observing the successes and failures of Christians in other times and places. No wonder, then, that Hodge has so little respect for the medieval Church and so much confidence in the perfections of Protestantism, as observed in the last chapter.

In conclusion, we see that Nevin and Schaff have a strong view of the interconnectedness of Church and history, growing out of their ecclesiology. Since the Church is necessarily a visible institution on earth, it necessarily undergoes changes and movements throughout history, and since it is animated by the Spirit and governed by Christ, these changes always point forward and lead the Church inexorably to its final triumph. Through all of its troubles and divisions, the Church is gradually progressing in its geographical spread over the earth, its institutional liberty and strength, and its conformity to Christ in life and doctrine. Hodge, on the other hand, sees change as a sign of impurity and imperfection, always a movement of decay. The invisible true Church, then, cannot be subjected to decay, though the visible church of course does undergo historical change, particularly doctrinal change. However, for Hodge, this change never really attains to the level of "historical progress": the visible church can as easily regress as progress, and insomuch as there is progress, Hodge isolates it to a limited number of elect individuals, who are not ultimately identifiable and thus not really objects of historical study.

96. Though even this, it might be objected, is undermined by the way in which Hodge denigrates medieval Christians as apostates.

97. Schaff, *What Is Church History?* 25–26.

Historical theology Hodge is content with: human thoughts change and progress, of course, and as long as the theology is allowed to govern the history, Hodge is happy to study that change. But true Church history, in which the Body of Christ is seen "as a historical fact, as a human society, subject to the laws of history, to genesis, growth, development," that Hodge cannot countenance, for the *true* Church, he is so fond of insisting, is not of this world.

What then have we found in this investigation? If nothing else, we have found that the differences we discerned in chapter 2 were not illusory or peripheral. It seems that Hodge really is that odd (or, if you're a Princetonian, Nevin really is that odd). The paradigms are diametrically opposed on issue after issue, and a consistent pattern manifests itself. Hodge's recurring dualism and nominalism force him to isolate divine and human in the Incarnation, and the incarnate Christ from the rest of the race. It forces him to separate the visible church from the invisible, and the changing church in history from the pure changeless doctrine that is true Christianity. And the whole time, grace is never incarnated, God never really comes down to earth. He raises the spirits of some men up to the heavenly sphere, but He dares not redeem them here on earth, in their true humanity, for that would mean entrusting the work of His Spirit to the changeful tides of history. Nevin has no such fear, for he starts with the Incarnation, and confesses it as radically as he can. God raised man up to the divine sphere, indeed, but only by truly taking man to Himself, only by truly entering creation and becoming visible within it. And so as redemption progresses, the life of God becomes ever more visible in the world, using history as its garment.

A fuller summary and evaluation will appear in chapter 7, but for now, let us turn our eyes to a wider horizon.

CHAPTER 4

The Dons Across the Pond
Mercersburg and the Oxford Movement

IN THE NEXT THREE chapters, the analysis shall take a somewhat different direction, as I bring the Mercersburg Theology into dialogue with
other traditions than its own. Whereas previously the purpose was to
establish difference and opposition, now I shall try to establish similarity and parallelism. So I shall take a chapter each to explore intriguing
points of comparison with Anglican theology (in the form of the Oxford
Movement), with Eastern Orthodox theology, and with Roman Catholic
theology (in the form of Henri de Lubac and the *nouvelle théologie*).
Of course, it would not be hard in any of these three chapters to establish plenty of differences as well, but that would hardly be interesting
or worthwhile, since these differences are generally taken for granted
(and overstated, often). So I will generally not focus on these, though
since Nevin and Schaff explicitly wrote on some of their differences from
Oxford, I shall spend some time on their remarks. Different topics shall
be covered in each chapter, though a fair amount of overlap shall appear,
both among these three chapters and with the discussions of chapters 2
and 3. Since I want to make sure the comparisons are clearly drawn at
each point, some discussions may briefly repeat ground that was covered
earlier, but hopefully this will prove helpful rather than tiresome.

First, then, let us explore how the Mercersburg Theology measures
up to the Oxford Movement. More than any other theological develop-

ment in the last two centuries, the Oxford Movement offers an intriguing and inviting comparison for the Mercersburg Theology. Not only were many of its central emphases the same, but it embroiled the Church of England in controversy at the very same time that Nevin was sparring with Hodge. The coincidence in time, aims, and shape of each movement are remarkable to say the least; indeed, Nevin believed that the widespread revival of high Church doctrine that both were a part of, spanning many nations and communions simultaneously, was no coincidence, but a "manifestly providential" movement.[1]

Here are just a few noteworthy parallels: the Oxford Movement began in the 1830s and reached its highest pitch of controversy in the early- to mid-1840s; the movement in Mercersburg began in the 1840s and reached its highest pitch of controversy around 1850. Both movements can be traced to a single sermon which brought the issues of the day into sharp relief and brought together two like-minded theologians to make common cause—for the Oxford Movement, it was John Keble's sermon "National Apostasy," which galvanized John Henry Newman to join the battle for England's soul; for Mercersburg, it was Schaff's sermon "The Principle of Protestantism," which helped galvanize Nevin to raise the banner of Reformed catholicity. Each movement began new publications specifically for the propagation of their views and to address the weaknesses they perceived in the Church (the *Tracts for the Times* and the *Mercersburg Review*). Each movement had two preeminent leaders— Edward Pusey and John Henry Newman for the one, Nevin and Schaff for the other.[2] The temptation to Catholicism was a major issue for the chief leaders of both movements, with Newman eventually converting and Nevin coming very close. Both movements prompted massive criticism and controversy in the religious press, and suffered accusations of Romanizing that were far out of proportion to their actual Catholic leanings. And not only the general air, but some of the specific issues of the controversy were remarkably similar, such as Pusey's and Nevin's experience after trying to revive Eucharistic doctrine.

But of course the parallels ran much deeper than these somewhat superficial similarities. James Hastings Nichols, the preeminent Mercers-

---

1. Nevin, "Anglican Crisis," 361.

2. If you really want to remark on funny coincidences, you might note the similarity between the names of the chief leaders for each movement: John Henry Newman and John Williamson Nevin—each going by all three names, each named John, and with similar last names.

burg scholar, draws attention to the shared roots of the two movements in his introduction to the anthology *The Mercersburg Theology*. He identifies the Oxford Movement (also known as Puseyism, Tractarianism, or Anglo-Catholicism) as an English parallel to a similar High Church Lutheran revival that was going on at the same time in Prussia and Denmark and which inspired much of Nevin and Schaff's theology.[3] Indeed, the Lutheran movement was certainly a greater influence on Mercersburg than Tractarianism ever was (as is evident in the number of articles in the *Mercersburg Review* that are simply translations of works by Martensen, Thiersch, and others of that movement), and naturally so, as Nevin and Schaff ministered in a German Reformed Church with continuing ties to German churches on the continent.

There are three reasons why the Oxford Movement, and not the High Church movement in Germany, receives attention in this book. The most simple, to be quite frank, is that I have had the opportunity to do much more research on the Anglican movement than the Lutheran. The second is that the Lutheran movement quickly dissolved in the face of liberalism, and seems to have produced little lasting effect on the history of the Church. Anglo-Catholicism, however, put an indelible stamp on the future history of the Anglican Communion, and ensured the survival of that Church by breathing new life into her. Nevin wrote at the time that the Oxford Movement was the greatest religious movement since the Reformation,[4] and while that seems like quite a brazen claim, it is a plausible one, at least until Vatican II and the recent reinvention of Roman Catholicism. To discuss Nevin's relationship to his German Lutheran contemporaries, then, would be of merely historical interest, a valid interest surely, but lacking the contemporary relevance I hope to maintain in this study. The Mercersburg Theology contains a strong ecumenical imperative, and while Mercersburg can supply no constructive ecumenical dialogue with the now-defunct High Church Lutherans, it may be provide a very timely and valuable discussion partner for the still-strong Anglo-Catholic tradition.

The third reason is based on Nevin's own assessment. Despite his heavy dependence on German sources, he evidently had more respect of

3. Nichols, *Mercersburg Theology*, 11. Note that although I call this movement "Lutheran," it was broader than that in Prussia at least, where the Lutheran and Reformed Churches had united in 1817.

4. Nevin, "Anglican Crisis," 359.

a kind for the English, and put the greatest hope for true High Church reformation in the Anglican Church, rather than the Lutheran. Nichols states it thus,

> Nevin's pessimism over Anglicanism was the worse because there was no other sect or fragment of Protestantism in which one could put more hope. He had a particular sympathy for Anglicanism, since along with his own denomination it fell at the churchly end of the Reformed spectrum, as opposed to Puritanism at the unchurchly limit. And the Tractarian leaders, whom he admired personally, had made an attempt which Mercersburg emulated to reassert the catholic continuity of the tradition.[5]

Nevin revered the catholic heritage and rejoiced to find that the Oxford men did so as well. On the theology of the ministry, Nevin frankly admitted to the Lutheran theologian Dorner that "our theology is more Anglican than German"[6] (more proof, incidentally, that he was not the slave to "Germanizing" that Hodge made him out to be).

However, Nevin's admiration was not without serious concern and disagreement. I shall discuss this further at the end of this chapter, but the sum of it is that he feared too much reverence for tradition, a reverence that could not turn around and face the future. Indeed, Nichols accurately pinpoints this difference:

> In this respect [the relationship of tradition and development] Nevin had more kinship with such high-church Lutherans as Lohe than with the Tractarians. The Oxford men represented a program of repristination simply, without any concern for, or probably even any understanding of, the Reformation. There was consequently little work to do save to weed out the distinctively Roman elements from the ancient Catholic heritage, and that was not really theological work. But for Nevin there was the task of clarifying the continuities on the one hand, and on the other, of interpreting the discontinuities, between the ancient Catholic Church and the Reformation, in relation to modern philosophy.[7]

Though he draws a good distinction here, Nichols is at times too anxious to highlight differences between Mercersburg and Oxford, always to the credit of the former and the discredit of the latter. He often makes it

---

5. Nichols, *Mercersburg Theology*, 26.

6. Nevin, "Our Relations with Germany," 265.

7. Nichols, *Mercersburg Theology*, 24.

out that the Tractarian theologians had no sense of church history at all (especially of the Reformation), but kept their heads buried in the sand of dogmatism that couldn't see beyond certain "authoritative" periods in Church history. Moreover, he claims,

> Though they accepted the idea of the church as the Body of Christ, the Tractarians were less interested in the church than in the exclusive prerogatives of the Episcopalian clergy based on their peculiar view of apostolic succession. They had a stronger sacramental interest than most Anglicans, but interpreted the sacraments still in largely individualistic terms.[8]

Repeatedly he portrays them as reactionaries who saw the Church as an external, mechanical institution, which magically transmits authority and sacramental grace, a picture that is more a caricature than a sober assessment.[9]

Of course, Nichols does, I think, accurately identify some of the weaknesses of the Oxford Movement, and the ways in which Mercersburg improved upon them, but these differences, I would suggest, are generally ones of degree, rather than absolute. The Tractarians did tend more toward the merely external, were more individualistic, and did not really embrace a principle of the development of doctrine, as Nevin and Schaff did. On apostolic succession and the sacraments, where Nichols repeatedly attempts to claim significant differences, I think a careful assessment will reveal otherwise. The central difference, I suggest, lies elsewhere, and is bound up with eschatology. Nevin was a constructive conservative who wanted to both retain the past and move forward into new frontiers; the Oxford men, he feared, were hyper-conservatives who only wanted the first. For Mercersburg, the Church was important for what it was bound to become; for Oxford, only for what it had been, a perspective that sometimes lent itself to a narrowly sectarian outlook that Nevin and Schaff could not tolerate. I shall come back to consider their concerns in more detail after surveying how close were some of the parallels between the two movements.

8. Nichols, *Romanticism*, 78.

9. Ibid., 79–82, 260, 268–69.

What Was the Oxford Movement?

But, before that, I should perhaps introduce the possibly bewildered reader to Tractarianism.[10] For, though I have just extolled its lasting influence, it is still, like so many other great periods in Church history, little known among most Christians today, especially outside of Anglicanism. Though its beginnings in a long-forgotten and ultimately inconsequential political dispute seemed to warrant little notice, the story of the Oxford Movement became a tale of high drama and bitter struggle. Animated by the fervent spirit of John Henry Newman, and supported by the famed Oxford dons John Keble and Edward Pusey, the movement was destined to shake England to its core.

The train of events that led to such a convulsion began with a bit of bureaucratic reshuffling—Parliament wanted to streamline the administration of the Church of Ireland by removing some surplus bishoprics. Appalled at the State's presumption to intervene in Church affairs (though, in truth, it had been doing the same sort of meddling ever since Henry VIII), a number of scholars and ecclesiastics raised a loud outcry, but to no avail. However, the outrage simmered in the hearts of men like Keble, Newman, and their friend Hurrell Froude, who lamented the low esteem in which Englishmen seemed to hold the great institution of the Church. While traveling in the Mediterranean in 1833, Newman was gripped with a strange sense of mission, and insisted on cutting the trip short, saying to his companions, "I have a work to do in England."[11]

Five days after he arrived back in Oxford, his friend John Keble preached a sermon entitled "National Apostasy," in which he called England to repentance for its disdain for the Church, manifested in the acts of Parliament and in the general indifference of the people and clergy. Though no movement has a perfectly clear-cut beginning, historians have generally followed Newman in marking this day, July 14th, 1833, as the beginning of the Oxford Movement. This is quite reasonable, for, though the sermon had no immediate effect on the English Church at large, it led to a gathering of like-minded Oxford leaders, including Keble and Newman's friend Hurrell Froude. Together, they decided to begin the publication of the *Tracts for the Times* to reassert the authority of the

10. Throughout this section I rely on Michael Chandler, *Introduction to the Oxford Movement*, 1–14.

11. Newman, *Apologia Pro Vita Sua*, 50.

Church and the honor of its traditions. Newman himself authored Tract 1, a call to remember the apostolic succession of the ministry in the Church of England. Many of the early tracts focused specifically on this issue of church authority and the ministry, but as the movement gathered steam, it quickly began to tap ever deeper into the richness of catholic tradition, especially on the sacraments, until it became a full-blown apology for the notion of the institutional Church as the living body of Christ, mediating His grace and presence sacramentally to His people.

Naturally this was going to ruffle a few feathers in a church that had settled comfortably into a mainstream Protestant mindset, largely forgetful of its original claims to being a *via media*, and viewing anything that smelled of Catholicism as the worst and most sinister of foes. It wasn't long before the movement provoked widespread outrage in England, with the first great eruption following Froude's premature death in 1836. In loving memory of his work, Keble and Newman published his journals as *Froude's Remains*, but unfortunately, the public was not moved to the sympathy and respect that Keble and Newman had expected. Opponents quickly seized upon passages in the *Remains* where Froude had complained against the Reformation, and began to paint the Tractarians as a sinister Trojan horse seeking to undo the Reformation and lead their church back to Rome. In spite of such opposition, however, new clergy and laity continued to stream to their banners, and the movement gained in confidence and influence, even as further controversies and rhetorical missteps threatened to unravel it. Much of this success was due to the support of Edward Bouverie Pusey, an immensely learned, pious, and respected Oxford professor, who had thrown in his lot with the Tractarians as early as 1835, and soon lent his name to the movement (hence Nevin, Schaff, and Hodge's references to "Puseyism").

By 1841, however, the increasing scope of the Movement's attempted reformation was beginning to provoke a storm of controversy at every turn. In that year Newman published his infamous Tract 90, "On the Thirty-Nine Articles," arguing for a more catholic interpretation of the Anglican confession and inciting so much opposition for its "Romanizing" that the publication of the Tracts was suspended and Newman was disgraced. This rejection drove him steadily out of his ecclesiastical responsibilities over the next few years, until, feeling like an unwanted alien in his own church, he converted to Rome in 1845. Meanwhile Pusey was weathering a storm of his own, over his 1843 sermon "The Holy Eucharist a Comfort to the Penitent," what he saw as a modest attempt to return to the Early Church and early Anglican doctrine of the sacrament. In a ridiculous trial that was an insult to sound doctrine and justice, Pusey's sermon was censored and he was stripped of his preaching privileges at the University. Further conflict in 1844 erupted over the open embrace of Rome by another leader, W.G. Ward, who was suspended from his professorship and shortly afterward joined the Roman Church.

But far worse than all these was the devastating loss of Newman, which seemingly gave the lie to all the Tractarians' protests that they were loyal sons of their Church. Yet through all this the Movement survived and indeed continued to grow, proof of the powerful lure of their doctrine, the charisma of their leaders, and the urgent need of their Church. Pusey's resolution, grace in conflict, and immense learning held their course true, and by the 1850s it was becoming clear that Anglo-Catholicism was not going anywhere, and indeed, was beginning to take root in other parts of the Anglican Communion such as the United States. The rich soil of tradition that Anglo-Catholicism had tapped into proved fertile, and provided the impetus for a wide-ranging liturgical and architectural renaissance that seems to have left a permanent mark on most corners of the Anglican Church. Though the Anglo-Catholics never obtained a majority or many positions of power in the Anglican Communion, they did come to make up a substantial portion, even till the present, and their reforms left the whole Church much stronger and richer than they found it in 1833.

Motivations

What was it in the Anglican Church of 1833 that seemed so dangerous, so in need of reform? There is no doubt that the Oxford men exaggerated the danger and the importance of their response to it somewhat, but there was just cause for concern. As mentioned earlier, the immediate cause for concern was the Parliamentary suppression of the Irish bishoprics, and more generally the increased Erastianism in the Church, whereby the State took charge of Church affairs, and many churchmen were content to let them. But these political concerns were part of a much more complex milieu of enemies, allies, and co-belligerents. For many of the opponents of Erastianism were theological liberals, who favored more openness of opinion and so desired the disestablishment of the Church and the relaxation of its traditional confessions. One of Newman's mentors, Richard Whately, held such opinions. But of course such a view was no solution at all to the Tractarians. It manifested the same disrespect for the Church that Erastianism embodied, indeed perhaps more so. For if the authority of the Thirty-Nine Articles could not be maintained, what could? Soon, it seemed, the faith would disappear under the rising tide of liberalism, which threatened to water down Christian faith and practice to the point of meaninglessness.

And yet the perceived enemy of liberalism, evangelicalism, presented no real solution either. While contesting the liberal indifference to right doctrine and orthodox practice, the evangelicals did not contest their fundamental assumptions about the Church, and countered liberalism with no stronger weapon than the insistence on a personal religious experience as the foundation of true Christianity. But of course, being rooted in subjectivism, this evangelicalism provided no real foundation or compelling obstacle to liberalism. It was apparent to Newman, Keble, and their allies that the root problem, underlying the political repression of the Church, the indifference to it among the masses, and the disdain for its teaching among academics, was a failure to see the Church as the divinely appointed mediator of grace.

Newman sums up his motivating views in *Apologia Pro Vita Sua*: "First was the principle of dogma: my battle was with liberalism; by liberalism I mean the anti-dogmatic principle and its developments."[12] Most important, then, for Newman at least, was the maintenance of the traditional teachings of the orthodox faith, against a growing indifference and rationalism that was becoming fashionable. Newman believed that he could speak confidently for the other leaders in affirming that this was "the fundamental principle of the Movement of 1833."[13]

The second principle, for Newman, defined where the Oxford men parted ways from others in their day who resisted the liberals: "that there was a visible Church, with sacraments and rites which are the channels of invisible grace."[14] Perhaps not in this affirmation as such, but in their development of it, the Tractarians found themselves and their attack on liberalism firmly at odds with the low-church conservative mainstream. For, by "visible Church," Newman does not merely suggest a voluntary

12. Ibid., 61.
13. Ibid.
14. Ibid., 61–62.

gathering together of believers as a visible body, but a continuing institution which descended directly from Christ, and had the Spirit's blessing. Likewise, by "sacraments and rites which are the channels of invisible grace," he does not simply mean the low-church doctrine that grace *might* come through the sacraments, but that it *does* flow through them—baptism and Communion really do accomplish what they signify. Also under this heading Newman contained his firm belief in the divine institution of the episcopate as the necessary form that the Church visible should take.

In these two principles we recognize, in less precise form, opposition to what Schaff identified as the "the diseases of Protestantism"—rationalism and sectarianism—and which he and Nevin fought unceasingly. Schaff insisted that these two errors were simply two sides of the same coin, and represented "one-sided theoretic subjectivism" and "one-sided practical subjectivism" respectively.[15] Both began from "the undervaluation of the church and her symbols" which, naturally, "led gradually to the undervaluation of the apostles and their writings, and terminated finally in a denial of the divinity of Christ himself."[16] Since both these great errors stem from the same source—a disregard of the objective, visible Church—their solution must a renewed confession of the power and authority with which the visible church has been entrusted.

Nevin makes this point even more clearly in "Antichrist," where he demonstrates the essential unity of the two great Christological heresies—Ebionitism and Docetism—and that these two lie at the root of the rationalist and sectarian errors. The third mark of "Antichrist," he says, is a "want of faith in the Church, as a real supernatural constitution always present in the world."[17] In discussing the fourth mark, he says,

> the want of faith in the Church, as the presence of a real divine life in the world, reveals itself always in a low view of the *ministry* and *sacraments*, and of Christian *worship* generally. If the Church be not the depositary of supernatural powers, made objective and constant in the world under this form, it is not to be imagined of course that the organs and functions of the Church can carry in them any greater value or force.[18]

15. Schaff, *Principle of Protestantism*, 130–55.
16. Ibid., 131.
17. Nevin, "Antichrist," 40.
18. Ibid., 41.

The fifth mark, "contempt for all *history* and *authority*," follows directly from all this. "Faith in a real Christ, felt to be always in the Church really to the end of the world, will make it impossible for Christians to undervalue and despise either the present Church or the Church of past ages."[19]

No doubt Newman, Pusey, and Keble would eagerly applaud this analysis, for, in their opposition to liberalism and the low-church tendency, they too saw the lack of respect for the Church as the fundamental danger, and a restoration of such respect as the only solution to the ebb of Christianity in their land. It is apparent then that the two movements, despite the very different situations that provoked them and the different contexts in which they expressed themselves, were animated by the same fears and turned to the same solution—a renewed confession of the one, holy, catholic, and apostolic Church. Even in Nevin's brief comments just quoted, we see, in his italicized keywords, a number of areas for fruitful comparison with the Oxford Movement. The Oxford men also insisted on the Church as a "real supernatural constitution"; they also sought to resurrect high views of the ministry, the sacraments, worship, history, and authority. But a complete analysis of these issues would require a book of its own, so in the next few pages, I will briefly survey just the first two.

The Sacraments and the Mystical Union

At first it might seem that there really isn't that much to say here, beyond noting the fact that both movements sought to regain a high view of the objective efficacy of the sacraments. But there is much more to say about the sacraments than this, more than simply determining whether one has a "high" view or a "low" view of their efficacy. Discussions of the sacraments have often tended to focus on certain narrowly defined loci, which waste most of the discussion time on questions of mode or proper reception, or hair-splitting debates on the nature of the efficacy. While there is much to be learned in studying how these theologians approached many of the traditional questions, that is not my purpose here. Rather, I want to survey how both Nevin and Pusey answered the question, "What do the sacraments mean for the relationship of Christ and the believer?" For the record, both theologians held to the objective efficacy of both sacraments, but denied an *ex opere operato* grace, and both held to some form of baptismal regeneration (though this requires a

19. Ibid., 43.

bit more demonstration in Nevin's case; see below) and the real presence in the Eucharist, although Pusey articulated this presence in more consecrationist terms, Nevin in receptionist terms. Having said this, however, what both theologians were deeply interested in was the mystical union between Christ and the believer, which was created and nourished by these two sacraments. In articulating this union, their accounts exhibit remarkable similarity.

First, then, each considered baptism to be the point at which the Christian is engrafted into Christ's life, while the Lord's Supper nourished, sustained, and strengthened the believer in that life. Pusey summarizes,

> Baptism containeth not only remission of sin, actual or original, but maketh members of Christ, children of God, heirs of Heaven, hath the seal and earnest of the Spirit, the germ of spiritual life; the Holy Eucharist imparteth not life only, spiritual strength, and oneness with Christ, and His Indwelling, and participation of Him, but, in its degree, remission of sins also.[20]

He elaborates this further, saying,

> Baptism gives, the Holy Eucharist preserves and enlarges life. Baptism engraffs into the true Vine; the Holy Eucharist derives the richness and fulness of His life into the branches thus engraffed. Baptism buries in Christ's tomb, and through it He quickens with His life; the Holy Eucharist is given not to the dead, but to the living. It augments life . . .[21]

Nevin concurs with this general representation, affirming in *The Mystical Presence,*

> Paul declares that we are members of Christ's body, of his flesh and of his bones. . . . The general thought is the close, constant communion in which Christ, as the Redeemer, stands with his Church. Reference is made first to Baptism, under this view, as the pledge and seal of the intimate relation. From this there is then an advance . . . to the other sacrament, in which the same mystery is still more strikingly exhibited and confirmed.[22]

---

20. Pusey, "Holy Eucharist," 7.

21. Ibid., 9.

22. Nevin, *Mystical Presence*, 240.

It is clear for Pusey that baptism objectively inaugurates a mystical union between the baptized person and Christ, by virtue of their ingrafting into His body, the Church:

> So then, it now appears that they who are baptized into Christ, are made members of the body of Christ; are joined on by a mystical union with Him their Head; are one mystical body, one with another, by being in Him, are in Him, by being clothed upon by Him; and so are sons of God by being members of Him.[23]

For Nevin, though he speaks much of the mystical union, it is not always clear what role baptism plays. In "Antichrist" he makes clear that there is a "objective efficacy" and "sacramental grace" in baptism,[24] but does not specify a doctrine of baptismal regeneration. In "The Anglican Crisis," he avoids committing himself to the specific terminology of "baptismal regeneration" but expresses full sympathy for the doctrine that the Tractarians were trying to uphold, considering it the universal doctrine of the Church pre-seventeenth-century.[25] So, in his article "The Old Doctrine of Christian Baptism," he cites Chrysostom, with full approval, to the effect that baptism was "an actual regeneration, by the grace of God, to the power of a new and heavenly life."[26] Moreover, he makes much of Paul's strong language about baptism, that "our baptism buries us into Christ's death," and makes this central to his notion of the mystical union.

However, we never really get a fully clear statement of Nevin's own baptismal theology and his view of baptismal regeneration until years later, when he is writing in defense of the baptismal liturgy he composed.

> Has the Church been wrong in believing, that such change of state, such transplantation from the kingdom of the Devil over into the kingdom of Christ, must in the nature of the case be a Divine act; and that as such a Divine act, it must be something more than any human thought or volition simply, stimulated into action by God's Spirit? Has the Church been wrong in believing, finally, that the Sacrament of Holy Baptism, the sacrament of initiation into the Church, was instituted, not only to signify this truth in a general way, but to seal it as a present actuality for all

23. Pusey, "Scriptural Views," 113.
24. Nevin, "Antichrist," 42.
25. Nevin, "Anglican Crisis," 369–72.
26. Nevin, "Old Doctrine," 196.

who are willing to accept the boon thus offered to them in the transaction?

Baptismal regeneration! our evangelical spiritualists are at once ready to exclaim. But we will not allow ourselves to be put out of course in so solemn an argument, by any catchword of this sort addressed to popular prejudice. The Liturgy avoids the ambiguous phrase; and we will do so too; for the word regeneration is made to mean, sometimes one thing, and sometimes another, and it does not come in our way at all at present to discuss these meanings. We are only concerned, that no miserable logomachy of this sort shall be allowed to cheat us out of what the sacrament has been held to be in past ages; God's act, setting apart those who are the subjects of it to His service, and bringing them within the sphere of His grace in order that they may be saved. We do not ask any one to call this regeneration; it may not at all suit his sense of the term; but we do most earnestly conjure all to hold fast to the thing, call it by what term they may. The Question is simply, Doth baptism in any sense save us? Has it anything to do at all with our deliverance from original sin, and our being set down in the new world of righteousness and grace, which has been brought to pass in the midst of Satan's kingdom all around it, by our Lord Jesus Christ?[27]

This quote explains Nevin's reticence to use the term "baptismal regeneration," but demonstrates that he is fully on board with the substance of the doctrine, and would have little to quibble with Pusey. Nichols's suggestion, then, that "the Mercersburg men themselves were not very decided"[28] on the issue of baptismal regeneration, and perhaps differed from the Tractarians on this point, is going too far.

This rich understanding of the power of baptism, and the intimacy of the union with Christ that it inaugurates, greatly affects the traditional Reformed conception of the *ordo salutis*. For, instead of viewing the various elements of salvation—regeneration, justification, adoption, sanctification, glorification, etc.—as discrete steps in a logical/temporal sequence, all of these are received, in seed form at least, definitively at the moment of baptism, for all of these inhere in Christ, and as we live in him, so we possess these.

Pusey is clear on this:

27. Nevin, *Vindication of the Revised Liturgy*, 397–98.
28. Nichols, *Mercersburg Theology*, 25.

And so, while we bear in mind the continued gifts of His goodness, in the life which He upholds; the fatness of the olive-tree,
which He imparts; the membership of the family, which He
continues; the stream, or the light, which He puts within us; still
there is eminently one date, from which all these present blessings are derived, differing from them in so far as it is one, the sun
rising, the engrafting, the adoption, the birth; one act, transitory
as an act, although abiding in its effects.[29]

Nevin makes the same point:

Every Christian may be said to be in Christ potentially from
the beginning, all that he is destined to become actually when
his salvation shall be complete. . . . And in view of this relation,
the apostle does not hesitate to add . . . "He hath quickened us
together with Christ, and hath raised us up together, and made
us sit together in heavenly places in Christ Jesus." All in the
past tense, not in the future. So Rom 8:30, not only the calling
of believers and their justification, but their glorification also, is
exhibited as something already complete.[30]

For both, the notion of the mystical union, mediated through the
sacraments, centers around the twin poles of Incarnation and Resurrection. Through the Incarnation, the Divine Word, possessing the life
which belongs only to God, has united to Himself human nature, and
thus enabled us, by receiving His human life, to be joined in communion
with the divine nature, and to be filled with the abundant life of the God-
Man. Speaking specifically of the Eucharist, Pusey closely links the grace
received to the reality of the Incarnation:

Such is undoubted Catholic teaching, and the most literal im-
port of Holy Scripture, and the mystery of the Sacrament that
the Eternal Word, Who is God, having taken to Him our flesh
and joined it indissolubly with Himself, and so, where His Flesh
is, there He is, and we receiving it, receive Him, and receiving
Him are joined on to Him through His flesh to the Father, and
he dwelling in us, dwell in Him, and with Him in God. . . . And
so is He also, as Man, truly the Mediator between God and Man,
in that being as God, One with the Father, as man, one with us,
we truly are in Him who is truly in the Father. He, by the truth
of the Sacrament, dwelleth in us, in Whom, by Nature, all the

29. Pusey, "Baptism," 155.
30. Nevin, *Mystical Presence*, 220.

fulness of the Godhead dwelleth; and lowest is joined on with highest, earth with heaven, corruption with incorruption, man with God.[31]

Again, he says, expounding the theology of the Gospel of John,

He is the Living Bread, because He came down from Heaven, and as being One God with the Father, hath life in Himself, even as the Father hath life in Himself; the life then which He is, He imparted to that Flesh which He took into Himself, yea, which He took so wholly, that Holy Scripture says, He became it, "the Word became flesh," and since it is thus a part of Himself, "Whoso eateth My Flesh, and drinketh My Blood," (He Himself says the amazing words,) "eateth Me," and so receiveth into Himself, in an ineffable manner, his Lord Himself, "dwelleth" (our Lord says) "in Me and I in Him."[32]

Later, he quotes Cyril of Alexandria saying, "And since the Flesh of the Saviour became life-giving, as being united to That which is by nature Life, the Word from God, then, when we taste It, we have life in ourselves, we too being united with It, as It to the indwelling Word."[33]

Nevin is, of course, full of this emphasis as well, beginning his systematic statement of Eucharistic doctrine in *The Mystical Presence* with a powerful development of the doctrine of the Incarnation. Because of his more detailed exposition, it is hard to find as neat a summary as we see in Pusey, but Nevin is quite clear about the new life made available to man by the Incarnation.

By the hypostatical union of the two natures in the person of JESUS CHRIST, our humanity as fallen in Adam was exalted again to a new and imperishable divine life. . . . An inward salvation of the race required that it should be joined in a living way with the divine nature itself, as represented by the everlasting Word or Logos, the fountain of all created light and life. The Word accordingly became flesh, that is assumed humanity into union with itself. . . . The object of the incarnation was to couple the human nature in real union with the Logos, as a permanent source of life.[34]

31. Pusey, "Holy Eucharist," 14.
32. Ibid., 11.
33. Ibid., 13.
34. Nevin, *Mystical Presence*, 156.

It is of this life, the life of the incarnate God, of divinized humanity, that we partake in the sacrament, as Nevin makes clear:

> Christ personally is this bread [of life] because it is only in his person, that the *Life* of the everlasting Word, which is the true *Light* of men, has revealed itself in the sphere of our common human existence. Only in this form, does he still the gnawing hunger of humanity, by supplying it with the very substance of life itself....The bread of life then, in this view, is Christ as slain for the sins of the world, received into the believer and made one with him by the power of the Holy Ghost. We must eat his flesh and drink his blood; otherwise we can have no life. His flesh is meat indeed—his blood drink indeed; *aleithos*, in reality, not in a shadowy or relative sense merely, but absolutely and truly in the sphere of the Spirit. The participation itself involves everlasting life; not in the form of hope and promise, but in the way of actual present possession; and not simply as a mode of existence of the soul abstractly considered, but as embracing the whole man in the absolute totality of his nature.[35]

This last point, that since we partake of Christ's glorified humanity, body and soul, we receive new life for our souls as well as for our bodies, is crucial for both Pusey and Nevin. In this they both closely follow (Pusey explicitly) the Christology of Cyril of Alexandria, the tenor of which is clear in Pusey's citation of him just above. The Incarnation, as a complete union of the divine and human, meant that the entire human nature of Christ, including His very flesh, is glorified by participation in the divine life; as partakers in the whole Christ, therefore, we should expect the same glorification of our bodies. Pusey says,

> This is (if we may reverently so speak) the order of the mystery of the Incarnation, that the Eternal Word so took our flesh into Himself, as to impart to it His own inherent life; so then we, partaking of It, that life is transmitted on to us also, and not to our souls only, but our bodies also, since we become flesh of His flesh, and bone of His bone, and He Who is wholly life is imparted to us wholly. The Life which He is, spreads around, first giving Its own vitality to that sinless Flesh which He united indissolubly with Himself and in It encircling and vivifying our whole nature, and then, through that bread which is His Flesh, finding an entrance

---

35. Ibid., 226.

to us individually, penetrating us, soul and body, and spirit, and irradiating and transforming into His own light and life.[36]

Nevin similarly insists,

> The process by which Christ is formed in his people, is not thus two-fold but single. It lays hold of its subject in each case, not in the periphery of his person, but in its inmost centre, where the whole man, soul and body, is still one undivided life. . . . Christ's life as a whole is borne over into the person of the believer as a like whole. . . . The power of Christ's life . . . works as a human life; and as such becomes a law of regeneration in the body as truly as in the soul.[37]

And later, "the glorification of the believer's body is the result of the same process that sanctifies his soul."[38]

This glorification of the body, of course, takes the form of resurrection, which, both Pusey and Nevin assert, is not simply a future event, but is possessed in seed form now through the sacraments, because by them we participate in Christ's resurrection and are united to His life which has already triumphed over death. Here the Johannine theology that has been so prominent thus far is enriched with many themes from Paul. Pusey quotes Paul profusely in relating baptism and resurrection.

> "We were all baptized into Christ," i.e., into a participation of Christ, and his most precious Death, and union with Him; "we," i.e., our old man, our corrupted selves, "were buried with Him by Baptism into death, that we also may walk in newness of life." Again, "we were planted in the likeness of His death"—that we may be "of His resurrection." Again, "our old man was crucified with Him"—"that the whole body of sin might be destroyed."[39]

He goes on to develop this further, saying,

> Our incarnate Lord imparted to our decayed nature, by His indwelling in it, that principle of life, which through Adam's fall it had lost: and when "by the Spirit of Holiness," which resided in Christ, He raised it from the dead, He made it not only "the first fruits," but the source of our Resurrection, by communicating

36. Pusey, "Holy Eucharist," 12.

37. Nevin, *Mystical Presence*, 162–63.

38. Ibid., 213–14.

39. Pusey, "Baptism," 94.

to our nature His own inherent Life. . . . He not only has obtained, purchased, wills, bestows, is the meritorious cause of, our Resurrection; He Himself is it; He gives it not, as it were, from without, as a possession, as something of our own, but Himself is it to us: He took our flesh, that He might vivify it; He dwelt in it, and obeyed in it, that He might sanctify it; He raised it from death by His quickening Spirit that He might give it immortality: the "first Adam" was "a living soul;" and that life being by sin lost, "the last Adam became a life-giving Spirit." And we in His Church being incorporated into Him, being made members of His Body, flesh of His Flesh, and bone of His bone, through His sacraments partake of His Life and immortality, because we partake of Him; we are made members of Him, He dwelleth in us, and is our Life; "Because I live, ye shall live also." . . . It is through the communication of that life, and so by belonging to Him, being joined to Him, that as many as live, have and shall have their life. . . . And this power of His Resurrection is imparted to us through Baptism.[40]

Similarly, Pusey is keen to emphasize that through the Eucharist, the partaker is filled with the life of Christ who has passed over from death to life, and are thus given a foretaste of their own resurrections:

Having Christ within him, not only shall he have, but he "hath" already "eternal Life," because he hath Him Who is "the Only True God and Eternal Life;" and so Christ "will raise him up at the last Day," because he hath His life in him. Receiving Him into this very body, they who are His, receive life, which shall pass over to our very decaying flesh; they have within them Him Who is Life and Immortality and incorruption, to cast out or absorb into itself our natural mortality and death and corruption, and "shall live for ever," because made one with Him Who Alone "liveth for evermore."[41]

And later, he says, "For since Christ is in us by His own Flesh, we must altogether rise, for it were incredible, yea rather, impossible, that Life should not make alive those in whom It is."[42]

Nevin too is full of similar statements, also relying on Paul to root the believer's participation in the resurrection in baptism:

40. Ibid., 101–2.
41. Pusey, "Holy Eucharist," 11.
42. Ibid., 13.

It is in [Christ] personally, as the bearer of our fallen humanity, that death is swallowed up in victory, by the power of that divine life of which he was the incarnation. From him, the same life, flows over to his people, in the way of real communication. He does not merely preach the resurrection. It is comprehended in his person. He hath in himself abolished death, and thus brought life and immortality to light through the gospel. . . . Baptism into Christ is baptism into his death, and so at the same time into his resurrection—the translation of the subject out of the sphere of the flesh into the sphere of the spirit. Christians are 'not in the flesh, but in the Spirit'—the new life sphere revealed in Christ. The resurrection power of Jesus dwells in them, at once the principle of a salvation, that will not rest till in their case too it shall have quickened the whole man into life and immortality.[43]

And of course, from John, Nevin can make the same connection between the Eucharist and resurrection, as we see in this passage which was quoted earlier:

We must eat his flesh and drink his blood; otherwise we can have no life. His flesh is meat indeed—his blood drink indeed; *aleithos*, in reality, not in a shadowy or relative sense merely, but absolutely and truly in the sphere of the Spirit. The participation itself involves everlasting life; not simply in the form of hope and promise, but in the way of actual present possession; and not simply as a mode of existence of the soul abstractly considered, but as embracing the whole man in the absolute totality of his nature, and reaching out to the resurrection of the body itself as its legitimate and necessary end. Christ once crucified, but now in glory, is the principle of immortality in every true believer. As the Resurrection and the Life, he will *raise him up at the last day*.[44]

Both of these theologians, as we have seen, develop a sacramental theology which rests on a similar (very Alexandrian) Christology. Both have creatively synthesized the Christological language of John's Gospel, and its repeated emphasis on the "life" that is in Christ and is sacramentally shared with believer, with the soteriology of Paul, who makes much of our participation in Christ's death and resurrection. Both thus offer a similar understanding of the benefits of the sacraments, which impart to

43. Nevin, *Mystical Presence*, 203–5.

44. Ibid., 226–27; see also 203, 213–14 for a fuller exposition of the mystical union as a participation in Christ's resurrection.

us all the benefits of redemption, from justification to glorification, and prepare our bodies for the Resurrection. These emphases are, of course, not unique among Protestant theologians, but they are certainly unusual enough to be noteworthy.

These remarkable similarities between Nevin's and Pusey's articulations of sacramental grace are thus quite revealing. For, if Nevin is primarily a Germanizing innovator, as Hodge charged, then we should expect his "German romantic" notion of the mystical union to contrast sharply with Pusey's approach. After all, Pusey firmly repudiated many of the theological developments in Germany, and even wrote a book against German theology. But instead we find Pusey voicing quite similar notions of the mystical participation in the life of Christ, suggesting that at least much of Nevin's thought springs from an older source than the recent developments in Germany. Of course, I am not denying differences of approach and emphasis, which reveal somewhat Nevin's greater taste for German theology, but these are undoubtedly outweighed by the similarities.

The similarity is also curious if Nevin is depending so heavily on Calvin, and is trying to uphold the Reformed tradition, as he states clearly in *The Mystical Presence*. For Pusey repeatedly, in both his essays on Baptism and on the Lord's Supper, repeatedly condemns the Calvinist position, even while saying things that strongly resemble Nevin's own statements. This suggests that even Pusey, great scholar though he was, was ignorant of the true Reformed teaching, and, like many high-church theologians, scorned Calvinist sacramentology as low and spiritualizing. Certainly so-called "Calvinist" sacramentologies by Pusey's day were radically different from Calvin's own views; after all, that was what Nevin was out to fix by writing *The Mystical Presence*. Of course, it is also possible that Pusey, being immensely learned, had accurate objections to Calvin's sacramentology; indeed, he backs up some of his critiques with actual quotes from Calvin. It would seem fair then to say that, though he was generally faithful to Calvin, Nevin's sacramentology was informed by patristic teaching as well, even when he was writing *The Mystical Presence*. Pusey's discussions of the sacraments are full of citations of patristic sources, and certainly we find similar interests in Nevin's later writing, so this shared source no doubt accounts for some of the similarity. This study suggests then that high-Church Anglicans ought to be able to enlist Reformed sacramentology as far more of an ally than they have generally supposed. Moreover, since the sacramentology of both the Anglo-Catholic and Reformed traditions has deep roots in patristic theology, closer attention to this shared foundation will point the way toward closer unity, as it does for Nevin and Pusey.

Ministerial Authority and the Apostolic Succession

A similar phenomenon can be observed in their doctrines of ministerial authority. It may surprise most readers to discover that, of all the emphases of the Oxford Movement, one that Nevin shared the most was the doctrine of the apostolic succession of the Christian ministry. This is surprising, both because the doctrine is so thoroughly associated in the minds of most Protestants with the Catholic and Anglican churches, and never with the Reformed, and also because it is on this point that Nevin and Schaff seem to target some of their strongest critiques of Tractarianism. I will survey these critiques and what to make of them in a bit, but first I will demonstrate that this similarity in fact exists.

Direct comparison here is in some ways even more difficult than it is with the sacraments, because, seminal as was the doctrine of the apostolic succession *to* the Oxford Movement, they produced no thorough survey and explanation of the doctrine (at least, until Charles Gore's *The Church and the Ministry*, which dates from a point so much later that it must be left to the side in this discussion). Rather, what we find are quite a number of brief, popular-level expositions in the Tracts for the Times (Tracts 1, 2, 4, 5, 7, 11, 15, 17, 19, 20, 24, 35, 47, and 74 are especially relevant) which each take slightly different but overlapping approaches, and none of which really tries to sketch anything like a definitive outline of the doctrine. However, direct comparison here is perhaps not so important, because we are not concerned, as with the sacraments, to demonstrate point-by-point similarities in the articulation of the doctrine, but the doctrine itself. Because the notion of the apostolic succession is so closely connected with high-church Anglicanism, but never with Reformed theology, it is very significant if we can show that Nevin insisted upon substantially the same doctrine, especially in view of his and Schaff's harsh remarks against it. It sounds at times as if they rejected the notion of a visible apostolic succession, but for Nevin, at least, I shall suggest, this was simply not so, and his apparent objection to Tractarianism at this point was actually the result of a rather different sort of disagreement.

For brevity's sake, this discussion will have to be rather oversimplified, and I shall omit a detailed exposition of the Anglo-Catholic teaching on this point, since a sketch of the general contours should suffice. So
I will first briefly provide such a sketch, then unpack a powerful sermon
by Nevin on the ministry to show its adherence to the sketch.

In summary, then, the Anglo-Catholic doctrine insists that, when
Christ commissioned His apostles and gave them the gift of the Holy
Spirit, He entrusted them alone with His authority to lead His Church
and minister to it. He did not simply entrust the Church as such with the
same commission and gift, for them to delegate to such authorities as they
would constitute. And, as this authority was given only into the apostles'
hands, none others could receive it but from their hands. Thus it was
necessary that all subsequent ministers must receive authority directly
from the apostles or their successors. Historically speaking, this succession took the form of bishops, upon which form the Catholic, Orthodox,
and Anglican all insisted on maintaining. As the ministry receives its gift
direct from God, not from the Church, the Church in a democratic capacity is never free to alter the authority of its ministry; rather, only the
apostolic ministers themselves can do this. Furthermore, this gift and authority is objective, so that, even if a particular office-bearer is unworthy
of the office, nonetheless, by virtue of the power of the office, his ministry
is still lawful and valid.

This understanding of Church authority, then, meant that no rebellion of dissenters from below in the church, nor any usurpation from the
state alongside, could ever rightfully interfere with the commission and
authority which the ministers had from above. The revival of the doctrine
of the apostolic succession was a linchpin of the Oxford Movement (indeed, Newman lists it among the foundational propositions in *Apologia
Pro Vita Sua*), as is evident enough from the fact that more than half of
the first twenty tracts focused on the doctrine. Obviously much more
could be said, but this should be enough to go on. For a more thorough
exposition, the Tracts mentioned above are valuable, as is Charles Gore's
The Church and the Ministry.

So did Nevin believe all this? In a sermon preached in 1854 (after
his decision to remain in the Protestant fold), Nevin articulated a surpris-
ingly strong doctrine of the ministry, which leaves little to be desired for
even the strongest advocates of the apostolic ministry like the Tractarians.
While he holds out against endorsing the episcopal structure *per se* as the

vehicle by which this ministry is perpetuated, it seems hard to avoid this implication, and, in any case, on every other point his argument either equals or surpasses the claims that the Oxford men and their Anglo-Catholic successors have tried to make for ministerial authority.[45]

He begins his exposition with Christ's promise of the Holy Spirit to His apostles, saying that

> This Gift now forms the origin and ground of the Christian Church, which by its very nature, therefore, is a supernatural constitution, a truly real and abiding fact in the world, and yet, at the same time, a fact not of the world in its natural view but flowing from the resurrection of Christ and belonging to that new order of things which has been brought to pass by his glorification at the right hand of God; a fact not dependent, accordingly, on the laws and conditions that reign in "this present evil world."[46]

This declaration is essential to the doctrine he is about to develop. For, because the Church, and with it the Christian ministry, stands over and above the authorities of this present age, and the vicissitudes of time, we may have confidence, surpassing that which mere history can provide, that this authority has indeed survived down in unbroken line through the ages. We may also have confidence that the authority of the ministry endures despite the unworthiness of any particular men who occupy it, and that it remains independent of the action of any monarch or secular authority.

This first statement, admittedly, refers to the Church generally, and not to its ministers *per se*, but he soon goes on to clarify this relationship, in light of the Great Commission:

> [The ministry] is, by the terms of this commission, identified with the institution of the Church itself. The two things are not just the same. The Church is a much wider conception than the ministry. But still they are so joined together that the one cannot be severed from the other. The idea of the Church is made to involve the idea of the ministry. The first is in truth constituted by the commission that creates the second; for it has its whole existence conditioned by an act of faith in the reality of this com-

45. While this sermon provides the fullest sketch of Nevin's mature understanding of the ministry, a few other remarks appear in other essays by Nevin and Schaff. For a fuller discussion, with attention to some of the distinctions between these articulations, see Nichols, *Romanticism*, 259–80.

46. Nevin, "Christian Ministry," 353.

mission, and this tested again by an act of real outward homage
to its authority.[47]

According to this conception, then, the visible Church flows out of the
authorization of its ministers; rather than its ministers being authorized
by the Church which is first instituted generally. This is a striking statement, though not as surprising as it might first seem when you consider
passages (as Nevin does) like Ephesians 2:20, where the Church is said
to be built on the foundation of the apostles. Nevin will expound this
further, and its applications, a bit later. For now he turns to consider the
nature of the ministry.

He makes it clear that the authority of Christian ministers is not
simply on a par with the authority of the magistrate, who is ordained
by God, or of parents, who clearly have divine authorization for their
headship. Nor is it even to be compared with the divine inspiration that
appears to have stood behind some of the great and charismatic leaders
in history, he says. All these, he says, lie in the realm of common grace;
they are "lodged in some way in the moral constitution of the world under its ordinary form, and [are] divine only in virtue of those general
relations to God, which this must be allowed on all hands to carry in its
bosom."[48] The ministry, however, is of another order, entirely, and holds
its authority directly from Christ through the Spirit. This means, among
other things, that the authority of the office is not dependent on the wor-
thiness of the man occupying it, a frequent emphasis of the Tractarians:
"It belongs to the institution of the ministry, and not to the men pri-
vately considered who may be charged at any given time with the sacred
trust. Their personal character may come in to enforce or to prejudice its
claims to respect; but the claims themselves are independent of this, and
rest upon other ground altogether."[49]

Many might be willing to grant all of this for the apostles themselves, but would deny that such authority flows over to their successors.
However, no distinction can be made, Nevin insists, between the authority of the apostles and later Christian ministers, "between the ordinary
and extraordinary forms of the office," as Nevin puts it.[50] Rather, he says,
there were "various classes and orders, some special and for a time only,

47. Ibid., 354.
48. Ibid., 356.
49. Ibid., 362.
50. Ibid., 357.

others for the ordinary use of the Church through all ages; but so far as their origin is concerned, all of precisely the same character and nature; since all alike are referred to the same Ascension gift. The source of the apostleship is the source also of the common pastoral episcopate."[51] This is a bold and important statement, a crucial part of the doctrine of the apostolic succession, which means not merely a succession beginning from the apostles, but one in which the fullness of their authority continues. While the apostles certainly had unique gifts that not all their successors have (such as the ability to work miracles and to mediate new special revelation), as far as authority, there has been no change, so that the Christian ministry now is as authoritative over the Church as the apostolate was in its day.

For Nevin as well as for the Oxford men, the doctrine of apostolic succession was a weapon against State encroachment.

> The office is ... founded in a power which has actually surmounted the order of nature, and reigns above it in its own higher sphere. On this ground it is that we declare the Church to be higher and greater than the State. . . . Governments have no right to place themselves at the head of the Church, or over it, in its own sphere, converting it into a department of state, as in Prussia, or making the civil power the source and fountain of ecclesiastical authority, as since the days of Henry the Eighth and Cranmer in England.[52]

But it was not merely the State that had no right to fashion the ministry as it saw fit—neither was it the democratic body of the Church as such.

> The people have just as little right here as parliaments and kings to shape the Church to their own ends, or to take the creation of its ministry into their own hands. The fond notion which some have of a republican or democratic order in Christianity, by which the popular vote, or the will of any mass or majority of men, shall be regarded as sufficient to originate or bring to an end the sacred office wherever it may be thought proper, and even to create, if need seem, a new Church, as they dare to prostitute that glorious name, for its service and use—is just as far removed from the proper truth of the gospel as any other that could well be applied to the subject.[53]

51. Ibid.
52. Ibid.
53. Ibid., 358.

One may well wonder where such a restriction leaves the Protestant churches, at least the non-episcopal ones, which seem to have indeed been the product of the will of men restructuring the Church and the ministry. This question continues to loom larger as Nevin's discussion continues, for he returns to his earlier discussion of the relation between the ministry and the Church and develops it further. He does not claim a distinction in temporal priority, but says there is reasonable question as to "inward priority," or what we might call "logical priority." He answers, as already pointed out, that the ministry is prior:

> The terms of that [apostolic] commission are such as of themselves plainly to show that the Church was to be considered as starting in the Apostles, and extending itself out from them in the way of implicit submission to their embassy and proclamation. They were to stand between Christ and the world, to be his witnesses, his legates, the representatives of his authority, the mediators of his grace among men. They were to preach in his name, not merely a doctrine for the nations to hear, but a constitution to which they were required to surrender themselves, in order that they might be saved. The new organization was to be formed, and held together, by those who were thus authorized and empowered to carry into effect officially its conditions and terms.[54]

This again is very strong language—Rome itself could hardly ask for more (indeed, Nevin goes on to mention Peter's unique commission). Because the ministers who succeed the apostles stand between Christ and the Church, and are alone responsible for the order and administration of the Church, their office cannot be modified from below, nor are their powers to be understood as delegated from below, as in most Protestant conceptions. Their powers are delegated from above only. Nevin adamantly disclaims any Protestant notion in which the Church as such is made the locus of authority, to shape the ministry as it sees fit:

> There is no room then for the theory by which the Church at large, or any particular part of it, is taken to be the depository, in the first instance, of all the grace and force which belong to the ministerial office, just as in a political organization the body of the people may be supposed to contain in themselves primarily the powers with which they choose to invest their own officers and magistrates. The order of dependence here is not ascending but descending. The law of derivation is downwards and not up-

54. Ibid., 358–59.

wards, from the few to the many, and not from the many to the few. . . . By whatever names they may be distinguished, apostles, prophets, presbyters, rulers, or pastors, their office is in its essential constitution episcopal. They are shepherds under him who is the Chief Shepherd, clothed by delegation with his authority, and appointed to have charge of the flock in his name.[55]

It would be no exaggeration to say that this militates against almost all contemporary Protestant conceptions, though it again dovetails very neatly with the agenda of the Oxford men. But Nevin perhaps goes even further than them in the strength and force of his conviction. For he goes on to say,

> To say that there can be a Church without a bishop . . . in other words, that the Church is before the ministry in the order of existence, and in no way dependent upon it, but complete without it . . . is a heresy which at once strikes at the root of all faith in the supernatural constitution of the Church, and turns both the apostolical commission and the gift of Pentecost into a solemn farce.[56]

Nevin then appears no less earnest than Newman in holding that just as there can be no remedy to liberalism and sectarianism without a revived sense of the supernatural and sacramental power of the Church, so there can be no true revival of this without a revived doctrine of the apostolic succession.

Nevin goes on to note at least two crucial features of this apostolic ministry: the first is the principle of a linear succession by laying on of hands, the second is the principle of unity or collegiality. Linear succession alone does not ensure authority, just as none of the Apostles could be assured that his authority continued if he was operating entirely of his own accord:

> The commission given to the Apostles implied that they were to act in concert. It was not an authority which each one of them was left to himself to exercise in his own way and for his own pleasure. It belonged to them only in their collective capacity. They were bound by it to the real and fixed constitution of grace with which it was concerned, in the capacity of a college or corporation. . . . As there can be, by the very conception of Christianity, but one

55. Ibid., 359.
56. Ibid., 360.

> faith, one baptism, and one Church, so can there be also but one
> ministry, and this unity must be taken to extend to all times and
> ages, as well as all lands.[57]

It is worth noting as an aside that, with such a strong emphasis on the
unity of the ministers (which he appeals to later as a necessary test or
mark of the true apostolic ministry), and given the state of the Church
at least since the Reformation, it seems impossible to maintain that any
Christian Church (including perhaps even the Roman) maintains the true
or full apostolic ministry. We should not be surprised then to find that
such an emphasis is much harder to find in the Tractarian discussions
of apostolic succession. According to Nevin's definition, the Anglican
bishops, operating outside of union with the rest of the Church, had no
authority to establish the independence of the English Church. So the
Tractarians put the emphasis more on the strict linear succession, since,
if this were all that were necessary, the schism of the Reformation need
constitute no mortal damage to the succession.

Nevin concludes with a fervent exhortation as to the importance of
this doctrine, as strong or stronger than anything we see from the pens
of the Tractarians:

> All are bound, as they value their salvation, to look well to the
> nature of the commission and character under which they pro-
> pose to secure this all important object. Indifference with regard
> to the matter is itself a just occasion for apprehension and alarm;
> for it implies at once serious infidelity towards the whole subject.
> . . . As every minister is bound to be well assured that he is a
> minister not merely of this or that sect, but of the true Church
> Catholic, and has part thus in that one great commission from
> which hangs the unity of the whole office; so also are all other
> persons under obligation to satisfy themselves, on good and suf-
> ficient grounds, that they are in the bosom of the Church in its
> true form, and under the guidance and care of a legitimate and
> true ministry.[58]

So, what are we to make of this? Here we have a German Reformed
theologian making a case for apostolic succession that Newman, Pusey,
or Keble would've probably loved to print off as Tract 91 if they'd ever
encountered it. And yet, throughout, Nevin maintains that he is not

57. Ibid.
58. Ibid., 370–71.

arguing for the episcopal structure *per se*, as the Oxford men were. He says, "The question is not of the episcopal office in some special given form, but of the office in its broad New Testament sense, as involving the idea of a real pastoral jurisdiction over the Church, representing in it immediately the authority of Jesus Christ."[59] This is consistent with his and Schaff's statements elsewhere, where they critiqued the Tractarians for their emphasis on the episcopal order. Nichols, indeed, draws a strong distinction between the Mercersburg doctrine of the ministry and the "external, mechanical" succession of the Tractarians.

However, we have seen that Nevin did make the external, linear succession indispensable, and it appears difficult for Nevin to consistently justify any distinction between the central idea of the doctrine, which is necessary, and the particular historical form, which is negotiable. For he himself said that all authority is given into the hands of the apostles and the successors they choose, not into the hands of the congregants or the Church generally. These latter, he says, have no authority to modify the form of the ministry. Therefore, even if he wishes to argue that the initial commission did not require that the ministry take the particular form of the threefold office, it seems that the Church, having adopted this form, is still bound to it, unless the ministers themselves decide to revise it. Moreover, because he insists that the ministers wield their authority in conjunction with one another, rather than as individuals, the action of certain Protestant ministers is not sufficient to authorize a new structure of Church authority.

But it remains a bit of an enigma why Nevin insists so strongly on views which appear to delegitimize Protestantism, especially when he is so forceful about the danger of being outside the proper succession. Nichols, in his commentary on this sermon, observes the ambiguity, but does not attempt to answer it.[60] The best answer, it seems, taking this sermon in conjunction with the essay "The Anglican Crisis," is to conclude that Nevin believed strongly in this ideal of the ministry, but did not believe that any current church had maintained this ideal in any sufficient form. Given that all had fallen short, then, the solution was not to jump to Rome or Canterbury, but to work within the Reformed Church for a

---

59. Ibid., 360.

60. Ibid., 349. He puts it this way in *Romanticism*: "Apparently Nevin never solved the doubt as to the validity of the ministrations of divided and independent successions in the ministry. Perhaps he felt he had discharged his responsibility to the best of his capacity when he laid the unanswerable problem formally before the church in his address" (280).

future reinstatement of the apostolic ministry.[61] Because of this future-orientedness, Nevin eschews the Tractarian emphasis on strict maintenance of the historical form of the ministry as being too past-oriented. It is not so much because he sees their episcopal form as incorrect, or even their "mechanical" view of the succession, but that, in thinking that all they must do to maintain the ideal is to maintain the historical form, the scope of their vision is reduced and the power of their call to action is weakened.

Mercersburg's Assessment of Oxford

It is time then to uncover, in a more systematic way, what Nevin and Schaff thought of their English counterparts, and where they did and didn't see their missions as the same. In his article "The Anglican Crisis," Nevin expresses, in dramatic tones, the tremendous significance of the Oxford Movement, and the power and timeliness of its proposed remedy to the ills of Protestantism. This declaration parallels in some ways the similar panegyric that Schaff offers in *Principle of Protestantism*, but Nevin goes on much longer, and his "but . . . " is more muted. It is apparent that, by this point, Nevin at least had come to view the movement with more favor (though still not unqualified favor). He saw that the central question that the Oxford men were trying to answer, and their essential mission, was the same as his own:

> The force of the question in the end is nothing less than this: Whether the original catholic doctrine concerning the Church, as it stood in universal authority through all ages before the Reformation, is to be received and held still as a necessary part of the Christian faith, or deliberately rejected and refused as an error dangerous to men's souls and at war with the Bible?[62]

He saw that the controversy over baptismal regeneration then going on in England was, at root, simply part of the debate over this greater question, and insisted that all who desired the good of the Church should understand that the whole concept of the Church as mediator of grace stood or fell on this point.

61. This reading fits well with Nichols's analysis of Nevin's struggle over conversion to Rome and the conclusions he reached that kept him in the Protestant fold. See chapters 8 and 9 of *Romanticism*.

62. Nevin, "Anglican Crisis," 369.

Having, however, so thoroughly expressed his sympathy with the cause of the Anglo-Catholic movement, he proceeds to sharply critique what he saw as the overly scrupulous stress on the externals—the proper institutional form of the Church—rather than the heart of the doctrine.

> What better is it than this [that is, Puritanism] to make Episcopacy, with its outward succession from the time of the Apostles, in and of itself the article of a standing or falling church . . . ? It is possible to take very high ground with this view, to be very aristocratic and very exclusive; but the view itself is low, and proceeds on the want of faith in the proper supernatural character of the Church rather than on the presence of such faith; on which account, the farther it is pushed it only becomes the more plainly empty and pedantic.[63]

What is crucial, he goes on to say, is an incarnational understanding of the Church, as a unique divine constitution on earth. Of course, "this does not imply," he goes on,

> that such organs and functions may be indifferently in any form, or in no form whatever . . . but it does mean certainly that the organs and functions make not of themselves the being of the body; they are parts only in any case, which owe their whole vitality and vigor to the general system in which they are comprehended, and away from this are of no worth whatever.[64]

One might suggest that Nevin's critique here is somewhat misguided, for in none of the leading writers of the Oxford Movement do we find this emphasis on the outward form divorced from an urgent sense of the importance of the inward power and significance of the Church. Indeed, in Wilberforce this is quite clear, as Nevin himself admits in "Wilberforce on the Incarnation."[65] However, it is true that in the *Tracts for the Times*, there is a disproportionate emphasis on the outward form of the Church and the doctrine of the apostolic succession separately considered (though it important to remember that these were meant as popular-level expositions, not theological treatises). One might also respond to Nevin's critique by pointing out that he himself seems to go too far the other way, emphasizing the "inward" to the detriment of the "outward" in Gnostic fashion: "all turns here on the idea of the Church, and this not only may,

63. Ibid. 376–77.
64. Ibid. 378.
65. See Nevin, "Wilberforce on the Incarnation," 155–63.

but must be settled to some extent in our minds, before we can go on to discuss to real purpose the obligation of Episcopacy, Presbyterianism, or any other polity claiming to be of such necessary force."[66]

Nevertheless, while wishing they would spend less time on episcopacy, he remains very happy with the stand they have taken on sacramental grace. But, here, he fears, their attempted reformation is in vain. The history of Anglicanism, its current temperament, and the harsh reaction to the Oxford Movement lead him to doubt that the Tractarians will ever be able to make their ideas generally acceptable within their communion. Their attempted liberation of the Church from State authority he considers almost impossible, given the long, entrenched history of the establishment Church. In this matter, he has to conclude, the Romanists have a better case to make, as having always remained constitutionally autonomous. Nevin foretold that, trying to move Anglicanism in directions that it simply was not able to go, the Anglo-Catholics would have to either form a secession body or move on into Romanism, as Newman had done.[67] "The result of the trial is sure to be," he sadly concludes, "that Anglicanism will be found wanting, having no power to make good its own high-sounding promises and claims."[68]

Having thus doubted that the Oxford Movement may ever successfully accomplish the necessary rejuvenation of Protestantism, may bring the Church back into the central position that belongs to it, Nevin suggests four alternatives that lie before Protestantism. The first is an abandonment of the high-church, sacramental position altogether, such as most of his contemporaries were doing; the second is a return to Rome; the third is hope in a new outpouring of the Spirit, resulting in a fresh new form of Christianity unlike anything before; the fourth is a belief that, by the historical development of the Church, Protestantism and Catholicism will both build off of the past and transcend it into a unity that is new and yet old.[69] And this is of course is where Nevin distrusts the Oxford Movement; for while he fixed his eyes forward, in constant hope for the Church of the future, they looked only to the past, seeking to do no more than hold fast to what they found there. This is Schaff's central critique in *The Principle of Protestantism*. There Schaff says,

66. Nevin, "Anglican Crisis," 378.

67. Ibid. 389.

68. Ibid. 390.

69. Nevin, "Anglican Crisis," 395–97.

As to Romanism, so to Puseyism also, there is wanting the true idea of development altogether. It regards the Church as a system handed down under a given and complete form, that must remain perpetually the same. . . . With all their historical feeling, the Puseyites show themselves with regard to the Reformation absolutely unhistorical. They wish to shut out of view the progress of the last three centuries entirely; to treat the whole as a negation, if possible; and by one vast leap to carry the Church back to the point where it stood before the separation of the Oriental and Western Communions.[70]

Mercersburg could view the Tractarians as co-belligerents then, perhaps even allies, but the movements were not identical in aim. While Nevin and Newman might tread the same path together for quite a distance, they must ultimately part ways and pursue their separate destinations. For, though Nevin had no interest in being an innovator, and repudiated Hodge's claims that he was creating a new theology, nor did he believe in slavish allegiance to the past. With the Oxford men, however, we hear only one note: "Tradition! TRADITION!" Though some like Newman were bold and creative thinkers, in every new teaching and practice we see only the motivation to regain a lost ideal from the past. This return *ad fontes* is surely a great and noble endeavor, but Nevin felt that it was only the beginning of the task. Though one may look at a map to figure out where one has been, normally this is so that one knows how to move forward, not so that one may drive back to the beginning. Where Mercersburg looked back to gain clearer sight for the forward march, the Oxford men looked backward and stayed that way. This fundamental orientation was ultimately an eschatological orientation; Keble, Newman, and Pusey are full of Stoic resolution to hold firm the course through this transient, troubled world, to come at last to heavenly bliss, while Nevin and Schaff are full of buoyant optimism that the Church will triumph over and transform this transient troubled world.

This interpretation explains, I think, Mercersburg's ambivalence regarding their counterparts across the pond, despite the remarkable theological similarity between the two movements. Both seek to recover much the same Patristic and early Reformation heritage, both attempt to graft themselves onto the old trunk of catholic tradition, and so it is no surprise that they seek to recover many of the same doctrines. On baptism,

---

70. Schaff, *Principle of Protestantism*, 160–61.

the Eucharist, and the function of the ministry, they occupy the same ground because they both turn to the same guides, Cyprian, Chrysostom, Augustine, the Cappadocians. And, as the early Reformers in many ways sought out the same ground, both Mercersburg and Oxford can appeal back to their Reformational roots. The similarity between Nevin and Pusey in their articulation of the sacraments is nonetheless striking, and suggests that perhaps Pusey is more Calvinist than he thinks, or Nevin is less Calvinist (depending on how you take Calvin), but a full discussion of this issue is out of the scope of this book. On the theology of the ministry, we have seen, despite his concerns and critiques of Anglican externalism, Nevin's view reduces to essentially the same doctrine. When it came to what Nevin pegged as the central question, whether the Church was the mediator of sacramental grace, both answered in the affirmative, and of course this determined their similarity on so many other questions.

Yet, where the Tractarians saw that Anglicanism itself could provide the answer, provided only that it grasped full hold of its proper history and tradition, Nevin and Schaff could never accept such a conclusion. For no historic church, no past however perfect, pointed the sure way into the future. The heritage of Anglicanism could and should be revived, Nevin agreed, but only provisionally, for the Church of the future would not be Anglican, nor Reformed nor Catholic for that matter. This also explains, at least partially, Nevin and Schaff's harsh reaction to the Oxford Movement's revival of episcopacy. It was not, as is clear from Nevin's sermon, a fear of an apostolic succession, even in episcopal form. However, if the Anglicans began to view their apostolic succession as a firm and sure rope stretching back to Christ, an anchor that they could grab hold of and rest secure in, then they were guilty of false complacency. The apostolic succession could not be thus restricted to the Anglican branch of the Church so easily, nor could it be used to legitimate its claims over any other form of Christendom. Such a view, Nevin and Schaff believed, was historically irresponsible, but more importantly, it stifled any genuine impetus for future reformation and reunion. While both Nevin and Newman extolled the apostolic succession in equally strong terms, Newman's point was to insist "We have it, so let's rest in that" (which of course he later found himself unable to do), but Nevin's was to suggest "We don't have it, any of us, so let's get to work."

As a summary evaluation then, I would suggest that the comparison of Mercersburg and the Oxford Movement suggests at least three crucial conclusions. First, though there were considerable divergences between the Mercersburg and the Oxford approach on many theological issues, the agendas were indeed quite similar. We might pinpoint the differences as stemming from the Anglo-Catholics' failure to reckon with the incarnational heart of the Church or with the notion of development in Church history; however, it seems that eschatology is more fundamental, and led to important differences where otherwise there need have been none. Second, it thus appears that a good high-church Reformed theology, and a good high-church Anglican theology, reduce to much the same thing—a rich patristic theology of Church and sacrament, enriched with a healthy dose of Reformational soteriology. This comparison shows us that high-church Anglicans and high-church Reformed may indeed make common cause across a wide spectrum of issues, even apostolic succession. Indeed, assuming a unified eschatological outlook, there seems no reason why the two cannot come to considerable unity of purpose. Third, although the Oxford Movement may have done well in avoiding too much of the influence of German theology, and hence gives us a purer view of catholic tradition, it seems that Nevin and Schaff did well in imbibing the German optimism. Certainly this optimism must be cleansed of its humanistic and pantheistic baggage, but, for Nevin and Schaff, it provided the optimistic eschatology necessary to constructively apply the riches of tradition to the needs of the Church today. Without this outlook, Anglo-Catholicism can provide nothing more than a temporary stopgap, trying in vain to halt the flow of Church history by tightening its grip on the past and never letting go.

CHAPTER 5

Facing East
Mercersburg and Eastern Orthodoxy

I N THIS CHAPTER, WE finally come to perhaps the most intriguing application of the Mercersburg Theology. Since the Great Schism of 1054, the rich, deep current of Eastern Orthodox theology has flowed far away beyond the knowledge of the Western Church. The twin calamities of the Fall of Constantinople in 1453 and the divisions prompted by the Reformation shortly afterward widened the divide still further. The Eastern Christians were weak and disunited in the wake of the Turkish invasions, and the Western Christians were so preoccupied with Protestant/ Catholic issues that they seemed to almost forget the existence of their Eastern brethren. Finally, in recent decades, with the resurgence of Eastern Orthodoxy, and the growing global consciousness of the Church, efforts at renewed dialogue have begun, both between the Orthodox and Catholic churches, and between Orthodoxy and Protestantism.

Unfortunately, many differences appear to remain irreconcilable. One place where such discussions consistently run aground is the arena of soteriology, where the Orthodox notion of *theosis*, or deification, seems quite repugnant to theologically conscious Protestants. Even when definitions are cleared up and the Orthodox clarify that deification does not mean any actual transformation into the divine nature, that the Creator/ creature distinction is still maintained, a real stumbling block persists. For, however they articulate the nature of the transformation involved in *theosis*, the fact remains that this is a transformational soteriology, while the Protestant doctrine, at least as widely understood today, is committed to an extrinsic, imputational soteriology.

We can observe this stumbling block in *Three Views on Eastern Orthodoxy and Evangelicalism*, where Michael Horton asserts that the two are incompatible, largely on the basis of soteriological differences: "The heart of our differences emerges over the material principle: justification by grace alone through faith alone because of Christ alone."[1] This is not because Horton is a hard-nosed Lutheran or a devotee of the *ordo salutis*. He acknowledges that the *ordo salutis* is "hardly the whole story"[2] and that there is much more to salvation than merely forensic justification.[3] He is willing to acknowledge, along with Orthodoxy, that Christology is foundational to soteriology, and affirms that "Reformed theology does set its exploration of justification in the context of its overarching covenantal scheme of 'union with Christ.'"[4] Nevertheless, he is only willing to bend so far. Though he agrees that "Orthodoxy has never bypassed the doctrine of justification," he holds firm that, "because it denies that this is a purely forensic declaration based on the imputation of Christ's 'alien righteousness,' we have historically regarded the Orthodox position, like Rome's, as constituting a denial of the doctrine as presented in Scripture."[5] Though forensic justification is not the whole picture, its integrity must be maintained as a unique part of the picture: "we insist that this forensic declaration, though foundational, is not all that is meant by 'salvation.' On the other hand, it seems that Orthodox theology does collapse all of soteriological reality into the category of transformation."[6]

Horton is consistently suspicious of the Eastern Orthodox soteriological framework and critiques it from a standpoint of radical monergism:

> It is true that a genuinely Pauline theology will emphasize both mystical union and the "summing up" of all things in Christ on the one hand, and individual justification and reconciliation on the other. However, how one relates the two is all-important. Any view of union and recapitulation that denies that the sole basis

1. Horton, "Eastern Orthodoxy and Evangelicalism," 128.
2. Horton, "A Response to Bradley Nassif," 90.
3. Ibid., 91–92.
4. Ibid., 91.
5. Ibid.
6. Ibid., 92.

> for divine acceptance of sinners is the righteousness of Christ and
> that the sole means of receiving that righteousness is imputation
> through faith alone apart from works is a denial of the gospel.[7]

Theosis, he insists, is semi-Pelagian, because man must be obedient to
the divine energies at work in him, and this is unacceptable. "Although it
will sound like a gross oversimplification, many of us will regard this as
a difference—although an important one—of degree. To what extent can
humans be said to contribute to their own salvation? Pelagians answer,
'Entirely'; Semi-Pelagians, 'In part.' Neither of these answers from a clas-
sical evangelical perspective, does justice to the biblical account of sin."[8]

Bradley Nassif responds by insisting that the differences here need
not be so great as Horton is making them. He refers to recent dialogues
between the Orthodox Church and the Scottish Reformed Churches,
which found "far greater compatibility between Orthodoxy and Calvin
than he himself [that is, Horton] has seen."[9] In Nassif's mind, the
Orthodox can maintain the integrity of justification (forensic, though
not purely forensic) so long as this is understood as simply a part of the
mystical union or *theosis*, which then continues with transformation and
deification, and the Reformed ought to be happy to accept the rest of the
redemptive package of which justification is only one piece.

It is my contention in this section that Nevin's creative unfolding of
the Reformed tradition vindicates Nassif's optimism in this area. In the
Mercersburg Theology, we see the articulation of a thoroughly participationist, transformationist Reformed soteriology that is, like Orthodoxy's,
rooted in the Incarnation and a *Christus Victor* emphasis on the atonement. No doubt many, Michael Horton not least, will protest that Nevin
is only able to provide such a bridge with Orthodoxy because he no longer stands on Reformed ground at all. The striking parallels that appear
between Nevin's conception and Orthodoxy's, such a protester will argue,
are evidence for nothing more than an abandonment of what it means to
be Reformed. Hodge certainly would have thought so. It will, of course,
be impossible to silence all such concern, but in Nevin's defense, I would
appeal back to the earlier chapters which sought to vindicate Nevin's version of "Reformed theology" over against Hodge's. More importantly,
Bill Evans's brilliant study of Reformed views of imputation and union

7. Horton, "Eastern Orthodoxy and Evangelicalism," 137.

8. Ibid., 140.

9. Nassif, "Response to Michael Horton," 147.

with Christ has revealed that Nevin was in close continuity with the early Reformed theologians on the central points of his soteriology.[10] Though the centrality of the Incarnation within his system is certainly more his own distinctive than a Reformed distinctive, it hardly seems that the emphasis should be irreconcilable with Reformed theology, whatever Hodge may have protested.

In any case, one certainly cannot maintain that Nevin must have been flirting with Eastern Orthodoxy or some such. The similarities that we find in this area of his thought are all the more remarkable because they are so clearly unconscious. There is scarcely a reference in all his writings to the Eastern Church, and even the few we can find are interested only in the period of the early Church; the contemporary Eastern Church is only ever mentioned in connection with the adjective "dead." Schaff makes the rather blunt pronouncement that the Eastern Orthodox Church had "passed over into a state of putrefaction, so as to present at best only the spectacle of a praying corpse."[11] Later, he feels confident enough in this evaluation to invoke the Eastern Church as a *reductio ad absurdum* of the idea that apostolic succession makes a Church: "How monstrous again is the position . . . that the dead Armenian and Greek [Nevin and Schaff appear to use the term "Greek" to denominate the entirety of Eastern Orthodoxy] denominations, because they have bishops, belong regularly to the Holy Church Catholic."[12]

I would not blame some of my Orthodox brothers for being offended at this arrogant pronouncement, and no doubt it was rather shortsighted even for that time (after all, this "state of putrefaction" was alive enough to produce the Christianity of Dostoevsky's *Brothers Karamazov*, a production rivaled by few eras and regions of Christendom). However, it is doubtless that the Orthodox Church of Schaff's day was not showing the same signs of life it is now. At any rate, these pronouncements make clear that the Mercersburg men had no thought of building off of or building toward Orthodox theology as such, so any connections we may discover must be referred to a deeper or older kinship.

While exploration of a number of areas of similarity would be fruitful, I will focus, as already suggested, on the area of soteriology, where the parallels are particularly close, and particularly significant given the tra-

10. See Evans, "Imputation and Impartation."

11. Schaff, *Principle of Protestantism*, 128.

12. Ibid., 162.

ditional rift between East and West on this issue. The Eastern Orthodox doctrine of *theosis* can be maddeningly difficult to pin down with any precision, both because of its innate mysteriousness, and because of Orthodoxy's historic aversion to dogmatic theology and its careful definitions. All Orthodox theologians agree that the doctrine is a central teaching of the Church, and dates back to the early Greek Fathers, but there is no standardized form of the doctrine in modern Orthodox theology. Indeed, the sketch of Orthodox soteriology in this chapter gives the deceptive illusion of a unified, agreed-upon Orthodox system of doctrine, and paves over many differences in emphasis or even paradigm. I attempt to note some of these differences in the footnotes, but no doubt this is still oversimplified.

Theosis, Creation, and Incarnation

However, we can start with a good working definition of *theosis* by Christoforos Stavropoulos: "It means the elevation of the human being to the divine sphere, to the atmosphere of God. It means the union of the human with the divine."[13] He goes on to add the crucial qualifier—that this divinization is not a change of nature, but the perfection and fulfillment of proper humanity.

> This union is not absolute. It is relative, for it is not the transformation of our essence. Rather, it is natural, ethical, and in accordance with grace. It is the union of the whole person with God as unrestricted happiness in the divine kingdom. Human nature becomes the outgrowth of divine nature. It is remade into its original beauty. It is reborn to a new life. It is re-created through divine adoption.[14]

Or, as Anastasius of Sinai puts it, "Theosis is elevation to what is better, but not the reduction of our nature to something less, nor is it an essential change of our human nature. . . . That which is of God is that which has been lifted up to a greater glory, without its own nature being changed."[15] This definition serves to point us toward a crucial feature of this doctrine, that is, the anthropology that is implied in it. The Eastern Orthodox understand *theosis* as far more than a merely soteriological

13. Stavropoulos, "Partakers of Divine Nature," 184.

14. Ibid.

15. Anastasius of Sinai, *Concerning the Word*, quoted in Stavropoulos, 184.

framework; rather, it reflects their entire understanding of man's created destiny. So let us first look at the Orthodox notion of creation and man.

Orthodox theology has traditionally distinguished between the "image" and the "likeness" of God. From the beginning, man had the image of God, that is, a unique spiritual predisposition toward God, but only by growth in maturity and faithfulness could he come to possess the "likeness" of God. Timothy (Kallistos) Ware describes it,

> Acccording to St. Irenaeus, man at his first creation was "as a little child", and needed to "grow" into his perfection. In other words, man at his first creation was innocent and capable of developing spiritually (the "image"), but his development was not inevitable or automatic. Man was called to co-operate with God's grace and so, through the correct use of his free will, slowly and by gradual steps he was to become perfect in God (the "likeness"). This shows how the notion of man as created in God's image can be interpreted in a dynamic rather than a static sense.[16]

Orthodoxy puts a lot of emphasis on this notion of a dynamic anthropology; man is not simply created happy and holy and perfect, to remain there (ideally), or to be restored there (after the Fall); man is to grow into fuller maturity and more perfect union with God his Creator. This emphasis works because the Orthodox here are thinking not so much in ethical categories (as we often tend to think of the created state—an ideal ethical purity), but in relational categories, and of course relationships are dynamic:

> The image and likeness signify orientation, relationship. . . . To believe that man is made in God's image is to believe that man is created for communion and union with God, and that if he rejects this communion he ceases to be properly man. There is no such thing as "natural man" existing in separation from God: man cut off from God is in a highly unnatural state.[17]

So, in the Eastern framework, man is created in relationship with God, and is commanded to grow into fuller fellowship.[18] The created

16. Ware, *Orthodox Way*, 52.

17. Ibid.

18. There appears to be some ambiguity, or perhaps a spectrum of viewpoints, on the question of this created relationship. Is there a seminal relationship from the outset that must grow and deepen? Or is there a capacity for a relationship that must be realized? Ware seems to quite clearly affirm the first; Lossky, seems to say the second: "Creatures, from

state is only a starting point, and *theosis* is man's original calling. This has radical implications for how we understand the rest of the history of redemption. For, if man was created at the beginning of a journey toward God, the Fall was not so much the loss of a state to be regained, but the wrong turn on the journey. Redemption in Christ, then, aims not to restore us to lost perfection, but to set us back on the road, thankfully much further along than we were when we lost it. Redemption in Christ, in fact, accomplishes that *theosis* for which we were created. Donald Fairbairn sketches it in terms of a three-act versus a two-act salvation scheme. The Western three-act scheme pictures first Creation, by which man is placed in perfect fellowship with God, then the Fall, by which he loses this fellowship, and finally, redemption, by which it is regained. However,

> In the Eastern model, the first act is that of creation, and God created humanity not so much in actual fellowship and union with God, as with the potential for such union. People were called to achieve *theosis*, to become partakers of the divine nature. In this mode, the fallen state is not drastically different from the original created state; the fallen state is the condition of people who have turned aside from the path they were to follow.[19] Accordingly,

the moment of their first condition, are separate from God; and their end and final fulfillment lies in union with Him or deification. Thus the primitive beatitude was not a state of deification, but a condition of order, a perfection of the creature which was ordained and tending towards its end" (Lossky, *Mystical Theology*, 99, quoted in Fairbairn, *Eastern Orthodoxy*, 66). The option you choose seems to me to make a great deal of difference. To borrow Western scholastic terminology; the second supposes the possibility of a state of "pure nature"; the first categorically denies it. In general, however, I believe that these seemingly contrasting viewpoints are not all that far apart. Most Orthodox construals of the image/likeness distinction seem to suggest that something like the first answer must be presupposed. Aghiorgoussis says, "Likeness with God is . . . becoming more and more what one already is: becoming more and more God's image, more and more God-like. The distinction between image and likeness is, in other words, the distinction between *being* and *becoming*." (Aghiorgoussis, "The Dogmatic Tradition," 150, quoted in Fairbairn, 68). Fairbairn comments on this quote, "One should notice here that the separation between God and people (to which Lossky refers in the earlier quotation) is not an absolute one. People were children of God from the beginning of their existence. Nevertheless, in a certain sense communion with God was not simply given to them at the beginning but was set before them as something to be obtained" (Fairbain, *Eastern Orthodoxy*, 68).

19. In this way of putting the matter, it sounds as if the Orthodox minimize the Fall too much. While Fairbairn's general picture is correct, we must be careful not to draw such a conclusion. For example, Stavropoulos says, "[Adam] took not the divine, but the demonic road. The immediate consequence of this apostasy was the fall, that is, separation from the living God. Humanity loses the divine gift. Human nature becomes distorted. Death comes. Our subjugation to the tyranny of the devil follows. And thus, we human beings

the fall does not constitute a separate act in the drama, the way it does in the western model. Rather, the second act is that of raising humanity to a new level altogether, a level of complete fellowship with God and sharing in divine life. This fellowship is the goal of the journey, not a state that people have possessed before. In this scheme, salvation is not a restoration, but an elevation to an entirely new sphere of life.[20]

Understood this way, it appears that the Incarnation must not be understood merely as the remedy for sin, but as a display of God's character that is built far more deeply into the framework of the creation. The Incarnation, it seems, is an essential part of man's journey to *theosis*, and so would have happened, somehow, even without the Fall. Ware rightly cautions against indulging in such hypotheticals, but still considers the question worthy of comment. Following St. Isaac the Syrian he hesitantly suggests that "Even had there been no fall, God in his own limitless, outgoing love would still have chosen to identify himself with his creation by becoming man."[21] Ware goes on to speak of the Incarnation in terms which echo Fairbairn's "two-act" model:

> The Incarnation of Christ, looked at in this way, effects more than a reversal of the fall, more than a restoration of man to his original state in Paradise. When God becomes man, this marks the beginning of an essentially new stage in the history of man, and not just a return to the past. The Incarnation raises man to a new level; the last state is higher than the first. Only in Jesus Christ do we see revealed the full possibilities of our human nature; until he is born, the true implications of our personhood are still hidden from us.[22]

Becoming more confident by the end, Ware appears to forthrightly affirm the prelapsarian necessity of the Incarnation, saying,

> The Incarnation, then, is not simply a way of undoing the effects of original sin, but it is an essential stage upon man's journey from the divine image to the divine likeness. The true image and like-

---

ourselves stand in the way of the divine grace which is poured out upon us. The image of God within us is weakened. We ourselves preclude the possibility of our union with God. We deny the human characteristic and possibility of divinization. The potential of becoming like God disappears and becomes impossible" ("Partakers of Divine Nature," 187).

20. Fairbairn, *Eastern Orthodoxy*, 76.

21. Ware, *Orthodox Way*, 70.

22. Ibid., 70–71.

ness of God is Christ himself; and so, from the very first moment
of man's creation in the image, the Incarnation of Christ was in
some way already implied. The true reason for the Incarnation,
then, lies not in man's sinfulness but in his unfallen nature as a being made in the divine image and capable of union with God.[23]

However, we would be over-hasty to take this conclusion as a distinctive of Orthodoxy *per se*; while Orthodox theology may tend in this
direction, it is not unanimous. For example, Stavropoulos treats the
person and work of Christ entirely in terms of a postlapsarian remedy:
"Incarnation-crucifixion-resurrection-ascension bridge the gap which
separates us from God. That chasm is death, sin, and fallen nature."[24]
In either case, the general picture of Christology is quite similar, which
Stavropoulos goes on to sketch in outline, "The chasm which our fallen
nature creates is bridged over by the Incarnation of the Divine Word. The
chasm which is created by our sin is bridged over by his crucifixion. And
the third chasm, death, is filled in by his resurrection. . . . And with his
holy ascension, Christ unites the earth with the heavens and unites the
two into one; he has made both one."[25] In this fourfold process, though,
the Incarnation receives special emphasis, not merely as a prerequisite
for the other three, but as profoundly efficacious in itself. It was "the basis
upon which the re-creation of humanity and their return to the road of
theosis . . . was to be realized."[26] It "brings us again to the Father and presents us with the potential of realizing the likeness of God in our lives."[27]
And Ware says,

> In his outgoing or "ecstatic" love, God unites himself to his cre-
> ation in the closest all possible unions, by himself becoming
> that which he has created. God, as man, fulfills the mediatorial
> task which man rejected at the fall. Jesus our Saviour bridges the
> abyss between God and man because he is both at once. . . . The
> Incarnation, then, is God's supreme act of deliverance, restoring
> us to communion with himself.[28]

23. Ibid., 71.
24. Stavropoulos, "Partakers of Divine Nature," 188.
25. Ibid.
26. Ibid., 187.
27. Ibid., 188.
28. Ware, *Orthodox Way*, 69–70.

It makes sense, within the general picture that Fairbairn sketched, that the Incarnation should receive greater emphasis than the atonement. In the Western picture, sin and the Fall are usually seen as *the* problem that needs to be fixed, so naturally, the atonement takes center stage. In the Eastern picture, sin and the Fall are more like a major complication to an existing problem, or, perhaps better, a grievous setback on a steep ascent that had to be made anyway. Pre-Fall or post-Fall, the fundamental need was the same: union with God. So while the atonement may remedy the setback of sin, the Incarnation (and its consummation in the Resurrection) springs us forward, brings the eschatological endpoint, as it were, into the present, in the person of Christ, so that, in Him, we may anticipate that end of union with God.

All of this, the attentive reader no doubt recognizes, is very close to Nevin's thought on creation, anthropology, and Christology. According to Nevin, man was created for communion with God. Indeed, all creation was meant to be lifted up into a kind of union with God, with man as the center and representative of the rest. This idea is of course very prone to misunderstanding, and can easily fall into a kind of pantheism—where nature is suffused with the divine and will come to realize its full divinity in a sort of Hegelian process. But Nevin, at least, is careful to avoid this pitfall. What Nevin sees instead is a creation that was intended to grow and mature from glory to glory, a nature that was never pure nature, but was suffused with grace, and longed ever to grow further into life with God: "Nature is only relatively true and real. It finds its actual sense . . . only as actualized in the mystery of the Incarnation . . . So all history becomes true at last only in Christ."[29] This notion of creation is developed further in the section on Nevin and the *nouvelle théologie*, but suffice it to say here that man's destiny, in Nevin's outlook, was far from static; Eden was but the beginning of the journey, in which man was to grow much further into communion with the life of God.

What this means, then, is that, for Nevin too, redemption is not simply a remedy for the Fall, but a raising up of mankind into fuller life with God. Redeemed and glorified man will be far more glorious and mature than unfallen man; will be, indeed, what unfallen man was intended to grow into. This of course raises the question, which Ware answered in the affirmative, whether the Incarnation would have happened without

29. Nevin, *Mystical Presence*, 195.

the Fall. Nevin grapples with this question directly in several articles,[30] and though he seems to leave the answer somewhat inconclusive, there is no doubt that throughout his work he leans very strongly toward the answer "Yes," and indeed seems to assume such a perspective in much of his talk of the Incarnation and redemption. Nevin is adamant, then, that the Incarnation not be understood simply as a means to the atonement, but as itself the beginning of an "at-one-ment"[31] between God and man, as has already been discussed in chapter 3. In *The Mystical Presence*, he says, "Here then [at the incarnation], as before said, we reach the central FACT, at once ultimate and primal, in the constitution of the world. All nature and all history flow towards it, as their true and proper end, or spring from it as their principle and ground.[32]

The incarnate Christ represents the perfect man, not simply because He was perfectly righteous, but because, by bringing human nature into intimate personal union with the divine, He pictured for us (and made possible for us to emulate) man as man was meant to be, united to God.

> He put on [human nature] truly and in the fullest sense. He was man more perfectly than this could be said of Adam himself, even before he fell; humanity stood revealed in his person under its most perfect form. Not a new humanity wholly dissevered from that of Adam, but the humanity of Adam itself, only raised to a higher character, and filled with new meaning and power, by its union with the divine nature.[33]

All that is lacking in this discussion for the parallels in anthropology and Christology to be perfectly lucid is the Orthodox terminology of "image" and "likeness." In comparison to Nevin's last statement, it is particularly interesting to quote Ware's similar description of Christ:

> Only in Jesus Christ do we see revealed the full possibilities of our human nature; until he is born, the true implications of our personhood are still hidden from us. Christ's birth, as St. Basil puts it, is "the birthday of the whole human race"; Christ is the first perfect man—perfect, that is to say, not just in a potential

---

30. See, for example, "Liebner's Christology," 55–72, and "Cur Deus-Homo?" 220–38.
31. Nevin, "Antichrist," 38.
32. Nevin, *Mystical Presence*, 192.
33. Ibid., 158.

sense, as Adam was in his innocence before the fall, but in the sense of the completely realized "likeness."[34]

Sharing in Christ

So Mercersburg and the East, so far, are in agreement. Creation looked toward the Incarnation as its proper fulfillment; man was called to grow into greater fellowship with the divine nature that had created him. Christ, by uniting in Himself human nature with the divine, anticipated in Himself the goal of mankind, and, as representative of the race, opened the door for the rest to follow Him. But in what sense does He open the door?

Here again, from the Orthodox side, we do not receive a univocal, standardized answer. Ware again offers one very helpful perspective. He says that "salvation is sharing," specifically, a sharing in the life of God, which is made available to us in Christ. He roots this notion in the doctrine of the Trinity: God Himself shares his life with Himself, and through Christ, we are invited in to share it as well. "God is not a single person dwelling alone, but three persons who share each other's life in perfect love. The Incarnation equally is a doctrine of sharing or participation. Christ shares to the full in what we are, and so he makes it possible for us to share in what he is, in his divine life and glory. He became what we are, so as to make us what he is."[35] Discussing Christ's great prayer in John 17, Ware says,

> Christ enables us to share in the Father's divine glory. He is the bond and meeting-point: because he is man, he is one with us; because he is God, he is one with the Father. So through and in him we are one with God, and the Father's glory becomes our glory. God's Incarnation opens the way to man's deification. To be deified is, more specifically, to be "christified": the divine likeness that we are called to attain is the likeness of Christ. It is through Jesus the God-man that we men are "ingodded", "divinized", made "sharers in the divine nature.[36]

---

34. Ware, *Orthodox Way*, 70–71. Note that Hodge and his ilk would tend to interpret Nevin's statement here (and other similar ones), as regurgitation's of the worst of liberal German theology, in which Christ becomes not the divine redeemer, but the "Ideal Man." However, I hope that Ware's statement provides more evidence that here, Nevin is at least largely influenced by patristic, not Hegelian, lines of thought.

35. Ibid., 74.

36. Ibid.

In this picture, what we receive in redemption is not merely the freedom from sin and death and hence the ability to live a proper human life anew, but life in abundance, a human life that is glorified by participation in divine life. As Nevin says,

> Christ does not exhibit himself accordingly as the medium only, by which the truth is brought nigh to men. He claims always to *be* himself, all that the idea of salvation claims. He does not simply point men to heaven. He does not merely profess to give right instruction. He does not present to them only the promise of life, as secure to them from God on certain conditions. But he says, "I AM the *Way*, and the *Truth*, and the *Life*; no man cometh unto the Father but by ME" (John 14:6). Men are brought to God, not by doctrine or example, but only by being made to participate in the divine nature itself; and this participation is made possible to us only through the person of Christ; who is therefore the very substance of our salvation, as here affirmed. "God hath given to us eternal life, and this life is IN his Son. He that HATH the Son, hath life; and he that hath not the Son of God, hath not life" (1 John 5:11, 12).[37]

Again, however, what is fairly clear in Nevin is a bit ambiguous on the Orthodox side. Does Christ accomplish this deification for us, for us to receive in union with Him, or does He simply make it possible for us to get back on the right track? The two need not be absolutely opposed, but there certainly seems to be an important difference. Ware seems clearly on the side of the former; Lossky, more toward the latter. According to Fairbairn,

> Lossky comments that the essence of Christianity is "an ineffable descent of God to the ultimate limit of our fallen human condition, even unto death—a descent of God which opens to men a path of ascent, the unlimited vistas of the union of created beings with the Divinity." Elsewhere he writes that after the fall, humanity's task is still deification and that Christ does not fulfill that task for people. Instead, his life, death, and resurrection serve to unite creation to God "in order to return to man the possibility of accomplishing his task.[38]

---

37. Nevin, *Mystical Presence*, 202.

38. Fairbairn, *Eastern Orthodoxy*, 85. The Lossky quote is from Lossky, *In the Image and Likeness of God*, 97.

This way of putting it almost seems to go back to the sort of Christology that Nevin so viciously critiques, in which Christ's person simply becomes a prerequisite for our salvation, rather than the medium of it. However, it is perhaps better to interpret Lossky as simply trying to emphasize that the Incarnation does not bring automatic universal redemption—we still have to come to Christ in order to achieve *theosis*, and many do not do so.[39]

In any case, the Orthodox soteriology emphasizes that salvation is a sharing in the divine life through Christ and the Spirit, and thus suggests a notion of grace quite different from that Protestants are familiar with. The grace of salvation, for the Orthodox, is the divine life, which begins to transform us into the divine likeness. This bears little resemblance to the typical Western understanding, in which grace is seen more as God's attitude toward us or gifts bestowed on us, a picture in which the divide between God and man remains more substantially in place. Fairbairn summarizes,

> In the Eastern understanding, therefore, to assert that salvation is by grace means that people are transformed as a result of God's communicating his energies, those aspects of his divine life that he chooses to share with people. . . . This belief that grace is the energies of God, which can be communicated to people and which lead them to union with God, contrasts markedly with the typical Western understanding. When we use the word "grace," we normally have in mind an attitude of God toward people, on the basis of which he grants salvation to us as a gift. We usually understand grace in contrast to merit or to humanity's natural capacities: God gives us what we do not deserve or does something

39. The apparent difference here—whether *theosis* is life in Christ or life enabled by Christ—is perhaps rooted more deeply in divergent expressions within the Orthodox heritage. The Greek fathers, from whom the Orthodox today still derive much of their theological inspiration, seem to see *theosis* in terms of a sharing in the life of Christ and thus in the life of the Holy Trinity—we are deified because we are made members of the divine family. More recent Orthodox tradition, rightly seeking to guard against blurring the distinction between our union with God and Christ's unique hypostatic union, formulated a strong distinction between the divine essence and the divine energies. The divine essence—God's being in Himself—is never shared with man, except in Christ alone, and even there, the Chalcedonian definition maintains the full integrity of the human nature. The divine energies, however—God's attributes or powers—can be transferred over to us in some way, and this is how *theosis* occurs. In the former model, everything turns on union with Christ, and participation in all that He possesses; in the latter model, the process can become more extrinsic, and the Spirit's work of imbuing us with the divine energies can be detached to some extent from Christ (a result, perhaps, of their rejection of *filioque*).

for us that we could not have done ourselves. In the East, grace is understood as God's giving us himself (that is, his own Spirit who communicates his own energies to us), so that we may be united to him.[40]

Note also that this typically leads Orthodoxy to a more progressive, transformational view of salvation than Protestants have generally been comfortable with. This of course is a major bone of contention for Michael Horton, mentioned earlier. Protestantism has always insisted that salvation (or at least the most important part of it, forensic justification, which tends to swallow up the rest) takes place in an instant (albeit a rather vague instant, since we dare not tie it to any particular action or ritual), and quite outside of us. But Orthodoxy sees salvation as taking place over a long period (albeit with crucial identifiable temporal moments), and as unfolding within us, transforming us. Fairbairn draws attention to this paradigm clash between West and East, which he describes as backward-looking vs. forward-looking and says,

> Aghiorgoussis explains this difference of emphasis by asserting that in Romans 8:28–30, when Paul writes of predestination, calling, justification, and glorification, these are all stages in one process, that of deification or sanctification. "In other words," he continues, "justification is not a separate act of God but the negative aspect of salvation in Christ, which is freedom from sin, death, and the devil; whereas sanctification is the positive aspect of God's saving act, that of spiritual growth in new life in Christ communicated by God's Holy Spirit."[41]

Fairbairn goes on to explain that while East is not altogether averse to talking about a definitive initial act in the process of salvation, it does steadily resist the use of juridical categories to describe this change. All centers on participation in the life of Christ and God. The crucial difference, then, is not between progressive vs. definitive views of salvation, but between extrinsic, juridical views and intrinsic, participationist views.

On this question, Nevin lands firmly on the Orthodox side of the divide. Every aspect of salvation, for Nevin, rests on participation in Christ. Like the Orthodox, too, he understands this participation to involve lifelong growth and transformation, without denying the centrality of the initial act of union. For Nevin, the "everlasting life" which we are

40. Fairbairn, *Eastern Orthodoxy*, 87–88.

41. Aghiorgoussis, "Orthodox Soteriology," 48–49, quoted in Fairbairn, 92.

promised in the Gospel is none other than the life of Christ Himself, who, glorified in the Spirit, has alone triumphed over death and been raised to communion with God. Salvation, then, for Nevin, cannot simply be a process of God's bestowing benefits that somehow radiate out from Christ or transferring over to us things He has earned, as much Reformed thought has seemed to suggest, for our mortal nature is unable to receive these benefits. That is why we must be born again to new life, a life which is a sharing in the nature of Christ Himself:

> We say of our union with Christ, that it is a new *life*. It is deeper than all thought, feeling, or exercise of will. Not a quality only. Not a mere relation. A relation in fact, as that of the iron to the magnet; but one that carries into the centre of the subject a form of being which was not there before. Christ communicates his own life substantially to the soul on which he acts, causing it to grow into his very nature. This is the *mystical union*; the basis of our whole salvation; the only medium by which it is possible for us to have an interest in the grace of Christ under any other view.[42]

In Christ are all the benefits of redemption, and they are ours not by outward transfer or imputation, but by actual possession through union with Him. And we receive not simply forgiveness of sins, but the immortal life of God and glorified humanity. In Christ, we receive this life, and are ourselves raised up, step by step, into a higher plane of existence. This progressive transformation Nevin insists upon, saying, "The new life of the believer includes degrees, and will become complete only in the resurrection. Only in this form could it have a true human character. All life, in the case of man, is actualized, only in the way of process of gradual historical development."[43] Baptism, then, is the beginning of this life, and is rightly called the "new birth" in John 3. In baptism,

> we are inserted into him by our regeneration, which is thus the true counterpart of that first birth that makes us natural men. We are not however set over into this new order of existence wholly at once. This would be magic. We are apprehended by it, in the first place, only as it were at a single point. But this point is central. The new life lodges itself, as an efflux from Christ, in the inmost core of our personality. Here it becomes the principle or seed of our sanctification; which is simply the gradual transfu-

42. Nevin, *Mystical Presence*, 159.
43. Ibid., 166.

sion of the same exalted spiritual quality or potence through our whole persons.[44]

This new life of Christ then, having regenerated and sanctified us, remains in us to glorify us at the last day.

The Work of the Spirit

At this point, Orthodoxy and Mercersburg seem to be in the same ball-park, but their theological idiom remains rather different (even if both are equally different from typical Western representations). From the foregoing, it appears that Nevin focuses most of his attention on Christ alone, the second person of the Trinity, and on union with Him, whereas the Orthodox theologians, while also highlighting the centrality of the Incarnation, speak often more in terms of "union with God" (rather than Christ specifically), and highlight the role of the Spirit more than Nevin seems to. This makes sense in light of the age-old *filioque* dispute; the Orthodox would seem more likely to separate the work of the Spirit from the work of Christ, while Nevin links the two inextricably. This apparent gap, however, is not so wide as we might expect, for Nevin reserves a central role for the Spirit in the soteriology he articulates in *The Mystical Presence*, and both he and Orthodoxy make the Spirit's work dependent on that of Christ.

Nevin roots our experience of the Spirit first in the role that the Spirit plays in Christ's glorification. It was in the Spirit that the divine life in Christ was made to triumph over the power of death that had swallowed up His mortal life, and thus the new resurrection life of Christ is life in the Spirit.

> In Romans 8:11, the resurrection of Christ is inseparably joined with the third person of the ever blessed and glorious Trinity, as one and the same life. . . . The resurrection state of the Saviour then, especially as made complete at his ascension, is itself *spirit*, in the way of distinction from the flesh or common mortal state in which he had appeared before. . . . The victory however must be understood to extend to the whole man, external as well as internal, transforming the every flesh itself into spirit. It is the full triumph of Christ's higher life over the limitations with which it had been called to struggle in its union with our fallen humanity.[45]

44. Ibid., 158.
45. Ibid., 210.

Through the Spirit, then, the entire human nature of Christ is raised up to a more glorified form, a more perfect unity with the divine. Since Christ is the Second Adam, this new form of existence is not restricted to Him alone, but in Him is made available to a new race. "He became for others, what he was thus shown to be within himself, a quickening or life-giving spirit (1 Cor. 15:45); from whom the power of a new creation was to be carried forward under the same form, in the world, by the Church, even as the fallen life of the first Adam had been transmitted in the course of nature to all his posterity."[46]

In union with Christ and by the power of the Spirit, then, new creation is accomplished in the body and soul of each believer. Each believer, then, does not merely have his or her sins forgiven, but is raised again to new life which transforms every corner of his or her existence. This transformation might indeed be termed a divinization, since in it, human nature enters into a deep and ever-deepening communion with the divine Trinity, and receives its life force from the direct power of the Holy Spirit Himself. Each believer, united to Christ, becomes another Christ, a son of God, alive by the Spirit, filled with the love and power of God. Again it is best put in Nevin's own words:

> The glorification of Christ then, was the full advancement of our human nature itself to the power of a divine life; and the Spirit for whose presence it made room in the world, was not the Spirit as extra-anthropological simply under such forms of sporadic and transient afflatus as known previously; but the Spirit as immanent now, through Jesus Christ in the human nature itself—the form and power, in one word, of the new supernatural creation he had introduced into the world. He shall *abide* with you, says the Saviour, forever (John 14:16). The Spirit then constitutes the form of Christ's presence and activity in the Church, and the medium by which he communicates himself to his people. But as such he is the comprehension in full of the blessed Redeemer himself; and the life he reveals, is that of the entire glorified person of the Son of Man, in which humanity itself has become quickened into full correspondence with the vivific principle it has been made to enshrine.[47]

Nevin calls this new life that believers possess a "pneumatic order of existence," and again, this Spirit-animated, Spirit-possessed life is not

46. Ibid., 211.
47. Ibid., 212–13.

simply ours after the resurrection, but, through Christ, fills us even in the present, transforming both soul and body.

> The last triumph of the Spirit is made to consist precisely, in the full transfiguration of the body itself into its own image. . . . As the subjects of this new creation, steadily advancing towards its appointed end, Christians are described as being already in the Spirit and not in the flesh—that is, as participant in the pneumatic order of existence, of which Jesus Christ is the principle and the Holy Ghost the medium, and not under the power simply of our nature as derived with a fallen character from the first Adam.[48]

This crucial role of the Spirit in our transformation into godlike-ness of course resonates well with Orthodoxy. While the Orthodox, as we have already seen, make the Incarnation central to opening for us the way to *theosis*, they emphasize perhaps even more the role of the Spirit in perfecting and applying Christ's work to us. Fairbairn summarizes,

> The Orthodox regard *theosis* as being, first and foremost, the result of the Holy Spirit's activity in people. Lossky writes, "The Son has become like us by the incarnation; we become like Him by deification, by partaking of the divinity in the Holy Spirit." . . . Thus, the Holy Spirit gives us God's own energies, granting us the transformation that Eastern Christendom associates with salvation.[49]

Stavropoulos also has a good deal to say on this theme:

> Our union with God, the theosis which is objectively offered to us by the incarnate, crucified, resurrected, and ascended God, can be realized only in the Holy Spirit. Only with the Holy Spirit will we be able to receive and taste redemption and theosis. Only in the Holy Spirit will we reach the point of becoming gods, the like-nesses of God. Only the Holy Spirit will transmit to us that which the Son and Word of God has offered to us. Our call remains only one: theosis through our Lord Jesus Christ in the Holy Spirit . . . the contribution of the Holy Spirit is always a finalizing action. God the Father, before all ages, conceives of the work of salvation and theosis. He realizes it in time, in the Son. The Holy Spirit completes and perfects and adapts this work to people.[50]

48. Ibid., 213–14.

49. Fairbairn, *Eastern Orthodoxy*, 86. The Lossky quote is from *In the Image and Likeness of God*, 109.

50. Stavropoulos, "Partakers of Divine Nature," 188–89.

This language shows that, despite the divergence we might expect because of the *filioque* controversy, Nevin and the East stand fairly close on this point. Of course their precise language and their emphases remain somewhat different, but the basic point is the same: Christ is the principle of new, divine life for the believer, and the Spirit is the medium who makes Christ present in the believer. Nevin tightly binds the Spirit's work to that of Christ, and the Orthodox do likewise—the Spirit cannot offer us anything that is not Christ's. Nevin and Orthodoxy are both able to maintain this framework because both Son and Spirit are held to reside in the same place—the Church.

You see, while Protestants today may have begun to think of the presence of the Spirit as a mere wind that blows where it wills, through the hearts and minds of believers, the Orthodox have always been careful to maintain a more focused conception of His work. The Spirit's ministry is tied inseparably to the Church, and mediated through the sacraments. Of course, "It is not the Church which, through the medium of its institutions, bestows the Holy Spirit, but it is the Spirit which validates every aspect of Church life,"[51] as Meyendorff clarifies. Stavropoulos puts it this way: "The Holy Spirit is the great resident of the church. It is there that the Holy Spirit exercises all of his sanctifying and deifying power."[52]

In the Church, the Spirit progressively unites believers to Christ and imbues them with divine life through the sacraments. Baptism is essential in beginning the path of *theosis*, and the other sacraments, chiefly the Eucharist, nourish and strengthen believers along that path. As Fairbairn summarizes,

> Baptism is the means by which God begins the process of *theosis* in a believer, since it brings him or her into the life that the Church possesses. Penance is the continual act by which a person returns to that life, and the supreme means of *theosis* is the Eucharist, because it is the sacrament through which people become the body of Christ, actualizing their union with the head of the Church through the Holy Spirit whom they receive.[53]

We have already seen that Nevin heavily emphasizes the role of the sacraments in creating and strengthening the mystical union between Christ and His members. The Church, of course, is also absolutely central

51. Meyendorff, *Catholicity and the Church*, 28, quoted in Fairbairn, *Eastern Orthodoxy*, 89.

52. Stavropoulos, "Partakers of Divine Nature," 188.

53. Fairbairn, *Eastern Orthodoxy*, 89.

for Nevin, as the true dwelling place of Christ, sustained by His Spirit. And of course, Nevin, like the Orthodox, is careful to clarify that the Church does not bind or contain the Spirit. There is no automatic transmission of grace in the Church as an institution. Though the life of Christ is carried on in the Church, it is not *contained* therein, in the sense of being locked up and dispensed at will. Rather, while each individual's rebirth and growth in divine life comes through incorporation into the Church through baptism and nourishment through the Eucharist, this whole process is carried on in the power of the Spirit. It is the Spirit who, in baptism, breathes into us Christ Himself, and His life-giving power, and it is the Spirit who, in the Eucharist, transcends the barriers between heaven and earth and makes Christ's glorified body available to us for vivification. It is the Spirit who, through all the long years of suffering and sanctification, helps us to live as little Christs, communing intimately with God Himself.

In the final analysis, both Nevin and the Orthodox maintain a similar understanding of the relationship of the second and third persons of the Trinity, and the Church which They animate. There can be no separation between the Church, Christ, and the Spirit. The Church is the body of Christ, but it is animated by the Spirit; Son and Spirit are undivided both in Their nature and Their work. Neither can Christ be communicated to His people without the Spirit, nor can the Spirit communicate anything that is not Christ's. As Nevin puts it,

> Where the one is, there the other is truly and really at the same time. . . . The Spirit was never brought near to men before, as now through the incarnate Word. It dwelt in him without measure. Humanity itself was filled completely with its presence, and appears at last translucent with the glory of heaven itself by this means. Forth from the person of Christ, thus "quickened in the Spirit," the flood of life pours itself onward continually in the Church, only of course by the presence and power of the Holy Ghost; for it holds in no other form.[54]

Orthodox theologians put it similarly. Florovsky summarizes, "He [Christ] lives and abides ceaselessly in the Church. In the Church we receive the Spirit of adoption. Through reaching towards and accepting the Holy Ghost we become eternally God's. In the Church our salvation is perfected; the sanctification and transfiguration, the *theosis* of the hu-

---

54. Nevin, *Mystical Presence*, 165.

man race is accomplished."[55] Stavropoulos, too, is careful to maintain the equal centrality of the incarnate Word and the Holy Spirit, and of the Church as the creation of both—the body of Christ that is united to its head by the Spirit:

> The essential place of the Incarnate Word of God is matched by that of the Holy Spirit. The divine Spirit that proceeds from the Father divinizes us. The Spirit is "divine and divinizing." The Holy Spirit is a divine bond which harmonizes and draws the mystical body of Christ, that is, the church, together with its Lord. It is the Holy Spirit who makes the faithful into other Christs, and thus creates the church. Our incorporation in the mystical body of Christ and our *theosis* are not exclusively the work of the incarnation of Christ. They are also the work of the creative Holy Spirit, who creates the church with his spiritual gifts.[56]

Despite, then, their radically different theological heritages, Mercersburg and Orthodoxy manifest a remarkably similar theological vision. Both begin with the same view of man's destiny: union with God. Man is created happy and holy, but not yet perfected, for his communion with God is only just beginning. Both, therefore, understand Christ's mission as not merely a reversal of the Fall, but as a fulfillment of man's original created destiny, making it possible for us, through Him, the God-man, to attain the divinization that we have been called to. This salvation that we receive is not merely the external imputation of Christ's benefits, but a sharing in His life which fills our whole being and raises us into fellowship with the Holy Trinity. Though, at baptism, we enter the life of salvation by being united to Christ, this life has much further to grow and develop within us, accomplishing a transformation from glory to glory through the power of the Spirit, who works in us to perfect and apply all that Christ has accomplished for us. Nevin and the East also find common ground in their expression of the relationship of the Son's and Spirit's work. Finally, both understand that this glorious process of *theosis* takes place only through incorporation into the Church and reception of its sacraments, since it is here that we find the Body of Christ and the temple of the Spirit.

These parallels are, of course, only a starting point, and Nevin is certainly not unique in confessing many of these things. Other fruitful areas

55. Florovsky, *Bible, Church, Tradition*, 37, quoted in Fairbairn, 88.

56. Stavropoulos, "Partakers of Divine Nature," 189.

of comparison suggest themselves, such as similar emphases in sacramental and liturgical theology, and perhaps also church polity. However, since this area of soteriology is one where the Reformed and the East have rarely seen eye-to-eye, and indeed, have usually considered these differences irreconcilable, this brief survey is very significant toward establishing a basis for dialogue and making common cause. Nevin here again proves that if we can take the discussion away from the juridical categories that have dominated Protestantism for centuries (while acknowledging their value in their proper place), our theological vision can open up to new horizons, and new opportunities to reunite with our estranged brothers and sisters, both East and West.

CHAPTER 6

The Church as "Catholic" and the Catholic Church
Mercersburg and the Nouvelle Théologie

Tʜᴇ ɢʀᴇᴀᴛᴇsᴛ ᴏғ ᴛʜᴇ three traditions covered in these chapters
is, of course, the Catholic Church itself, with its rich history, lofty
claims, and highly developed theological tradition. The relationship of
Catholicism to Mercersburg is not, as in the case of Anglo-Catholicism,
that of close parallelism, nor, as in the case of Orthodoxy, great distance
and seeming irrelevance. There was of course no great movement within
Catholicism, in the nineteenth century or any other time, that bears close
resemblance to the particular vision and experience of the Mercersburg
Theology, yet Catholicism was never far from Nevin's mind as he studied,
wrote, and debated. Unlike most of his Protestant contemporaries (and
indeed, predecessors and successors), Nevin felt the weight and majesty
of the Catholic Church and its claims, and sought to teach Protestants to
see that Church as an erring sister, not a foe.

As the so-called Mercersburg Theology grew and matured, and
the controversies it prompted also grew, Nevin felt the need to yield the
ground to Rome on many points where he had once hoped Protestantism
could maintain itself. At last he was convinced that, at least as a historical fact, the Early Church had not been Protestant in any recognizable
sense, but basically Catholic. His subsequent struggle over whether or
not to convert to Rome marks one of the most fascinating, yet mysterious, phases in Nevin's life. His ultimate decision to remain in the German

147

Reformed Church seems to have resulted not from any especial faith in Protestantism, as much as a lack of faith in Catholicism and some of the most difficult Romish doctrines.[1] My purpose here is not to analyze the ins and outs of this struggle and Nevin's assessment of Catholicism; however, it is clear that Nevin had a fervent desire for Protestants to learn from Catholics and for both to find theological common ground to work toward cooperation and unity. I believe Nevin would have been very gratified by many of the developments in that direction in the last century, and by many of the recent dramatic developments in Catholic theology. No doubt some his lingering concerns about Catholic teaching would have been assuaged by post-Vatican II teachings, and he would have been greatly encouraged by the theological riches produced by men like Henri de Lubac and Joseph Ratzinger (Benedict XVI).

In particular, I believe, Nevin would have felt great sympathy with de Lubac and the *nouvelle théologie* movement with which he is closely identified. His struggle, after all, was not all that different from Nevin's in many ways. De Lubac confronted a Church whose theology had in many ways degenerated into an ossified orthodoxy defined in opposition to Protestantism and other errors. Much of the original life-force of its theology was gone, and in fighting the obvious enemies so vigorously, it had allowed others to sneak in through the back door. The result was a theology that had succumbed to much the same individualism that characterized its enemies, modernism and Protestantism, and which, like them, increasingly separated the "spiritual" calling of the Church from the "natural" calling of man. Nevin, of course, was fighting a Protestantism which likewise subsisted as little more than an orthodoxy defined against Romanism and liberalism, and which was crippled by the influences of individualism and dualism. De Lubac's seemingly innovative (but really very ancient) proposals engendered at least as much controversy as Nevin's, though de Lubac was fortunate enough to be vindicated at last by the Second Vatican Council, while Nevin still awaits vindication from any Second Westminster Assembly yet to come.

On many points, the theological agenda which de Lubac advanced resonated deeply with that of Mercersburg. Both movements involved a decisive turn back to patristic sources, an emphasis on the inherently

---

1. Nichols offers the most helpful summary available of this period in Nevin's life in chapter 8 of *Romanticism*; Hart's biography also devotes chapter five to the subject, but is somewhat less helpful on the whole.

social character of the Church, as opposed to the modern conception which sees it as a mere collection of individuals, a call to hold visible and invisible together as two aspects of a single church, with an appeal to the hypostatic union as the foundation of this unity, a focus on the Eucharist as that which constitutes the Church, and an attempt to describe the Church as a supernatural body that fulfills nature, rather than a supernature alongside or against nature.

In this chapter, however, I wish to focus particularly on how both men answer the question, "What is 'catholicism'?" (and in so doing, touch on a number of the points just mentioned). One of Nevin's greatest and most revealing articles, entitled "Catholicism," seeks to uncover what exactly the Creed means by "one, holy, *catholic* Church." De Lubac, likewise, in one of his masterpieces, also entitled *Catholicism,* attempts to demonstrate what it means for the Catholic Church to be "catholic."

Nevin begins by offering a terminological distinction which will help clarify the direction of the discussion here. The adjective "catholic," he says, has often been replaced by skeptical Protestants with the weak substitute "universal." This, he fears, is insufficient and potentially misleading, for "there are two kinds of generality and universality, and . . . only one of them answers to the true force of the term catholic . . . the two kinds of universality to which we refer are presented to us in the words *all* and *whole.* These are often taken to be substantially of one and the same meaning. In truth, however, their sense is very different."[2] The universality of "all," he says, is an abstract totality of individual particulars, "something secondary to the individual existences from which it is abstracted." It is a nominalistic universality, no more than the sum of its parts, if not, indeed, less. The universality designated by "whole," however, "is not abstract, a mere notion added to things outwardly by the mind, but concrete; it is wrought into the very nature of the things themselves, and they grow forth from it as the necessary and perpetual ground of their own being and life." The whole is not merely the sum of the parts; it is something much greater, and indeed, rather than depending on them for its existence, he says, they depend on it, "and subsist in it and from it as their proper original." This universality is realist, not nominalist. Nevin summarizes,

> the *all* expresses a mechanical unity, which is made up of the
> parts that belong to it, by their being brought together in a purely

2. Nevin, "Catholicism," 2.

outward way; the *whole* signifies on the contrary an organic
unity, where the parts as such have no separate and independent
existence, but draw their being from the universal unity itself in
which they are comprehended, while they serve at the same time
to bring it into view.[3]

Nevin concludes that for the Church to be "catholic" means that it
constitutes the proper wholeness of mankind and creation; it is no mere
universal convocation of men from all over the world, but the renewal
of the human race as a whole. The renewal of the race, moreover, is not
merely "extensive" but "intensive"; that is, every field of human endeavor,
all that belongs to man's created calling, is taken up into the Church's
mission and renewed by her. He concludes,

When christianity [*sic*] is declared to be *catholic*, the declaration
must be taken in its full sense to affirm, that the last idea of this
world as brought to its completion in man is made perfectly
possible in the form of christianity, and in this form alone, and
this power therefore can never cease to work until it shall have
actually taken possession of the world as a whole, and shall thus
stand openly and clearly revealed as the true consummation of
its nature and history in every other view.[4]

De Lubac concurs with the definition Nevin sets forth. If "catholic"
means universal, de Lubac clarifies,

a universal is a singular and is not to be confused with an aggregate. The Church is not Catholic because she is spread abroad
over the whole of the earth and can reckon on a large number of
members. She was already Catholic on the morning of Pentecost,
when all her members could be contained in a small room. . . .
For fundamentally Catholicity has nothing to do with geography
or statistics. . . . Like sanctity, Catholicity is primarily an intrinsic
feature of the Church.[5]

Augustine, he says, understood this, and "sees her including the whole
orbis terrarium because he is aware that all, whatever their origin, race
or condition, are called on to become one in Christ, and that thencefor-
ward the Church is fundamentally that unity."[6] Moreover, as catholic, the

3. Ibid., 3.
4. Ibid., 5.
5. De Lubac, *Catholicism*, 48–49.
6. Ibid., 50.

Church does not merely embrace mankind as a whole, but the whole of what it means to be human: "The Church in each individual calls on the whole man, embracing him as he is in his whole nature."[7]

If this is what it means for the Church to be catholic, then what implications does this have for ecclesiology, and for theology as a whole? For both Nevin and de Lubac, it means that we must see continuity, rather than separation, between nature and grace, the natural and the supernatural; it means that we must see man as inherently social, sharing one common life; and finally, it means that the Church is fundamentally a visible body, simultaneously natural and supernatural, rather than a bifurcation into an invisible, supernatural body and a visible, natural body.

Supernatural at the Source

So first, what is this issue of natural and supernatural? De Lubac has received a great deal of attention for his work on the supernatural, in *Surnaturel* and *The Mystery of the Supernatural*, where he attempted to tear down the barriers between natural and supernatural in traditional Catholic theology. Nature was no self-sufficient realm on top of which supernatural grace could just be slapped on, like icing on a cake. For de Lubac, it was crucial to understand that man was never created in a state of "pure nature," where his only desires were for natural, immanent ends, and where his only mode of realizing those ends was through his own powers. De Lubac argued that natural man is not oriented to purely natural ends—rather, his fundamental orientation is determined by a supernatural end—the vision of God. He quotes Aquinas to this effect: "every intellect naturally desires the vision of divine substance."[8] So a transcendent desire, the desire for God, is part of man's natural desires, from the beginning of its creation. Or, as he puts it in *The Splendor of the Church*, "Man's nature is twofold—he is animal and spirit. He lives on this earth and is committed to a temporal destiny; yet there is in him something that goes beyond the terrestrial horizon and seeks the atmosphere of eternity as its natural climate."[9] This quest for eternity is not something additional to man's created nature, but is completely native to him, as natural as the

7. Ibid., 49.

8. Aquinas, *Summa Contra Gentiles*, Bk. 3, c. 57, quoted in de Lubac, *Mystery of the Supernatural*, 56.

9. De Lubac, *Splendor of the Church*, 166.

desire for food. Grace, then, does not come to man as something foreign and hostile to nature; rather, as de Lubac's axiom would have it, "grace perfects nature." More specifically, grace is "a perfection given to nature in the same direction toward which its own tendencies are working."[10] That is to say, when God's economy of redemption makes itself present in the world, it does not give it a fundamentally new orientation, but brings creation to a completion toward which it was already straining and for which it was yearning, what scholasticism called "the vision of God." While this may seem uncontroversial when so stated, such a framework has been hotly contested by many Catholic theologians, and, inasmuch as they deal in these categories, by many Protestants as well.[11]

Nevin without question finds himself running up against this same issue, though, because these questions were rarely posed explicitly in Protestant theology as they were in Catholic scholasticism, we never see him addressing it in such a systematic way as de Lubac does. Nevertheless, it stretches through all of Nevin's theology like a hidden thread, and once you begin to look for it, you see that the relationship of natural and supernatural comprises a key structuring theme of Nevin's theology. What de Lubac treats in a somewhat abstract, philosophical manner, Nevin approaches via a more historical route, asking how the Incarnation, the union between God and man, fit into the flow of history—as intrusion or as fulfillment. His answer, of course, is the latter; which is to say, in de Lubac's terms, that nature was properly oriented toward, and perfected in, a supernatural end. As mentioned in the last chapter, Nevin leaned toward the Orthodox and patristic view that the drama of mankind consisted not merely the redemption from sin, but in the growth of the race into union with God, and that therefore, the very creation of the world assumed Incarnation as its proper fulfillment.[12]

---

10. De Broglie, "Autour de la notion thomiste de la beatitude," 222, quoted in De Lubac, *Mystery of the Supernatural*, 31.

11. Now is not the place to discuss the ins and outs of such debates. Suffice to say that the concern of many such objectors is that the spontaneous, gracious quality of grace be preserved, and this seems to be lost if nature presupposes grace. More problematically, many, influenced by Enlightenment dualism, believe it is theologically desirable (or perhaps, philosophically necessary) to maintain the autonomy of nature. In Reformed Protestant circles, bicovenantal theology has insisted that grace is a post-Fall phenomenon, and is not part of the picture for natural unfallen man, who relies on the so-called covenant of works.

12. It should be noted here that just because Nevin leans toward the patristic view here does not mean that he arrived at this view entirely from reading Patristic sources; more

For Nevin, all of the lower creation found its perfection in man, and mankind found its perfection in union with God, fulfilled in the Incarnation. That is to say, nature was never sufficient unto itself, but was designed for union with the supernatural; fall or no fall, human nature longed for a more complete union with God, only made possible by the Incarnation. As Nevin puts it in *The Mystical Presence*, "Humanity itself is never complete, till it reaches his [Christ's] person. . . . Our nature reaches after a true and real union with the nature of God, as the necessary complement and consummation of its own life. . . . The incarnation then is the proper completion of humanity."[13] Though the theological idiom is different, this claim essentially parallels de Lubac's claim that, from creation, man is oriented toward the goal of seeing God. There is no "pure nature" for Nevin either, a state in which man is sufficient as he is, and in which his history can progress as a closed immanent system, without needing to lie open to the transcendent. There is only an immature, incomplete nature, a creation waiting until the supernatural has come to take its rest within the natural, so that nature, thus united with supernature, might be more fully itself. "Nature is only relatively true and real. It finds its actual sense . . . only as actualized in the mystery of the Incarnation."[14]

For Nevin, Christ's Incarnation and resurrection, as an act of new creation, constituted the historical goal toward which the whole creation was striving. The Incarnation, he says, forms

> the inmost and last sense of all God's works. The world, from its extreme circumference, looks inward to this fact as its true and proper centre, and presses towards it continually, from every side, as the end of its entire constitution. All is one vast prophecy of the Incarnation.[15]

One way in which the Incarnation brings all prior history to fulfillment is by providing the answer to all man's prior religious endeavors, as mentioned above in chapter 3. The desire for proper union with God, according to Nevin, can be seen in all the striving of the ages prior to Christ. Pagan religions and mythology aimed for it, but were misguided, and

---

often he received these views through the mediation of contemporary German theology, and turned later to Patristic sources for confirmation.

13. Nevin, *Mystical Presence*, 188.

14. Ibid., 195.

15. Ibid., 189.

ended in the attempt to divinize man by his own efforts. Even Judaism
was in itself incomplete:

> God drew continually more and more near to men in an outward
> way. But to the last it continued to be only in an outward way.
> The wall of partition that separated the divine from the human,
> was never fully broken down . . . the revelation to the end, was a
> revelation of God *to* man, and not a revelation of God *in* man.[16]

When this revelation of God in man comes, it reveals the true nature and intent of creation, and raises it to its proper maturity. Christ
comes not as a mere redeemer from sin, but as the hermeneutical key to
all science, philosophy, and history, as the full flowering of the life of the
world and of the human race:

> Here then, as before said, we reach the central FACT, at once
> ultimate and primal, in the constitution of the world. All nature
> and all history flow towards it, as their true and proper end, or
> spring from it as their principle and ground. The incarnation, by
> which divinity and humanity are joined together, and made one,
> in a real, inward and abiding way, is found to be the scope of all
> God's counsels and dispensations in the world. The mystery of
> the universe is interpreted in the person of Jesus Christ.[17]

In another place he says that there is "nothing *so* natural, as the supernatural itself in the Saviour's person."[18]

Though the Incarnation does not constitute the center of de Lubac's
theological reflection as it does for Nevin, de Lubac unquestionably shares
Nevin's emphasis on the New Creation as ever constituting the goal of the
first creation, the perfection for which it was ever intended. He speaks of
this by quoting a passage from *The Shepherd of Hermas*:

> "Who is this aged woman, think you, from whom you re-
> ceived the little book?" . . . .
> "The Church."
> "Why is she aged?" I then asked.
> "Because," he answered, "she was created first, before all else;
> that is why she is aged. It was for her that the world was made."[19]

16. Ibid., 191.
17. Ibid., 192.
18. Ibid., 196.
19. De Lubac, *Catholicism*, 71.

This beautiful affirmation represents of course the patristic conviction that the Incarnation and the Church were not merely the result of the Fall, but a crucial part of the framework of creation. On this view, then, when the Church as new creation came into the world, it could only come as the inner fulfillment of the world as it was created, not in any sense as a contingent add-on. All of history, then, is a preparation for the final perfection of man in union with God. De Lubac says nothing less:

> Christianity alone continues to assert the transcendent destiny of man and the common destiny of mankind. The whole history of the world is a preparation for this destiny. From the first creation to the last end, through material opposition and the more serious opposition of created freedom, a divine plan is in operation, accomplishing its successive stages among which the Incarnation stands out as chief.[20]

This fact, he says, gives meaning and direction to Creation and its history, which would else be but a sequence of phenomena. It also reveals, as it did for Nevin, all the prior centuries of pagan thought as imperfect strivings toward the truth revealed in Christ, which Christianity can christen and adopt.[21] The two great works of God, redemption and creation, are too often seen in some kind of semi-Marcionite opposition. De Lubac is adamant that we see the second as the completion of the first, rather than a separate work of an entirely different nature:

> The Creator and the Redeemer, the Church adds, are one and the same God; therefore there can be no conflict between their works, and it is to stray from the true path to believe the second can be magnified at the expense of the first. The Word that became incarnate to renew and complete all things is also he who 'enlighteneth every man that cometh into this world'. *Dominus naturalia legis non dissolvit, sed extendit et implevit.* Just as he did, his messengers come not to destroy but to accomplish; not to lay waste, but to raise up, transform, make holy.[22]

Against a Gnostic Supernaturalism

In thus insisting on the continuity of Creation and Redemption, natural and supernatural, nature and grace, both Nevin and de Lubac are con-

20. Ibid., 140–41.
21. Ibid., 284.
22. Ibid.,

cerned to guard the truly "catholic" nature of Christianity, a Christianity that has "actually taken possession of the world as a whole, and shall thus stand openly and clearly revealed as the true consummation of its nature and history in every other view."[23] Otherwise, our faith will tend towards a form of Gnosticism, in which Christ comes not to redeem the world in its wholeness, but to redeem us (or perhaps just our souls) from the world. In *Catholicism*, de Lubac spells out at length what he sees as the dangers:

> For about three centuries, faced by the naturalist trends of modern thought on the one hand and the confusions of a bastard Augustinianism on the other, many could see salvation only in a complete severance between the natural and the supernatural. Such a policy ran doubly counter to the end which they had in view. For on the one hand they failed to observe that the more you separate the less do you really *distinguish*. . . . Thus the supernatural, deprived of its organic links with nature, tended to be understood by some as a mere 'super-nature', a 'double' of nature. Furthermore, after such a complete separation what misgivings could the supernatural cause to naturalism? For the latter no longer found it at any point in its path, and could shut itself up in a corresponding isolation, with the added advantage that it claimed to be complete. No hidden dissatisfaction could disturb the claim of its splendid equilibrium. . . . Such a dualism, just when it imagined that it was most successfully opposing the negations of naturalism, was most strongly influenced by it, and the transcendence in which it hoped to preserve the supernatural with such jealous care was, in fact, a banishment. The most confirmed secularists found in it, in spite of itself, an ally.[24]

There are some fascinating points in this quote. As de Lubac diagnoses the problem, once you separate the supernatural from the natural, confining the two to a merely extrinsic relationship, then there is no need to distinguish their mode of operation anymore, since they operate in totally different spheres. Indeed, it was against something of this sort in late medieval Catholicism that Protestantism was reacting. Catholic theology, by narrowly confining the supernatural within the substance of the sacraments, represented them as something which could be applied to us in a beneficial way, but not so as to transform the whole man.

23. Nevin, "Catholicism," 5.
24. De Lubac, *Catholicism*, 313–14.

The natural man could go on living his life as he wished, as long as he received his weekly dose of the supernatural. This tendency in Catholic theology (though recurrent in Protestant theology as well) comes out vividly in a movie like the *Godfather*, where the natural world of violence and power is left unaffected by the operations of a separate supernatural world which runs parallel to it. Moreover, de Lubac is also pointing out here that, in separating the supernatural, theology made it into a double of nature that could be explained and manipulated according to the same principles as the natural could be—hence a mechanical, Aristotelian sacramentology ensued. De Lubac explains this further in *The Mystery of the Supernatural*:

> Modern theology . . . sees nature and supernature as in some sense juxtaposed, and in spite of every intention to the contrary, as contained in the same genus of which they form as it were two species. The two were like two complete organisms; too perfectly separated to be really differentiated, they have unfolded parallel to each other, fatally similar in kind. Under such circumstances, the supernatural is no longer properly speaking another order, something unprecedented, overwhelming and transfiguring: it is no more than a "super-nature," as we have fallen into the habit of calling it, contrary to all theological tradition; a "super-nature" which reproduces, to what is called a "superior" degree, all the features which characterize nature itself.[25]

By some curious transformation, the supernatural, having once been separated from the natural, begins to look more and more natural, and what began with a claim to exalt the supernatural ends by being indistinguishable from mere naturalism:

> Everything that now comes to us by the grace of God is thus withdrawn from the "supernatural" properly so-called of our present economy, and "naturalized"—at the risk of being attributed afresh to some special intervention by God according to a different "mode."[26]

Salvation is conceived in more and more humanistic terms, union with God is reinterpreted as a universal human possession, revelation becomes simply another product of private experience.

25. De Lubac, *Mystery of the Supernatural*, 48.
26. Ibid., 52.

Nevin offers a remarkably similar critique, which will perhaps shed further light on this theme. Throughout his writings, Nevin ceaselessly decried the innovations of revivalism and nineteenth-century American Christianity in general as no more than the products of rationalism. This was a shocking charge, since rationalist theology had no use for the supernatural, it seemed, and revivalist theology seemed to focus entirely on the supernatural. The revivalists, though, shared the rationalist desire to keep the supernatural out of the natural, particularly when it came to things like the sacraments. For them, the supernatural must be preserved as a separate realm, not one that interpenetrates the natural. Nevin identified the problem this way: "Its conception of the supernatural was always external and abstract; placing it thus in the same false relation precisely to nature and humanity, which was established by Rationalism itself."[27] He saw, like de Lubac, that the root problem was the severance of an organic union between the natural and the supernatural. He explains himself further,

> For one who has come at all to understand the constitution of this abstract supernaturalism, it can produce no surprise to find the sect system marked universally by a *rationalistic* tendency. A rationalism that denies the supernatural altogether, and a Supernaturalism that will not allow it to enter into any concrete union with the natural, are at bottom much of the same nature; and the last needs only the force of true consecutive thinking always, to pass over peacefully into the arms of the first. Sects start usually in abstract supernaturalism, with an affectation of hyper-spiritual perfection. But the rationalistic element comes at once into view, both in their thinking and practice.[28]

The problem, then, is that supernatural and natural are linked only outwardly, rather than by inner necessity. This problem, according to Nevin, stemmed from a more fundamental inability to rightly discern redemptive history, to understand the inseparability of old creation and

---

27. Nevin, *Mystical Presence*, 138.

28. Nevin, "Sect System," 528. Nevin points out in many of his writings the tendency of the revivalists to treat supernatural grace in a naturalized way, as something they can manipulate mechanically. His work *The Anxious Bench* exposes how the supposedly "supernatural" religion of revivalism actually relies on all kinds of contrived methods to channel its supernatural grace. This, of course, connects with de Lubac's point about the supernatural, once divorced from the natural, being naturalized.

new creation, as expounded upon above. He contrasts the "sect system's" conception of Christianity to his incarnational approach, saying

> The relation of the new creation to the old, is felt always to be abrupt, violent, chasmatic; as though the first stood in no organic connection with the last, but were only joined to it in an outward way. Christianity is not viewed as the form in which the world itself becomes finally complete; the resolution of the inmost secret of humanity; the last scope of all God's ways in the vast process of creation. It is a factitious system, rather, the product of infinite skill combined with infinite love, mysteriously superadded to the constitution of the world's proper life, for the purposes of redemption. It is above this life, beyond it, over against it, as another order of existence; but comes to no real reconciliation with it, by taking it up in its own sphere, and penetrating it with its own divine power.[29]

In contrast to such an opposition of the two spheres of physical and spiritual, natural and supernatural, Nevin insists again upon the fundamental unity of the two, a unity which only Christianity can do full justice to.

> Christianity is emphatically a spiritual religion; but it is at the same time real, and in this respect conformable to the actual nature of man. It is the spiritual in true union with the natural, as the necessary basis of humanity, and a necessary element also in its constitution. Its Christ is one who has come in the flesh.[30]

What then does it mean for the Church to be truly "catholic"? For Nevin and de Lubac, we must not suppose that the mission of the Church is merely to offer supernatural "grace" as a remedy for sin and an escape from the temptations of the world; if this were the point, it would leave most of man's nature and his created faculties untouched. Rather, as Christ sums up and renews in Himself the entirety of the world and its history, so the Church, His Body, is the perfect synthesis of the divine and human, natural and supernatural, charged with the task of bringing mankind and the whole cosmos into this union. Nevin summarizes in "Catholicism," "The proper wholeness even of nature itself, ideally considered, lies ultimately in the power of Christianity. . . . Christianity is catholic, and claims to be so received by an act of faith, inasmuch as it

29. Nevin, "Antichrist," 48.
30. Ibid., 47.

forms the true and proper wholeness of mankind, the round and full symmetrical *cosmos* of humanity."[31]

The Irreducibly Social Nature of the Church

Both Nevin and de Lubac also realize that if the Church is to be thus "catholic," comprehending the whole of human nature, it is necessary that we rightly characterize this human nature that is to be redeemed. Nevin's anthropology has been mentioned briefly in earlier chapters, but I will here give it more attention and compare it to de Lubac's. In defining the term "catholic" above, Nevin distinguished between the universality of "all" and the universality of "whole," a distinction he regularly employs in characterizing the nature of man. As quoted above, Nevin says,

> the *all* expresses a mechanical unity, which is made up of the parts that belong to it, by their being brought together in a purely outward way; the *whole* signifies on the contrary an organic unity, where the parts as such have no separate and independent existence, but draw their being from the universal unity itself in which they are comprehended, while they serve at the same time to bring it into view.[32]

The latter, he says, is how we are to understand the unity of the human race. Mankind does not simply consist of the sum total of all men, but of the universal life of the race from which individual men spring: "the human race is not a sand-heap. It is the power of a single life. It is bound together, not outwardly, but inwardly. Men have been one before they became many, and as many, they are still one."[33] To illustrate this, Nevin invokes the idea of a forest of oak trees, derived in the beginning from one single acorn. The life of that one acorn lives now in the whole forest, which are thus not merely a collection of separate trees, but constitute a true organic unity.

In Adam, therefore, we can say not merely federally, but truly, that the whole human race is comprehended.

> His individual personality of course was limited wholly to himself. But a whole world of like separate personalities lay involved in his life, at the same time, as a generic principle or root. And

31. Nevin, "Catholicism," 5.
32. Ibid., 3.
33. Nevin, *Mystical Presence*, 155.

all these, in a deep sense, form at last but one and the same life. Adam lives in his posterity as truly as he has ever lived in his own person. They participate in his whole nature, soul and body, and are truly bone of his bone and flesh of his flesh.[34]

While his theology is not couched in the same philosophical idiom as Nevin's, de Lubac has a similar view of the objective reality and unity of the human race. Indeed, it is only upon such a basis that we can suppose an objective unity of the body of Christ: "The unity of the Mystical Body of Christ, a supernatural unity, supposes a previous natural unity, the unity of the human race." He goes on to cite the Church Fathers, who

> delighted to contemplate God creating humanity as a whole. "God," says St. Irenaeus, for example, "in the beginning of time plants the vine of the human race; he loved this human race and purposed to pour out his Spirit upon it and to give it the adoption of sons." For Irenaeus . . . the lost sheep of the Gospel that the Good Shepherd brings back to the fold is no other than the whole of human nature. . . . The Fathers designated this nature by a series of equivalent expressions, all of a concrete nature, thus demonstrating that it was in their view a genuine reality. They seemed to witness its birth, to see it live, grow, develop, as a single being. With the first sin it was this being, whole and entire, which fell away, which was driven out of Paradise and sentenced to a bitter exile until the time of its redemption. And when Christ at last appeared, coming as the "one bridegroom," his bride, once again, was the "whole human race."[35]

This natural unity of man is based upon the image of the united and indivisible God in man, and as such, it suffers along with that image a serious blow at the Fall. The race is still one, but its unity has been grievously compromised. Christ's redemption, therefore, aims to heal the race by uniting it anew within Himself.

> Christ from the very first moment of his existence virtually bears all men within himself—*erat in Christo Jesu omnis homo.* For the Word did not merely take a human body . . . He incorporated himself in our humanity, and incorporated it in himself. . . . In making a human nature, it is *human nature* that he united to himself, that he enclosed in himself . . . Christ the Redeemer does

34. Ibid., 152.
35. De Lubac, *Catholicism*, 25–27.

not offer salvation merely to each one; he effects it, he is himself the salvation of the whole.[36]

Christ as Redeemer thus redeems a new race, the Church, "one living being [that] grows under the action of a single life-force, and vivified by the one Spirit attains to the stature of perfection."[37] This is the "one new man" that Paul speaks of in the Epistle to the Colossians. Again citing the Fathers, he says,

> "The whole Christ, if we may be allowed the phrase, the total Christ, is not divided, for he is neither barbarian, nor Jew, nor Greek, nor man, nor woman, but the new man, wholly transformed by the Spirit." St. Augustine, in his turn, faithfully following St. Paul, speaks of "this new man spread about over the whole world" and made up of the body of the Christian faithful. . . . God cannot be worshiped save in one edifice, and his straying children can only find the way to the Father if they are gathered together in one Body, the new man whose head is our Redeemer.[38]

The Church then is a new humanity, sharing a common life, which contains all that was proper to man as created, but raised to a higher level of existence. This is a thought which pervades Nevin's *Mystical Presence* as well.

> By the hypostatical union of the two natures in the person of Jesus Christ, our humanity as fallen in Adam was exalted again to a new and imperishable divine life. That the race might be saved, it was necessary that a work should be wrought not beyond it, but in it; and this inward salvation to be effective must lay hold of the race itself in its organic, universal character, before it could extend to individuals, since in no other form was it possible for it to cover fully the breadth and depth of the ruin that lay in its way. . . . Humanity dwelt in his [Christ's] person as the second Adam, under a higher form than ever it carried in the first.[39]

The redeemed race, of which Christ is the Head, lives of course within his Body, the Church, as Nevin goes on to describe in terms similar to de Lubac's.

36. Ibid., 37–39.
37. Ibid., 47.
38. Ibid., 46.
39. Nevin, *Mystical Presence*, 156–57.

The chief point of all this (at least for de Lubac, and Nevin would be quick to concur) is to establish the inherently social nature of the Church. That is to say, by its very nature, the Church must comprise a gathering together of men, united in a whole that transcends the sum of its parts. The Church is not merely incidentally social, as if the purpose of the Gospel were to redeem individuals, who then gather together in groups for edification, and who can be added together and referred to as the abstract sum, "the invisible Church." God did not merely create a collection of individual men; so he does not redeem a mere collection of individual men. This social unity of the Church, as is clear from both Nevin and de Lubac, is far more than merely visible, but it is clearly no less—it is manifest as a visible unity of all the redeemed who call on the name of the Lord, and in whom we can discern a deeper unity—their participation in the one life of Christ by the Spirit.

The Visibility of the Church

Thus far, then, we have established two main tenets of Nevin's and de Lubac's ecclesiology: the redemption accomplished in the Church does not destroy nature or leave it behind, but transforms and perfects it, leaving out nothing that is proper to mankind. Moreover, it certainly does not leave out the intrinsic unity of mankind which derives from creation, and is renewed in Christ. The Church is a visible unified body of renewed humanity. Taken together, these tenets demand a certain understanding of the visibility and invisibility of the Church, as already hinted at. Any view of the Church which disparages its visible embodiment, suggesting instead that the truest form of the Church is the invisible, destroys any understanding of the Church as truly "catholic." Such a view would suggest that Christ redeems not a new humanity, but only a piece of humanity—men's souls; that redemptive grace leaves behind nature and takes men into another sphere of existence, rather than transforming them within every sphere in which they work and live. Moreover, it suggests that the Church is a mere collection of individuals, each attracted to God and then counted among his invisible host; it is not a gathering together, on this earth, of mankind into a single Body.

We should not surprised to find, then, that Nevin and de Lubac both take time to clarify the proper understanding of the Church in its visibility and invisibility.

De Lubac devotes an entire chapter to the subject in *The Splendor of the Church*, entitled "The Two Aspects of the One Church," a phrase which sums up the view he will argue for. He begins,

> There have always been visionaries and rebels against the burden-some conditions of Catholic unity who have made a distinction between the visible, temporal, hierarchic church that exists among us and a sort of invisible Church—wholly 'interior', wholly 'spiritual', 'the luminous community of God dispersed throughout the universe'. On such a view, the title 'Church of God' could only be applied, properly speaking, to this vast *communio sanctorum*, the theoretical common ground of all Christian communities and all good men. It alone would be divine; the first Church, the 'bodily' Church, would be a 'human creation' and no more.[40]

This is primarily a polemic against Protestantism, of course, and we see that de Lubac perceives that, as soon as an invisible Church is introduced as a separate reality, it necessarily supplants and nullifies the visible Church, whatever the claims of those who pretend to maintain both entities side-by-side as equally important. He likewise sees the attempt to root the unity of various churches, however visibly disconnected, in an invisible Church, as simply "Platonizing."[41] Invisible unity cannot exist without visible, organic unity, he argues. De Lubac appeals to the example of the Incarnation to explain his point, saying, "If the Church is real, she must be an organism which we can in some sense 'see and touch' just as we could have seen and touched the God-Man during his life on earth."[42] The human and divine, visible and invisible natures of Christ, insepara-bly indwelling each other, provide a picture of how Christ's ecclesial body should appear: "There, then, is the Church—human and divine at once even in her visibility, 'without division and without confusion', just like Christ Himself, whose body she mystically is."[43]

If we are not to divide the Church into visible and invisible then, how are we to characterize it? De Lubac wants to speak of two "aspects" of the one Church, as opposed to those who imply two separate entities, and he avoids visible/invisible terminology. The first aspect, the "ideal," is given by God and is inherent in the Church from its very inception, in

40. De Lubac, *Splendor of the Church*, 85.

41. Ibid., 87.

42. Ibid., 88.

43. Ibid., 102.

which she appears as the Bride of Christ, "entirely holy and unfailing. . . . Her doctrine remains perpetually pure and the spring of her sacraments perpetually fresh."[44] The second, the "concrete," "which is the end and fruit of the first, is a treasure which each man can lose; a Christian must simply hope, in all humility, for the single divine gift of final perseverance. . . . In this world the Church is a mixed community and will stay like that to the very end."[45] But he emphasizes again, it is not as if the ideal Church was the true Church and the concrete was not—rather, the one, visible body of Christ was the true Church, while possessing these two seemingly contradictory characters.[46]

> Under both aspects it is still the same body which St. Paul holds up to our contemplation and our participation. He shows us this body which is the Church, which lives and develops in this world and has a history to be followed, in the process of building itself up and growing until the day when it has reached full stature.[47]

This emphasis on breaking down the divide between visible and invisible Church does not simply appear because de Lubac is a Catholic. It is deeply rooted in the themes we have already touched on. To suggest that the true realm of grace is to be found in some invisible body, separate from the visible Body of Christ and indeed even seducing us away from it, is to deny that the supernatural penetrates the natural. It is to deny that the natural—the seemingly commonplace four walls and bread and wine—can be oriented toward and become a bearer of the supernatural. De Lubac rightly links this up with the Incarnation, which is the ultimate proof of the unity of natural and supernatural—if that is how Christ Himself was constituted, then his Body in the Church cannot be different.

Nevin's argument in all this is strikingly similar, and we have already seen much of it in chapter 3. I will cover much of the same ground again here, so the reader may see the parallels with de Lubac without having to flip back and forth. We may remember Schaff's excellent summary statement from *The Principle of Protestantism* (apparently conceiving that principle rather differently than de Lubac did!):

44. Ibid., 112.
45. Ibid., 112–13.
46. Ibid., 116.
47. Ibid., 123.

> [The Church] possesses, like her Founder, a divine and human,
> an ideal and a real, a heavenly and an earthly nature; only with
> this difference, that in her militant stage, freedom from sin and
> error cannot be predicated of her in the same sense as of Christ;
> that is, she possesses the principle of holiness and the full truth,
> mixed, however, still with sin and error.[48]

This quote touches on both of the points we made above—the connection between the Incarnation and the nature of the Church, and the
distinction of two natures of a single body, rather than treating them as
two separable bodies. On the first point, Nevin had much to say. He is
even more forceful than de Lubac in critiquing those Christians who saw
in the invisible Church something truer and more real than the visible
body, for he sees this as fundamentally a denial that Christ had come in
the flesh. He expounds this critique in his essay "Antichrist." Sectarians,
believing that whatever the state of their visible churches, they had access
to the invisible Church, were implicit docetists, he said, seeing Christ
as an essentially spiritual, divine being, with only a show of humanity.
Nevin traces this problem, too, back to their conception of the relationship of supernatural and natural; the Christians of his day saw the two as
completely separate and accordingly saw no true unity of the two even in
Christ Himself. Accordingly,

> As the Savior himself had no real being in the world, stood among
> men only in the form of an unsubstantial phantasm, or in the
> show of a human life which was after all but the sign or symbol of
> his invisible nature, not the very presence of this nature itself; it
> was not possible of course to attach any different idea of reality to
> the new life which he introduced into the world.[49]

Against this, Nevin argued that if Christ is to be truly the God-man, a
genuine union of divine and human, Spirit and flesh, then the Church, as
His Body, that which carries forward His life, must likewise be a union of
divine and human, Spirit and flesh, visible and invisible.

This unity Nevin also conceived as involving two "aspects"—the
"ideal" and "actual."[50] The ideal Church he characterized as follows:

48. Schaff, *Principle of Protestantism*, 220.

49. Nevin, "Antichrist," 41. Note that what is cited here is only the tip of the iceberg of
a long and fascinating discussion of the various heresies concerning Christ's person, how
they manifest themselves in terms of various understandings of the Church and of natural
and supernatural, and how they were at work in the Church of his day.

50. Nevin, "The Church," 57–58.

It is a living system, organically bound together in all its parts, springing from a common ground, and pervaded throughout with the force of a common nature. In its very conception, therefore, it is catholic, that is, one and universal. . . . In her Ideal character . . . the Church is absolutely holy and infallible, free from error and sin . . . the Church is represented to be the organ and medium by which the world is reclaimed from the power of error, and transformed into a holy life.[51]

It is not, however, an invisible Church, a supposition that Nevin considers as absurd as an invisible family, or an invisible man.[52] "The Idea of the Church," he maintains, "includes visibility, just as the Idea of man supposes a body." Moreover, this visibility is not merely the visibility of individuals within the Church, but "the visibility of the Church as an organic body, in whose presence alone all individual Christianity becomes real."[53] Of course, as visible, the fullness of the ideal Church can only be glimpsed, until we come to the consummation. In the meantime, we can only see clearly the "actual Church."

The "actual Church" is the historical body that we see, yet is one in all times and places where we see it. Of course, it cannot live up to its ideal perfection, but is always struggling with "opposition, contradiction, and conflict, disturbing forces, foreign elements, corruptions, distortions, aberrations." "The historical Church," he confesses, "is always the true church, but never a pure or perfect Church. It is by no means free either from error or sin."[54] Here he identifies the mistake of Rome, which seems to think that if the visible Church is the true Church, it must be an infallible Church. But the solution, of course, is not to, in seeking an infallible Church, give up on the visible Church. We must see, says Nevin, that the Church's struggle with error "lies in its very conception. The Church is a new creation for the world, complete from the first in Christ, but requiring a process of historical evolution, according to the law of all life, to actualize itself with final, universal triumph in the world as a whole."[55] When we understand this, we will see that "the actual Church and the Ideal Church . . . are in the end the same";[56] the actual Church is simply

51. Ibid., 59–60.
52. Ibid., 60.
53. Ibid., 61.
54. Ibid., 62.
55. Ibid.
56. Ibid., 64.

the Ideal Church as we behold it now, before; in the fullness of time, it shall be manifested in its mature form.

Like de Lubac, Nevin applies his theology of natural and supernatural to his understanding of how the Church manifests itself in the world. Creation has required since the beginning that it be brought into union with the supernatural, and this has at last been accomplished in the new creation of Christ and His Church. As the fulfillment of all nature and the body of her incarnate Head, it is unthinkable that the Church could be no more than an invisible spiritual society, a supernatural floating on top of nature. No, the Church is the place where the supernatural has been made visible, and penetrates that natural realm. "The creation itself becomes complete only in the Church, the life of nature in the life of the Spirit."[57] Thus she is inescapably, fundamentally visible, though, since she has not yet attained to her final end, she remains, in the present time, invisible in a sense.

Reformed and Catholics as Allies?

As with Eastern Orthodoxy, then, we have discovered that, in some of Nevin's most creative reflections, he takes Reformed theology into close dialogue with a former adversary, Roman Catholicism. Though it is perhaps less surprising to find parallels here, since Nevin did directly engage with Catholic thought (as he never did with Orthodoxy), I have focused on points in his theology where he expected to find an enemy, not an ally, in Catholic theology, and where de Lubac seems to have felt likewise toward Protestantism. Of course, Nevin would not necessarily have been wrong in supposing this, back in the 1850s. But de Lubac's thorough research in the Patristics unearthed many ideas that had been neglected at best, rejected at worst. While many Reformed would disown Nevin's theology, and many Catholics would still disown de Lubac's theology (though with a disciple of his on the throne of St. Peter, that's getting more difficult), I would suggest that the comparisons displayed in this chapter can point these two traditions toward much more dialogue than they have previously enjoyed.

Of course, none of these points of comparison (nature and supernature, visibility of the Church, etc.), taken alone, are particularly remarkable in themselves, we have seen a remarkably similar thought process at work in Nevin's and de Lubac's development of these themes. Certainly

---

57. Nevin, *Mystical Presence*, 204.

at points these similarities are obscured by very different methodologies; for all his talk of the supernatural fulfillment of the natural, de Lubac says little explicitly of the Incarnation, and for all his talk of the Incarnation and creation, Nevin says little explicitly of the proper relationship of natural and supernatural. However, I think we can accurately discern that both men felt that the construal of this relationship stood as one of the most pressing problems of theology. Both felt that the supernatural must be understood as the proper fulfillment of the natural, Incarnation as the proper fulfillment of creation. If this was true, then the Church's task was clearly to redeem and transform all that belongs to nature, especially human nature, rather than merely offering some spiritual way out of nature. This meant that since men were created as a social whole, a united race, salvation must redeem men as social whole, not as individuals each drawn to God on his own. Finally, if this were so, the Church must be fundamentally visible in its very nature. Of course invisible divine power shone through the outward visible Body, but this visible Body could never be replaced with a mere invisible communion of saints, or mere voluntary gatherings of individual saints, without ceasing to be the Church. In the Church, as "catholic," the whole of mankind and all of his endeavors are raised up from their fallen state, beyond even the created state, into a new age that brings all to completion.

This common vision of the Church and her calling provides a common theological language for Mercersburg and the *nouvelle théologie*, and perhaps, indeed, for Reformed theology and Catholic theology. By creatively, self-critically examining their own traditions, with an eye always to the heritage of the early Church, both Nevin and de Lubac manage to highlight some of the most glaring failings of both Protestantism and Catholicism. At the same time, they also point a way out of the dualism that has bedeviled both and show how both bodies may return to a more proper understanding of the Church's calling. Hopefully, in the process, they may also come to a fuller understanding and appreciation of one another.

CHAPTER 7

Lessons from Mercersburg

THE PRECEDING PAGES, I hope, have begun to introduce the reader to the enormous treasures the Mercersburg Theology has to offer. It is certainly odd that it should prove so, that a dinky little German seminary, and its two underpaid and unrenowned teachers, should have something to offer to us today. And yet they surely do, and not merely to the Reformed, but to many other branches of the Church—to evangelicals who may be able to learn from their critiques, and rediscover a more ancient understanding of the Church; and to Anglicans, Orthodox, and Catholics, who may be encouraged to see in Reformed Protestantism perhaps an unruly brother, rather than a second cousin twice removed. The theology of Mercersburg, whatever its imperfections, may hold a mirror up to Reformed churches today, forcing them to ask whether they are really heirs of the Reformation, and of the historic Church, or of some version of the "modern Puritanism" which preaches scarcely the same Gospel. By exposing the presuppositions of Hodge's system of doctrine, Mercersburg may show many how their "Reformed" doctrine is more a product of the Enlightenment than the Bible or the Reformation. Above all, it may point Reformed Christians, who are often quite narrow-minded, to see themselves as part of a larger tradition, a Church that is one, holy, catholic, and apostolic, and to recognize and learn from their brothers in the Anglican, Catholic, and Orthodox traditions.

Conversely, hopefully Mercersburg's contributions can help to serve as a Reformed welcome mat to those other traditions. To Anglicans, and especially Anglo-Catholics, Nevin's theology offers an excellent reminder of the common high church, high sacramental heritage, grounded in the best of patristic theology, that Reformed and Anglicans once shared. Nevin shows that a rich theology of the sacraments and the ministry can thrive in Calvinist soil as well as in Cranmerian. To the Orthodox, Mercersburg Theology offers a firm rebuttal to the idea that Reformed and Protestant soteriology is bound to extrinsic, juridical categories and has no use for the Orthodox teachings of *theosis*. Nevin argues that the Reformed heritage is quite receptive to an Incarnation-centered, participationist account of salvation, and begins to build bridges across the chasm that has separated East and West. To the Catholics, especially those influenced by de Lubac, Nevin shows that, despite remaining differences, many misconceptions may be laid to rest and much common ground may be covered together. The dualisms of nature and grace, matter and spirit, visible and invisible, so often attributed to Protestants, are as much a stranger to the Mercersburg Theology as to the *nouvelle théologie*, and if these are once purged from theology, many other dangers and divisions will disappear.

Any of these areas, so briefly sketched in this book, will provide, I think, a rich ground for further study and discussion. Mercersburg's theology does not provide any simple answers, however. If Mercersburg vs. Princeton is seen as a clash of interpretations as to what the Reformation really stood for, we may be convinced that Princeton was innovating, but that only begins to answer the question. The issues raised by Nevin and Schaff unveiled tensions that had been inherent in Protestant theology since the days of the Reformers. Though they were able to show that the Reformers had not meant to despise, but to embrace, the heritage of the preceding centuries of the Church, had not meant to subjectivize and spiritualize the Church and the sacraments, they recognized an ambivalence on these points from the very beginning, which made subsequent developments unsurprising. Nevin feared that, even in the best of the Reformers, he could not find a consistently catholic, ecclesial, sacramental theological vision, and this fear led him to question his allegiance to Protestantism. The questions with which he wrestled should prove instructive for Protestants (Reformed or otherwise), who are struggling to decide what Protestantism stands for, and against what precisely it is protesting. All may not agree with his answers, but his questions and his keen perceptions about Protestantism may not be ignored.

When it comes to the philosophical questions which underlay Mercersburg and Princeton's clash, these may seem irrelevant to many of us today. However, though Scottish Common Sense Realism and German Idealism are all but extinct in their nineteenth-century forms, they still embody approaches to theology which remain common today. The answers which Nevin and Hodge gave to questions of general vs. particular, ideal vs. actual, spiritual vs. physical, are highly relevant and instructive for theologians within and without the Reformed tradition.

Of course the Mercersburg men were not perfect, and their teachings are no timeless encapsulation of truth; they, more than anyone, would refuse such an assessment as unhistorical. They were, as much as any theologians, products of their time and place, and, if we are to learn from them, we must be able to separate the truths—biblical, catholic, and Reformed—that they discovered from the foreign conceptions which they imported into them. To attempt such a task is far beyond the scope of this book. A full survey of scriptural teaching on the issues above, covering as they do a very wide scope of Christian theology, would take several full-length books, even without addressing some of the questions of hermeneutics that must necessarily precede such a study. However, to completely sidestep the question would be cheating. Perhaps it is not necessary for chapters four through six, where the main concern is to show parallels; whether Nevin and Pusey were both right about sacraments or both wrong matters less than the fact that, either way, they agreed. But in chapters two and three, where the point is to show the stark contrast between Mercersburg and Princeton, many readers, especially Reformed, may be asking, "Ok, so who was right?" Of course, even if they are asking, they may not simply take my opinion on it, which I have hardly sought to disguise throughout, but I should perhaps take a few pages to offer a more explicit evaluation.

So I will offer a brief recap of the two systems of theology which were sketched in chapters two and three, along with a few remarks about what Scripture has to say on these issues.

Evaluating Mercersburg and Princeton

The overarching emphasis of Mercersburg thought, whether in theology, anthropology, or history, is *continuity*. To the nominalism of Ockham, the dualism of Descartes, the noumenal/phenomenal division of Kant, Mercersburg answered with an account of reality that insisted on the continuity between mind and matter, finite and infinite, nature and supernature, faith and reason. They made as their starting point the Incarnation, in which the infinite became finite, the natural became supernatural, Spirit took on matter, the deathless died and the mortal became immortal. After such a radical intrusion upon history, the world could not continue as before. Humanity was renewed into the Church, in which God through Christ was united to His people, and transforms the world. Since men are not independent units, but are part of an organic whole, the very concept of individual and immediate communion with God is ruled out—members of the new humanity commune with God by virtue of their membership in it, the Church. Likewise, as the Church is the body of Christ and Christ the life of the Church, believers receive spiritual life through the Church, particularly through the ordained means of the sacraments, in which Christ and the benefits of His divine-human life are made present to believers. History, then, since the Incarnation, is in a real sense the story of Christ's life. And just as there was an invisible, divine dimension to that life while He was on earth, so there is also in the Church, yet it remains one life, and despite all trials and divisions, it is one life and one story. All this stems from Nevin's and Schaff's emphasis on continuity and unity in theology, and determines for them a radically different destination than we find in Hodge's theology.

For Hodge and the theological tradition he represents, division, distinction, and discontinuity were the order of the day. Theology was a science, and hence had to follow clear rational distinctions and proceed on the basis of logical consistency, as defined by Common Sense Realism. For the Incarnation, this meant that divine and human must be kept at arm's length from one another. Certainly the union brought about in the Incarnation could not be made the principle of new life for New Covenant believers, lest we should risk falling into pantheism. It was the righteousness Christ earned, not the life within Him that saves believers; justification, therefore, was not about becoming part of a new people or receiving a new life, but was about receiving the imputed righteousness of Christ. To be sure, the believer was steadily transformed by grace, but as Nevin charged, this was for Hodge a transformation wrought from without, not unfolding within.[1] Moreover, since salvation was a matter

1. This is ironic, since it is Hodge who emphasizes the preeminence of the inward and

of the spirit, believers could receive grace only by being immediately united to Christ, and only thus could constitute the Church. A mediate union with Christ through the Church could only be outward, and hence meaningless and baseless. For Hodge, the Church, like man, was in effect divided into divine and human, spirit and flesh, and these two were also kept at arm's length from one another. The Church as a physical body on earth was transitory, unreliable, and insignificant. Only as the pure assembly of the elect, invisible and timeless, could the Church be considered the Body of Christ. Thus, since history consists of visible events in time, the true Church as such had no real history. There was only history of the various external societies of believers, and as these have been legion throughout the history of Christianity, there is nothing that we can point to as *our* history, the story of *our* people. We stand not as members of a Spirit-animated organism, looking back upon the long and glorious growth of the body of which we are a part, and forward to its final glorification, but as isolated units, lost in a whirl of conflicting groups and opinions, with no clear view of our origin or destination.

Hodge's view thus appears to undermine many key scriptural doctrines and emphases. Much time could be spent demonstrating that Scripture presents an essentially integralist anthropology, in which soul and body are inseparable. Good exegesis has consistently shown that Paul's "spirit-flesh" dualism is not intended to set the body and soul of man at odds with one another, as if one was good and valuable, and the other worthless. Instead, Paul contrasts a way of life lived according to the desires of the flesh and of the world and a way of life animated by the Spirit. But to make this point thoroughly would far exceed the limits of this study.

One brief point, worth making because Nevin and Hodge explicitly debated over it, concerns the question of the future state. If our existence is supposed to continue in the spirit after the body is dead, and is indeed, supposed to be better after death, does this not show that spirit and body are not necessary for one another, that the spirit is better off by itself? To this suggestion Nevin replies in *The Mystical Presence*:

> The whole argument in the 15th chapter of 1st Corinthians, as well as the representation [of] 1 Thess. IV.13–18, proceeds on the

---

spiritual over the outward and physical. Yet by separating the two so decisively, he not only loses a proper conception of the outward work of grace, but also a proper conception of the inward unfolding of new life.

assumption that the life of the *body*, as well as that of the soul, is indispensable to the perfect state of our nature as human. The soul then, during the intermediate state, cannot possibly constitute, in the biblical view, a complete man; and the case requires besides, that we should conceive of its relation to the body as still in force, not absolutely destroyed but only suspended. The whole condition is interimistic, and by no possibility of conception capable of being thought of as complete and final.[2]

If there is any doubt about Scripture's attitude towards the relationship of body and soul, there is certainly none regarding the relationship between men. For Hodge, as we will remember, men are independent units, bound together by common desires and needs, to be sure, invariably joining in associations and societies for various purposes, but not, by their nature, united to one another. Nevin, however, insisted there is no such thing as an isolated man; humanity transcends all individual men, who are all bound together with a common life by virtue of being members of humanity. Scripture certainly appears to stand closer to the latter view. Throughout the Bible, God never acts with men as individuals, but as communities. Even when he does appear to be covenanting with an individual man, such as Abraham, it is with the purpose of creating a new community, a new humanity bound together by a common life. It is this understanding, that men are intrinsically united to their ancestors and their posterity, that underlies the whole biblical conception of imputation, and indeed of covenant. Adam's sin is not our sin because God made it so by the terms of His federal agreement with man, as Hodge would have it, but because it really is our sin, because Adam is in us and we are in Adam; as he is the head of the race, so the whole race acts in his acts. Nor is Scripture unclear about making this same organic unity to underlie the relationship of Christ, the Last Adam, to His new humanity. Nevin expounds this in one of the strongest sections of the *Mystical Presence*, appealing to Rom 5:12–19 and 1 Cor 15:21, 22, 45–49:

> "By one man sin entered into the world, and death by sin, and so death passed upon all men, for that all have sinned." They were constituted sinners by that first act of disobedience itself. They sinned in Adam, and fell with him, in his first transgression. He stood in the case as their federal head, because he was their true organic head. . . . Christ too is the federal head and representative

2. Nevin, *Mystical Presence*, 162, note.

of humanity as a whole. "As by one man's disobedience many were made sinners, even so by the righteousness of one shall many be made righteous." Not in the way of a mere outward imputation, of course, in the last case, more than in the first; for this would destroy the parallel; but on the ground of a real community of life. As the world fell in Adam organically, so it is made to rise in Christ in the same way, as the principle of a new spiritual life.[3]

This organic conception of humanity leads for Nevin, as we have seen, to a high view of the mystical union between Christ and the believer, which, taking place through the Church and her sacraments, is a true life-giving union in which Christ is imparted to believers. The doctrine of union with Christ, as Bill Evans argues, had been central to Reformed theology early on, but had steadily weakened with the rise of federal theology. What had been seen as an intimate union between Christ and the believer, through which the believer received all spiritual blessings, became a mere legal union, in which the righteousness of Christ was extrinsically declared to belong to the believer, who then clung to Christ in some vague spiritual manner through faith.[4] Nevin attempted to revive the older model, adamantly affirming that it was the incarnational life of Christ shared with the believer, not the benefits of redemption outwardly considered, that were the basis for new life in the Christian. He appeals to John 6:51–58, Rom 6–8, 2 Cor 5:17, Gal 2:20, Phil 3:9–12, Col 3:1–4, and a host of other passages, demonstrating how scripturally, it is union with Christ Himself, not merely reception of His righteousness, which constitutes salvation. "In whom also ye were circumcised with the circumcision made without hands, in putting off the body of the sins of the flesh by the circumcision of Christ: buried with Him in baptism, wherein also ye are risen with Him through the faith of the operation of God," declares Paul in Col 2:11–12. On this point at least, Nevin's appeal to Scripture is convincing and leaves the Princetonian paradigm of union with Christ looking unsatisfactory at best.

Further, Nevin's view of the Church as the agent of this mystical union is substantiated by Paul's rich theology of the Church: "And [He] hath put all things under His feet, and gave Him to be the head over all things to the Church, which is His body, the fulness of Him that filleth all in all" (Eph 1:22–23). "For we are members of His body, of His flesh and

---

3. Ibid., 198–99.

4. See Evans, "Imputation and Impartation," chapter 2.

of His bones. . . . This is a great mystery: but I speak concerning Christ and the Church" (Eph 5:30, 32). Nor is it legitimate for Hodge to take refuge in his doctrine of the invisible Church, claiming that this mystical bond between Christ and the Church applies only to the invisible body of the elect. Paul moves seamlessly between talking about the blessings given to "us" and to "you" and the blessings given to the "Church." When he writes to a church, he writes to a visible body of saints and assures them that it is they, that visible body, who are the Body of Christ, who have all the blessings and obligations of the Church.

Hodge, on the other hand, insists that the word "Church," even when applied to a particular city, only applies to the elect in that city: "the Church of God is the whole number of the elect; the Church of Corinth is the whole number of the called[5] in that city. . . . The multitude of believers in Corinth, organized or dispersed, is the Church of Corinth, just as the whole multitude of the saints in heaven and on earth is the Church of God."[6] But of course, if the true Church is an indeterminate, unrecognizable, unchangeable body of the elect, rather than the visible organization of believers who worship and practice the sacraments and minister in their communities, then much of the New Testament's teaching concerning it becomes nonsense. For example, if the Church in Corinth to whom Paul is speaking consists only of the elect, as Hodge would have us believe, why does Paul say, "Do not ye judge them that are within [the church]? . . . Therefore put away from among yourselves that wicked person" (1 Cor 5:12–13). Or why does he warn these elect that they might be lost? "Wherefore let he which thinketh he standeth take heed lest he fall" (1 Cor 10:12). "Be not highminded, but fear: for if God spared not the natural branches, take heed lest he also spare not thee. Behold therefore the goodness and severity of God: on them which fell, severity; but toward thee, goodness, if thou continue in his kindness: otherwise thou also shall be cut off" (Rom 11:20–22). Why, particularly, does John threaten the "church" at Ephesus, presumably all the elect in that city, that they may be destroyed wholesale? "Remember therefore from whence thou art fallen, and repent, and do the first works; or else I will come unto thee quickly, and will remove thy candlestick out of his place—except thou repent" (Rev 2:5). Even beyond such problem passages, of which

5. Note that Hodge carefully defines the word "called" as referring to the truly elect and regenerate.

6. Hodge, *Discussions in Church Polity*, 9–10.

there are many more, we might ask the more basic question: what does it mean to write a physical letter to an invisible body? How were the true recipients of the New Testament epistles to be identified? It is all but impossible to reconcile Hodge's definition to Scripture.

On the other hand, if the visible Church is granted to be the true Church, as Scripture appears to say, then all the promises and commands which Scripture gives to the "Church" apply, at least to a large extent, to the visible historical body of believers. Thus, Nevin and Schaff's view of Church history necessarily follows from Scripture's promises of the continuity and triumph of the Church: "On this rock I will build my church, and the gates of Hades shall not prevail against it."

In short, then, not only is Nevin's position more consistent with itself than Hodge's (which often seems torn between lip service to the ecclesiology of the Reformation and allegiance to a newer semi-revivalistic ecclesiology), but it appears to be far more consistent with the teaching of Scripture. To demonstrate this in full is, of course, impossible here, but the points sketched above are clear enough and show Hodge and the Reformed tradition he represents to have fallen away significantly from the emphases of the Reformers, as Nevin charged, and from Scripture itself.

As mentioned earlier, in many ways the divide between Mercersburg and Princeton fell along philosophical lines. For this reason, it might be complained that often, Hodge's theology was motivated by Scottish philosophy rather than good biblical exegesis, and Nevin's by German philosophy rather than good biblical exegesis. And if this is the case, is either one really doing good theology; is either one worth listening to? But this objection could be raised against any theology in any age. We must dispense with the notion that there is such a thing as "good biblical exegesis" unaffected by philosophical precommitments, or even by the temperaments and life circumstances of the particular theologian. So it is somewhat naïve to complain that a theologian came to the right conclusion for the wrong reason, just because there were philosophical influences on his exegesis. Nevertheless, the practical impossibility of pure exegesis should not deter us from the attempt. As the Church matures in her study and understanding of the Scriptures, theologians should seek more and more to understand the biblical text on its own basis and let it speak for itself, while importing as few outside assumptions as possible.

On this basis, the Mercersburg Theology warrants some critique. Hodge, of course, accuses Nevin of importing Schleiermacher's system wholesale and of merely restating the liberal, semi-pantheist theology of nineteenth-century Germany in an American setting. Nevin defended himself against this charge, saying. "Am I not a teacher in the German church, and as such bound, in common honesty, to cultivate a proper connection with the theological life of Germany, as well as with that of Scotland and New England?"[7] and in other places, spells out at some length his relation to the German theologians to prove his orthodoxy. There was indeed, as Nevin was quick to point out and as Hodge seemed unable to notice, a huge diversity of thinkers and theologies in Germany at that time, even as there were in America. Some were full-blown Hegelians, others were more Schleiermacherian, still others eschewed both for a more orthodox alternative. Nevin and Schaff followed none slavishly, but critically and discriminatingly borrowed from several of them, as well as from other traditions, such as the Anglican.

Nevertheless, they were probably not as critical and discriminating as they should have been. Nor, for the most part, do they seem to have clearly subordinated their philosophical notions to biblical exegesis; in many cases, they seem to take for granted certain notions of anthropology or history before approaching the biblical text. This results in some vague and potentially confusing articulations of theological concepts. Nevin is right to emphasize the "mystery" inherent in Christian theology,[8] and Hodge and his allies are wrong to insist that all must be perfectly rational and transparent; but Nevin's use of German philosophical concepts often creates mysteries where there shouldn't be, or at least, in ways that there shouldn't. His constant use of the term "organic" provides a case in point. While we can get a general feel for its meaning in Nevin's usage, sometimes he seems content to use it as in any context as a vague general term of approval. The word "abstract," likewise, can function in almost any context for Nevin as a vague undefined term of disapproval. These possible weak points, however, do not seem to have led Nevin down the road of German liberalism and pantheism, as Hodge had feared; he remained conservative and orthodox his whole life.

The greatest potential weakness in the Mercersburg Theology stemmed from one of their greatest strengths, their Hegelian notion of

---

7. Nevin, "Antichrist," 14, note.

8. It is certainly an emphasis he shares with St. Paul (cf. 1 Cor 2:7, Eph 3, Col 1:26–27).

historical progress. While, carefully applied, this notion enabled them to give a convincing, unified, and strongly postmillennial account of Church history, it also carried within it the seeds of relativism, as Søren Kierkegaard argued in *Concluding Unscientific Postscript*.[9] The difficulty lies in the assertion that each age of history was important for what it had to contribute, and was true and good in its own way, but had to be superseded by a new era which was also important and good and true for what it had to contribute. This has a tendency to make the truth of each period something passing and provisional, creating skepticism in the pessimists and overweening confidence that it is theirs to bring in the new era in the optimists. Schaff, indeed, grew increasingly ecumenist in his thought, and by his later life, had joined forces with many early liberals (though he never embraced liberalism himself), helping to organize the World Parliament of Religions in 1893. Nevin, however, was so thoroughly imbued with a deep respect for the authority of the teachings of the early Church, that he never allowed his catholicity to morph into proto-liberalistic ecumenism.[10]

Indeed, Nevin's approach to Protestant catholicity was undoubtedly more valuable and potentially effective than the approach Schaff eventually took, and along with him, the mainstream of Protestant churches. Ironically, Nevin's catholicity was more historically centered than Schaff's, the great historian. For Nevin sought to find unity by returning to common sources (though never in mere slavish imitation), rather than, as

9. "According to Hegel, truth is the continuing world-process. Each generation, each stage of this process, is valid; and yet it is only a moment of the truth. Unless we here allow ourselves to introduce a dash of charlatanry, which helps out by assuming that the generation in which Professor Hegel lived, or the generation which after him plays the role of *Imprimatur*, is the last generation, we are all in a state of skeptical uncertainty. The passionate question of truth does not even arise, since philosophy has begun by tricking the individuals into becoming objective. The positive Hegelian truth is as illusory as happiness was in paganism. The individual could not know whether he was happy until all was at an end, and so here: only the next following generation can know what the truth was in the preceding generation. The great secret of the System . . . is pretty much the same as the sophism of Protagoras, that everything is relative, except that here, everything is relative in the continuing world-process." (Kierkegaard, *Concluding Unscientific Postscript*, 34). For an incisive (though not always entirely orthodox) critique of Hegelianism and the whole system of German theology of the day, Kierkegaard is easily the best source. See especially *Fear and Trembling* (1843), *Philosophical Fragments* (1844), *Concluding Unscientific Postscript* (1845), and *Attack on Christendom* (1854).

10. Indeed, he carefully distinguishes between *catholicity* and *ecumenism* and roundly denounces the latter. See his article "Catholicism."

modern liberal ecumenism, abandoning the past and embracing a common future, purged not only of the traditions that divide us, but those that unite us as well. This means returning to great unifying traditions of the historic faith, like the incarnational theology of the early Greek Fathers, or the historical understanding of the divine power of the visible Church.

Of course, this defense will not satisfy many, who may have a more fundamental objection to the presentation of the Mercersburg Theology here. "That's all well and good that they're more biblical than Hodge," the objector may say, "and that they have a safeguard against liberalism, but they're simply not Reformed, so how can they represent a Reformed catholicity?" The presentation of parallels between Nevin's Reformed theology and the theology of their Anglican, Orthodox, and Catholic counterparts certainly invites the objection that these parallels are only possible because, at the crucial points, Nevin has abandoned Reformed theology. His sacramental theology, one will say, though not Romanist, is at least too preoccupied with the incarnate flesh of Christ, rather than His Spirit and His benefits. His theology of the ministry is an abandonment of the Calvinistic marks of the Church for a magical visible transmission of grace. His preoccupation with the Incarnation, one will say, is an unhealthy obsession, more at home in Eastern Orthodox theology than Reformed, and his soteriology abandons the crucial Reformation distinctives. Even his resolution of nature/grace and visible/invisible church dualisms owes more to idealist philosophy than to Reformed theology, the objector may insist. And, if these charges are at all true, how does Mercersburg really bring Reformed Protestantism into dialogue with other branches of the Church, since it has to abandon that Protestantism to accomplish the link?

Two different types of objector may be asking these questions. One is the reader who is convinced that it is more important to be Reformed than to be catholic, and thus is not willing to abandon Reformed teaching for any dialogue, who feels that no theology deserves consideration unless it sports a Reformed pedigree that can pass the strictest inspection. For such a reader, I have no reply, except to say that he has picked up the wrong book (and apparently wasted several hours reading it by now). I cannot establish the kind of strict Reformed pedigree desired for some of Nevin's doctrines, nor should I wish to. But there may be another sort of objector. He may be more than willing to engage in ecumenical dialogue, to push his thinking in some new directions and look for areas of common ground, even when it takes a stretch, but he wants to do so from a Reformed standpoint. He wants to make sure that he doesn't build bridges so aggressively that he loses firm home turf to stand on. "I'm all for catholicity," he may say, "but I want it to be a genuinely *Reformed* catholicity, not a headlong dive into catholicity by someone who perhaps was once Reformed but now is nothing recognizable." This is a fair position. Faithfulness to our own traditions is the only sure way to start out on the rocky road of ecumenical discussions with other traditions.

However, I think that the Mercersburg Theology should be able to satisfy such an objector, at least on the vast majority of points. I would not go so far as Darryl Hart in claiming that Nevin's main concern was to be Reformed; nor would I embrace Wentz's conclusion that he is only interested in being catholic. Nevin was very interested in being both, and that meant that while he freely pursued lines of theological inquiry that took him beyond the Reformed tradition, he did not seek to embrace doctrines that went contrary to that tradition. When he urged new emphases and perspectives, he saw in them complements to Reformed theology, new ways of looking at an issue that could enrich, improve, and augment the Reformed perspective, but not contradict it and nullify it. We see this, for example, in his appropriation of certain themes in German theology, and in his strong incarnational focus, which, while in some ways strangers to Reformed theology, could easily be adopted and made to feel at home there. On questions of the purpose of the Reformation, the visibility of the Church, and the presence of Christ in the sacrament, scholarship since his time has consistently proven that Mercersburg lay close to the minds of the original Calvinistic Reformers. His whole understanding of the grace-bearing Church, her ministry and sacraments, while marking a shift in emphasis from certain Reformation polemics, can certainly be shown to square with their theological vision. On soteriology, his more participationist, Eastern Orthodox model was actually very consistent with early Calvinistic paradigms, as scholars such as Bill Evans have shown. His view of the nature/grace distinction and what it means for the Church to be "catholic," though he does not put it this way, is really but a consistent outworking of the insights of covenant theology, with its emphasis on the unity of Creator and Redeemer.

Any of these points would require long chapters of documentation to fully substantiate, but I hope the idea is satisfactorily clear. Nevin and Schaff unearthed the treasures of their Reformed heritage to construct a paradigm of Protestantism that was far more catholic (in every sense of the word) than Princeton could imagine or ever consent to, but which was nevertheless authentically Reformed. If fidelity to Scripture and the testimony of the historic Church compelled them to revise or augment a part of the Reformed tradition, they gladly did so, for to be a Christian, and in unity with the one, holy, catholic, and apostolic Church was more important than being distinctively Reformed. They knew better than to suppose that Reformed theology had all the answers, and should take up its lectern and teach all their erring brothers, as Princeton did; they preferred to take more time to listen and learn. But in none of this did they lightly abandon their heritage, for how could they be faithful to the Church of all ages if they did not even know how to be faithful to the Church of their childhood, as Nevin showed in his courageous decision to remain German Reformed.

Perhaps in this—their demonstration of how to be Reformed because they were catholic, catholic because they were Reformed—even more than in their fascinating doctrines, Nevin and Schaff have a thing or two to teach us today.

Appendix

A Timeline of Key Dates

1797: Charles Hodge is born

1803: John Williamson Nevin is born

1816: Hodge graduates College of New Jersey, enters Princeton Seminary

1821: Nevin graduates from Union College

1822: Hodge appointed professor of Biblical and Oriental Literature at Princeton Seminary

1823: Nevin enrolls at Princeton Seminary

1824: Charles Finney begins his revivalistic preaching

1825: Hodge founds *The Biblical Repertory and Princeton Review*

1826–28: Hodge studies in Germany; Nevin fills his professorship

1830: Nevin begins teaching at Western Theological Seminary in Pittsburgh

1833: Beginning of the Oxford Movement

1835: Pusey joins the Oxford Movement

1837: Presbyterian Church in the U.S.A. divides into Old School and New School

1840: Nevin accepts position as head of Mercersburg Seminary, transfers to German Reformed Church; Hodge accepts Chair of Didactic Theology at Princeton

1841: Nevin becomes president of Marshall College; Newman publishes infamous "Tract 90"

1843: Nevin writes *The Anxious Bench*

1844: Schaff joins Nevin at Mercersburg, delivers "The Principle of Protestantism" at Synod of the German Reformed Church

1845: Nevin translates *The Principle of Protestantism*; Hodge publishes his review in *The Biblical Repertory and Princeton Review*; Newman secedes to the Roman Catholic Church

1846: Nevin publishes *The Mystical Presence*

1848: Hodge publishes his scathing review of *The Mystical Presence*; Nevin responds with *Antichrist*

1849: Nevin and Schaff found *The Mercersburg Review*

1850: "Gorham affair"—controversy over baptismal regeneration—rocks the Church of England

1851: Nevin resigns post at Mercersburg Seminary

1853: Nevin resigns post at Marshall College

1854: Schaff publishes the first volume of his *Church History*, is negatively reviewed by Hodge; Robert Wilberforce secedes to the Roman Catholic Church

1866: Nevin becomes president at Franklin and Marshall College

1867: Liturgical controversy in the German Reformed Church; German theologian Isaak Dorner debates with Nevin

1869: Old School–New School schism healed

1870: Schaff accepts post at Union Theological Seminary in New York

1871: Hodge publishes his *Systematic Theology*

1878: Charles Hodge dies, after 56 years of professorship at Princeton

1886: Nevin dies

1893: Schaff speaks at World Parliament of Religions in Chicago, dies later that year.

Bibliography

Chandler, Michael. *An Introduction to the Oxford Movement.* New York: Church Publishing, 2003.

Chapman, Raymond, editor. *Firmly I Believe: An Oxford Movement Reader.* Norwich: Canterbury, 2006.

Clendenin, Daniel, editor. *Eastern Orthodox Theology: A Contemporary Reader.* Grand Rapids, MI: Paternoster, 2003.

———. *The Mystery of the Supernatural.* Translated by Rosemary Sheed. New York: Herder and Herder, 1998.

———. *The Splendor of the Church.* Translated by Michael Mason. San Francisco: Ignatius, 1986.

Evans, William Borden. "Imputation and Impartation: Union With Christ in 19th-Century Reformed Theology." PhD diss., Vanderbilt University, 1996. Now published as William B. Evans, *Imputation and Impartation: Union with Christ in American Reformed Theology.* Milton Keynes, UK: Paternoster, 2008. Page citations are from the dissertation.

Fairbairn, Donald. *Eastern Orthodoxy: Through Western Eyes.* Louisville: Westminster John Knox, 2002.

Hart, D. G. *John Williamson Nevin: High Church Calvinist.* Phillipsburg, NJ: P. & R. Publishing, 2005.

Hodge, Charles H. *The Constitutional History of the Presbyterian Church in the United States of America.* Philadelphia: Martien, 1840. Reprint, New York: Westminster, 2000.

———. *Discussions in Church Polity.* New York: Scribner, 1878. Reprint, New York: Westminster, 2001.

———. "Doctrine of the Reformed Church on the Eucharist." *The Biblical Repertory and Princeton Review* 20 (1848) 227–78.

———. "Dr. Schaff's Apostolic Church." *The Biblical Repertory and Princeton Review* 26 (1854) 148–92.

———. "Schaff's Protestantism." *The Biblical Repertory and Princeton Review* 17 (1845) 626–36.

———. *Systematic Theology.* 3 vols. New York: Scribner, 1873. Reprint, Peabody, MA: Hendrickson, 1999.

———. "What is Christianity?" *The Princeton Review* 32 (1860) 118–61.

Kierkegaard, Søren. *Concluding Unscientific Postscript.* Translated by David F. Swenson. Edited by Walter Lowrie. Princeton: Princeton University Press, 1941.

Lubac, Henri de. *Catholicism: Christ and the Common Destiny of Man.* Translated by Lancelot C. Sheppard and Elizabeth Englund. San Francisco: Ignatius, 1988.

Marsden, George M. *The Evangelical Mind and the New School Presbyterian Experience.* Eugene, OR: Wipf & Stock, 2003.

Mathison, Keith. *Given for You.* Phillipsburg, NJ: P. & R. Publishing, 2002.

Murray, Iain H. *Revival and Revivalism: The Making and Marring of American Evangelicalism, 1750–1858.* Carlisle, PA: The Banner of Truth Trust, 1994.

Nevin, J. W. "The Anglican Crisis." *The Mercersburg Review* 3:4 (1851) 359–97.

———. *Antichrist: The Spirit of Sect and Schism.* New York: Taylor, 1848. Reprinted in *The Anxious Bench, Antichrist, and Catholic Unity.* Edited by Augustine Thompson. Eugene, OR: Wipf & Stock, 1999.

———. *The Anxious Bench.* 1844. Reprinted in *The Anxious Bench, Antichrist, and Catholic Unity.* Edited by Augustine Thompson. Eugene, OR: Wipf & Stock, 1999.

———. "Catholicism." *The Mercersburg Review* 3:1 (1851) 1–26.

———. "Cur Deus-Homo?" *The Mercersburg Review* 3:3 (1851) 220–38.

———. "Early Christianity, Article 2." *The Mercersburg Review* 3:6 (1851) 513–62.

———. "The Heidelberg Catechism." *The Mercersburg Review* 4:2 (1852) 155–86.

———. "Liebner's Christology." *The Mercersburg Review* 3:1 (1851) 55–72.

———. *The Mystical Presence: A Vindication of the Reformed or Calvinistic Doctrine of the Holy Eucharist.* 1846. Reprint, edited by Augustine Thompson. Eugene, OR: Wipf & Stock, 2000.

———. "The Old Doctrine of Christian Baptism." *The Mercersburg Review* 12:2 (1860) 190–215.

———. "Our Relations with Germany." *The Mercersburg Review* 14:4 (1867) 627–33.

———. "Sartorius on the Person and Work of Christ." *The Mercersburg Review* 1:2 (1849) 146–69.

———. "The Sect System, Article 1." *The Mercersburg Review* 1:5 (1849) 482–507.

———. "The Sect System, Article 2." *The Mercersberg Review* 1:6 (1849) 521–39.

———. *Vindication of the Revised Liturgy.* Philadelphia: Rodgers, 1867. Reprinted in *Catholic and Reformed: Selected Theological Writings of John Williamson Nevin.* Edited by Charles Yrigoyen, Jr., and George H. Bricker. Pittsburgh, PA: Pickwick, 1978.

———. "Wilberforce on the Incarnation." *The Mercersburg Review* 2:2 (1850) 164–95.

Newman, John Henry. *Apologia Pro Vita Sua.* 1865. Reprint, edited by Ian Ker. New York: Penguin, 1994.

Nichols, J. H, editor. *The Mercersburg Theology.* New York: Oxford University Press, 1966. Reprint, Eugene, OR: Wipf & Stock, 2004.

———. *Romanticism in American Theology.* Chicago: University of Chicago Press, 1961. Reprint, Eugene, OR: Wipf & Stock, 2007.

Proudfit, John. "The Heidelberg Catechism and Dr. Nevin." *The Biblical Repertory and Princeton Review* 24 (1852) 91–184.

Pusey, Edward Bouverie. "Scriptural Views of Holy Baptism." 4th ed. *Tracts for the Times,* vol. 2. London: Gilbert and Rivington, 1840.

———. "The Holy Eucharist a Comfort to the Penitent." *Nine Sermons Preached Before the University of Oxford.* Oxford: Parker, 1859.

Schaff, Philip. *The Principle of Protestantism.* Vol. 1 of *Lancaster Series on the Mercersburg Theology.* Chambersburg, PA: German Reformed Church, 1845. Reprinted, edited by Bard Thompson and George H. Bricker. Eugene, OR: Wipf & Stock, 2004.

———. *What is Church History?: A Vindication of the Idea of Historical Development.* Philadelphia: Lippincott, 1846. Reprinted in *Reformed and Catholic: Selected Theological Writings of Philip Schaff.* Edited by Charles Yrigoyen, Jr., and George H. Bricker. Pittsburgh, PA: Pickwick, 1979.

———. *History of the Apostolic Church with a General Introduction to Church History,* vol. 1 (Edinburgh: T. & T. Clark, 1854), reprinted in *Reformed and Catholic: Selected Theological Writings of Philip Schaff.* Edited by Charles Yrigoyen, Jr., and George H. Bricker. Pittsburgh, PA: Pickwick, 1979.

Stamoolis, James, editor. *Three Views on Eastern Orthodoxy and Evangelicalism.* Grand Rapids: Zondervan, 2004.

Ware, Kallistos. *The Orthodox Way.* Crestwood, NY: St. Vladimir's Seminary Press, 1995.

Wentz, Richard E. *John Williamson Nevin: American Theologian.* New York: Oxford University Press, 1997.

Index